Review of the Regulation of Freight Transport in Mexico

OECD
BETTER POLICIES FOR BETTER LIVES

This work is published under the responsibility of the Secretary-General of the OECD. The opinions expressed and arguments employed herein do not necessarily reflect the official views of OECD member countries.

This document and any map included herein are without prejudice to the status of or sovereignty over any territory, to the delimitation of international frontiers and boundaries and to the name of any territory, city or area.

Please cite this publication as:
OECD (2017), *Review of the Regulation of Freight Transport in Mexico*, OECD Publishing, Paris.
http://dx.doi.org/10.1787/9789264268364-en

ISBN 978-92-64-26827-2 (print)
ISBN 978-92-64-26836-4 (PDF)

The statistical data for Israel are supplied by and under the responsibility of the relevant Israeli authorities. The use of such data by the OECD is without prejudice to the status of the Golan Heights, East Jerusalem and Israeli settlements in the West Bank under the terms of international law.

Photo credits: Cover © Suat Gursozlu/Shutterstock.com

Corrigenda to OECD publications may be found on line at: *www.oecd.org/about/publishing/corrigenda.htm*.

Foreword

Governments create and issue regulation to reach a public policy objective, such as protecting lives, minimising the impact of economic activity in the environment, or informing consumers. Well-designed, high-quality regulations can not only help achieve these goals, but generate more benefits than costs for society.

In any jurisdiction, the transport sector is subject to a myriad of rules and regulations with different policy objectives, such as: road safety, tax collection, promoting industries, and restricting the market power of firms. Mexico is no exception. Furthermore, the horizontal nature of the transport industry makes it a sector whose performance has a direct impact on other industries, affecting the availability, quality and price of products and services in these sectors. Ultimately, a badly regulated transport sector can have a ripple effect across the economy, hampering growth and economic development.

The *2012 Recommendation of the Council on Regulatory Policy and Governance* recognising the need to have regulations that are "fit-for-purpose" invites OECD countries to "conduct systematic programme reviews of the stock of significant regulation against clearly defined policy goals, including consideration of costs and benefits, to ensure that regulations remain up to date, cost justified, cost effective and consistent, and deliver the intended policy objectives".

This report *Review of the Regulation of Freight Transport in Mexico* is a response to this recommendation. Mexico's Ministry of Economy and Federal Commission for Better Regulation (COFEMER) asked the OECD to carry out a review to identify regulatory barriers, obstacles, implementation flaws or inefficiencies affecting the freight transport sector in Mexico. The objective of this review, therefore, is to generate recommendations for improvement using as basis good international practices. These recommendations will be used to prepare a set of legal reforms for the road transport, rail, civil aviation, ports and border management sectors. The goal is to promote economic efficiency, productivity and growth. This study is carried out as part of a broader programme of co-operation among the Ministry of Economy, COFEMER and the OECD to strengthen competitiveness in Mexico through regulatory improvement.

The *Review* finds several regulatory challenges across the different means on transport. For instance, on road transport the modification of regulation on limits on weigh and dimensions should be based on empirical evidence and on a clear indication that the benefits of any regulatory restriction outweighs the potential costs. In rail transport, the *Review* suggests that authorities should develop the capacity to collect and analyse data needed to form judgements on competition issues. Similarly, on issues on ports, the *Review* finds that the lack of infrastructure coupled with legal controls and administrative procedures create unnecessary bottlenecks in the release of cargo, hence affecting efficiency of transport and increasing costs for businesses.

The link between regulation that inhibits economic activity, either by creating barriers to entrepreneurship or by restricting competition in the marketplace, and lower productivity has been studied by the OECD using an indicator on product market regulation and related research (see https://www.oecd.org/eco/growth/indicatorsofproductmarketregulationhomepage.htm). Therefore, this review can contribute to Mexico's efforts to bolster economic growth.

Most of the main regulatory issues in this review were identified through a series of meetings with public officials and regulators of the transport sector, as well as business and private associations and chambers of industry in the transport sector. Meetings were held between officials of the Regulatory Policy Division of the OECD, the International Transport Forum (ITF) at the OECD, the Ministry of Economy, COFEMER, and several departments of the Ministry of Transport and Communications of Mexico, including the General Directorate for Road Transport, the General Directorate for the Merchant Marine, the General Directorate for Civil Aviation, and General Directorate for Rail and Multimodal Transport; as well as industry and academia representatives.

ACKNOWLEDGEMENTS

The report was prepared by a multidisciplinary team, led by Manuel Flores Romero, Senior Economist in the OECD Regulatory Policy Division, and Stephen Perkins, Head of Research and Policy of the International Transport Forum at the OECD under the guidance of Rolf Alter, Director, Public Governance and Territorial Development Directorate, and Nick Malyshev, Head, Regulatory Policy Division. The review team was composed of economists from the OECD and the International Transport Forum together with international regulatory experts: Aimee Aguilar Jaber, International Transport Forum; Monica Alcala, Regulatory Policy Division, OECD; Andres Blancas, Regulatory Policy Division, OECD; Alberto Morales, Regulatory Policy Division, OECD; Olaf Merk, International Transport Forum; Michele Acciaro, Kuhne University, Hamburg, Germany; Michael Tretheway, InterVISTAS, Canada; and David Widdowson, Charles Sturt University in Australia. Andrea Uhrhammer and Luiz de Mello from the Public Governance and Territorial Development Directorate provided valuable comments to improve the draft. Jennifer Stein from the OECD Regulatory Policy Division co-ordinated the editorial process.

We thank Ildefonso Guajardo Villarreal, Minister of Economy of Mexico and Rocio Ruiz Chavez, Vice-minister for Competitiveness and Regulation of the Ministry of Economy, for their valuable support, empowerment and intense work to improve regulatory governance in Mexico, and for providing the facilities to complete this report.

We express our gratitude to Jose Eduardo Mendoza Contreras, head of the Unit for the Design and Implementation of Public Policies for Productivity of the Ministry of Economy, and his team that includes David Lopez Victoriano, Gustavo and Rodrigo Perez Valdespín, and Alin Martinez Morales, for their support to complete this report, and for the comments provided.

We thank Mario Emilio Gutiérrez Caballero, head of the Federal Regulatory Improvement Commission of Mexico, and his team, for their comments on earlier versions.

This report on potential improvements to the regulation of freight transport in Mexico was prepared on the basis of interviews held with stakeholders in Mexico City throughout 2014. The team is grateful for the assistance of the stakeholders consulted with: General Administration of Customs Tax Administration Service (*Administración General de Aduanas del Servicio de Administración Tributaria*, SAT); Port Authority of Manzanillo (*Administración Portuaria Integral de Manzanillo* S.A. de C.V.); Port Authority of Veracruz (*Administración Portuaria Integral de Veracruz S.A. de C.V.*); Mexican Association of Shipping Agents (*Asociación Mexicana de Agentes Navieros*, AMANAC); Mexican Railway Association (*Asociación Mexicana de Ferrocarriles*, AMF); Mexican Association of Intermodal Transport (*Asociación Mexicana de Transporte Intermodal*, AMTI); National Private Transport Association (*Asociación Nacional de Transporte Privado*, ANTP); Harbourmaster of the State of Colima (*Capitanía de Puerto del Estado de Colima*); Harbourmaster of the State of Veracruz (*Capitanía de Puerto del Estado de*

Veracruz); Federal Competition Commission (*Comisión Federal de Competencia Económica*, COFECE); Federal Regulatory Improvement Commission (*Comisión Federal de Mejora Regulatoria*, COFEMER); Deputy General Directorate on Maritime Port Projects, Ministry of Communications and Transportation (*Dirección General Adjunta de Proyectos Marítimo Portuarios, Secretaría de Comunicaciones y Transportes*); Directorate General of Federal Auto Transport, Ministry of Communications and Transportation (*Dirección General de Autotransporte Federal, Secretaría de Comunicaciones y Transportes*); Directorate General of Civil Aviation, Ministry of Communications and Transport (*Dirección General de Aviación Civil, Secretaría de Comunicaciones y Transportes*); Directorate General of Promotion and Port Administration, Ministry of Communications and Transportation (*Dirección General de Fomento y Administración Portuaria, Secretaría de Comunicaciones y Transportes*); Directorate General of Merchant Marine, Ministry of Communications and Transportation (*Dirección General de Marina Mercante, Secretaría de Comunicaciones y Transportes*); General Directorate of Standards, Ministry of Economy (*Dirección General de Normas, Secretaría de Economía*); Directorate General of Railways and Multimodal, Ministry of Communications and Transportation (*Dirección General de Transporte Ferroviario y Multimodal, Secretaría de Comunicaciones y Transportes*); Mexican Transport Institute (*Instituto Mexicana del Transporte, IMT);* Ministry of Agriculture, Livestock, Rural Development, Fisheries and Food (*Secretaría de Agricultura, Ganadería, Desarrollo Rural, Pesca y Alimentación*, SENASICA); Ministry of Economy (*Secretaría de Economía*); Productivity Unit, Ministry of Finance and Public Credit (*Unidad de Productividad, Secretaría de Hacienda y Crédito Público*, SHCP).

Table of contents

Tables

Figures

Acronyms and abbreviation

AAR	Association of American Railroads
AEO	Authorized Economic Operator
AETR	European Agreement concerning the Work of Crews of Vehicles engaged in International Road Transport
AFAC	Federal Agency of Civil Aviation (*Agencia Federal de Aviación Civil*)
ANPACT	National Association of Buses, Trucks and Trailers of Mexico (*Asociación Nacional de Productores de Autobuses, Camiones y Tractocamiones, A.C*)
API	Integral Port Administration (*Administración Portuaria Integral*)
APMT	APM Terminals
ARTF	Railway Transport Regulatory Agency of Mexico (*Agencia Reguladora del Transporte Ferroviario*)
ASA	Airports and Auxiliary Services (*Aeropuertos y Servicios Auxiliares*)
ASUR	Southeast Airports (*Aeropuertos del Sureste*)
ATI	Anti-Trust Immunity
CANACAR	National Chamber for Road Freight Transport (*Cámara Nacional del Autotransporte de Carga*)
CETA	Comprehensive Economic and Trade
CFI	International Phytosanitary Certificate
CGPMM	Ports and Merchant Navy General Coordination (*Coordinación General de Puertos y Marina Mercante*)
C-TAPT	Customs-Trade Partnership Against Terrorism
COFECE	Federal Economic Competition Commission (*Comisión Federal de Competencia Económica*)
COFEMER	Federal Commission for Regulatory Improvement of Mexico (*Comisión Federal de Mejora Regulatoria*)
COH	Operation and Schedule Committee (*Comité de Operación y Horarios*)
SRGT	Continuing Survey of Road Goods Transport
DGAC	General Direction of Civil Aviation (*Dirección General de Aviación Civil*)

DGAF	General Direction of Federal Road Transport (*Dirección General de Autotransporte Federal*)
DGDFM	General Direction of Rail and Multimodal Development (*Dirección General de Desarrollo Ferroviario y Multimodal*)
DGTFM	General Direction of Rail and Multimodal Transport (*Dirección General de Transporte Ferroviario y Multimodal*)
DoJ	Department of Justice of the United States of America
DoT	Department of Transport of the United States of America
FAA	US Federal Aviation Administration
FMCSA	Federal Motor Carrier Safety Administration
FMVSS	Federal Motor Vehicle Safety Standards
FNM	National Railways of Mexico (*Ferrocarriles Nacionales de México*)
GATT	General Agreement on Tariffs and Trade
GACM	Airport Group of Mexico City (*Grupo Aeroportuario de la Ciudad de México*)
GAP	Pacific Airport Group (*Grupo Aeroportuario del Pacífico*)
GBP	Great Britain Pounds
GDP	Gross Domestic Product
HPH	Hutchison Port Holdings
IASGO	IATA Safety Audit for Ground Operations
IATA	International Air freight Transport Association
ICAO	International Civil Aviation Organization
ICTSI	International Container Terminal Services Inc.
IDB	Inter-American Development Bank
IMT	Mexican Transport Institute (*Instituto Mexicano del Transporte*)
INEGI	National Institute of Statistics and Geography (*Instituto Nacional de Estadística y Geografía*)
ITF	International Transport Forum
ITM	Mexican Infrastructure and Transports (*Infraestructura y Transportes México*)
ITOC	Integrated Targeting and Operations Centre of New Zealand
JOC	Journal of Commerce
KCSM	Kansas City Southern Mexico
LA	Law of Airports (*Ley de Aeropuertos*)
LAC	Law of Civil Aviation (*Ley de Aviación Civil*)

LCPAF	Federal Law on Roads, Bridges and Motorised Transport (*Ley de Caminos, Puentes y Autotransporte Federal*)
LFMN	Federal Law of Measurements and Technical Standards (*Ley Federal de Metrología y Normalización*)
LGBN	General Law of National Properties (*Ley General de Bienes Nacionales*)
LGCPQ	Federal Law to Control Chemicals Precursors, Essential Chemical Products and Machines to Elaborate Capsules, Pills and Tablets (*Ley Federal para el Control de Precursores Químicos, Productos Químicos Esenciales y Máquinas para Elaborar Capsulas, Tabletas y Comprimidos*)
LGPGR	General Law to Manage and Prevent Residuals (*Ley General para la Prevención y Gestión Integral de Residuos*)
LIE	Law of Foreign Investment (*Ley de Inversión Extranjera*)
LNCM	Law of Navigation and Maritime Commerce (*Ley de Navegación y Comercio Marítimo*)
LP	Law of Ports (*Ley de Puertos*)
LRSF	Law of Rail Service (*Ley Reglamentaria del Servicio Ferroviario*)
LRPV	Law of the Public Register of Vehicles (*Ley del Registro Público Vehicular*)
LSN	Law of National Security (*Ley de Seguridad Nacional*)
LVGC	Law of General Communication Routes (*Ley de Vías Generales de Comunicación*)
MAF	Ministry of Agriculture and Forestry of New Zealand
MRA	Mutual Recognition Agreement
MVSS	Motor Vehicle Safety Standards
NAFTA	North America Free Trade Agreement
NEEC	New Scheme of Certified Enterprises (*Nuevo Esquema de Empresas Certificadas*)
NOM	Mexican Official Standards (*Norma Oficial Mexicana*)
OE	Office of Economics of the STB
OECD	Organisation for Economic Co-operation and Development
OMA	Centre North Airport Group (*Grupo Aeroportuario Centro Norte*)
PASA	Pre-Authorization Safety Audit
PCS	Port Community Systems
PROFEPA	Federal Procurement of Environment Protection (*Procuraduría Federal de Protección al Ambiente*)
PSO	Public Service Obligations

RAB	Regulatory Asset Base
RLA	By-law of the Law of Airport (*Reglamento de la Ley de Aeropuertos*)
SAFE	Framework of Standards to Secure and Facilitate Trade
SAC	Stand Alone Cost
SAGARPA	Ministry of Agriculture, Livestock, Rural Development, Fisheries and Feeding (*Secretaría de Agricultura, Ganadería, Desarrollo Rural, Pesca y Alimentación*)
SENASICA	National Service of Sanity, Safety and Agro food Quality (*Servicio Nacional de Sanidad, Inocuidad y Calidad Agroalimentaria*)
SIIF	Phytosanitary Inspections Information System (*Sistema de Información de Inspecciones Fito zoosanitarias*)
SCT	Ministry of Communications and Transport of Mexico (*Secretaría de Comunicaciones y Transporte*)
SME	Small and Medium Enterprises
SPS	Sanitary and Phytosanitary
STB	US Surface Transportation Board
TEU	Twenty-foot Equivalent Unit
TRS	Time Release Study
ULSD	Ultra-Low-Sulphur Diesel Fuel
UNECE	Economic Commission for Europe
USD	United States' Dollars
VUCEM	Mexican Single Window (*Ventanilla Única de Comercio Exterior Mexicana*)
WCO	World Customs Organization
WSG	World Scheduling Guidelines
WTO	World Trade Organization

Executive summary

The *2012 OECD Recommendation of the Council on Regulatory Policy and Governance* states that OECD members should "Conduct systematic programme reviews of the stock of significant regulation against clearly defined policy goals, including consideration of costs and benefits, to ensure that regulations remain up to date, cost-justified, cost-effective and consistent and delivers the intended policy objectives". This report contributes to this objective by assessing regulation of freight transport in Mexico, and whether they represent obstacles in the pursuit of their underlying policy objectives. Therefore, other elements of governance, such as institutional design or integrity issues, are not part of the scope of this report.

Regulation of road transport in Mexico

Transport by road is the most important mode of transport in Mexico in terms of production, volume and employment. More than half of Mexico's international trade by value is carried by road, most of it across the border with the United States.

The most important regulatory instruments for road transport concern safety, weight and size dimensions, the import of used vehicles and emissions.

Fatigue is a factor in a significant proportion of road crashes. Almost all OECD countries regulate driving hours and rest times for commercial drivers, but there are no legal national limits on continuous driving times in Mexico.

Much of the sales of heavy vehicles in Mexico are in the form of used imported vehicles, particularly from the United States, that are often old and likely to be equipped to lower standards in terms of safety and emissions control technology.

Mexico has one of the poorest road safety records in OECD countries in terms of people killed and seriously injured per capita and per vehicle. Lack of resources for enforcement and inadequate co-ordination amongst agencies are a common feature in Mexico.

The regulation on weight and dimensions in Mexico was recently revised and updated. Changes to truck weight and dimension limits tend to be controversial across OECD countries, as there are strong views from stakeholder wielding opposite views.

Recommendations:

- increase the resources available for enforcement
- complete and adopt, as a matter of priority, regulation on hours of service
- introduce emissions standards in the regulation for imported second-hand vehicles
- base any change on the limits of weigh and dimension on empirical evidence that should allow for a cost-benefit analysis of the proposed changes.

Regulation of rail transport in Mexico

Demand for Mexico's railways has grown substantially since their privatisation in 1995, and productivity in the sector has also shown a marked increase. Rail services represent the main transportation mode for a number of sectors in Mexico; the automotive industry, in particular, is dependent on it for integrated production on either side of the US-Mexico border.

The current regulatory framework grants exclusive rights in the provision of rail freight transport services through concessions. Concessionaires need to negotiate compensation for interconnection services and access rights, but if they do not reach agreement after 90 days of negotiations, the Mexico's Ministry of Communications and Transport (SCT) can establish compensation and conditions of such services and trackage rights, but the basis on which terms should be established is unclear.

Prices for freight, passenger and auxiliary services are set freely, and the rail network was privatised to promote competition. However, a number of shippers have claimed that railway rates are too high. The government does not presently collect the data or conduct the analysis required to determine access conditions and tariffs, or where trackage rights are disputed.

Recommendations

- develop capacity to collect and analyse the data needed to form judgements on competition issues
- establish timelines for the development of analytical capacity for determining conditions for the use of trackage rights in cases where agreement is not reached voluntarily
- enhance efforts to gather and report available information in accessible formats to assess rail performance and evaluate possible public policy changes.

Regulation of air freight transport in Mexico

Demand for air freight is largely driven by the economic climate, and as a result, air freight transport in Mexico has grown broadly in line with both GDP and the number of passengers carried by airlines.

The Mexican air freight market is open to entry from national and foreign companies. Regulatory challenges facing by the air freight sector concern:

- Landing and take-off slot allocation at congested airports: In Mexico, auctioning, rather than rationing, is used to distribute slots. This approach is a major departure from the internationally recognised guidelines
- Transposition of international regulations into national one: in fields such as aviation the resources required to establish standards are so large that often these standards can only be developed by international co-operation Furthermore, some of the international standards for aviation stipulate an official language to be used
- Limits to market development imposed by restrictive air service agreements: Open skies agreements relax the controls on routes, frequencies of service and

size of aircraft operating services, which can produce strong economic benefits for tourism and trade, as well as reduced air fares.

Recommendations

- facilitate the implementation of auctions for primary slot allocation or replace the auction mechanism with international standards on airport slot allocation
- publish aviation standards immediately in their original language in the Official Gazette, with acknowledgement that they are legally binding until replaced by official translations
- consider the adoption of a policy that seeks open skies agreements with other nations, in order to accrue benefits in trade and tourism of expanded air service, and enable Mexican air carriers to enter into alliances with antitrust immunity.

Regulation of ports in Mexico

Mexico has 117 ports and terminals that handled 288 million tonnes of goods in 2013. Four ports are considered to be national hubs: Manzanillo, Lazaro Cardenas, Altamira and Veracruz.

The SCT has the legal authority to grant concessions, permits and authorisations for building, establishing, administrating, operating and exploiting works and goods in ports, maritime terminals and port installations.

Mexico suffers of lack of capacity of hinterland connections with ports; and road connections appear more developed than rail. Main bottlenecks in ports are linked to the release of cargo due to various controls and administrative procedures, which increase burdens for companies and restrict transport activity.

Recommendations

- develop an integrated logistics strategy for the main four Mexican ports to increase the volume of containers that could be carried on railroads
- increase port efficiency by: establish a dedicated area free of border controls for coastal shipping; introduce a specific regime to facilitate transhipment; expand opening hours of customs and other inspection agencies; simplify port gate operations.

Chapter 1

Regulation of road transport in Mexico

Transport by road is the most important mode of transport in Mexico in terms of production, volume and employment. More than half of Mexico's international trade by value is carried by road, most of it across the border with the United States. The most important regulatory instruments for road transport refer to a safety, weight and size dimensions, import of used vehicles and emissions. Road transport faces important challenges: the resources available for enforcement should be increased; the regulation in preparation to regulate hours of service should be completed and adopted as a matter of priority; emissions standards should be introduced in the regulation for imported second hand vehicles; and any change on the limits of weigh and dimension should be based on empirical evidence that should allow for a cost-benefit analysis of the proposed changes.

Overview of road transport in Mexico

Market organisation

Road transport in Mexico is extensively used by freighters and passengers, in contrast with air transport that focus on passengers, or rail that concentrates on freight. SME firms account for the majority of the business in road transport, but larger firms, however, own most of the units operating in the market. This segmentation impacts the competitiveness of the sector, because most of the SME firms have old trucks and in consequence old technology in their vehicles. In contrast, big firms have more new generation transport trucks. The difference between SME and big firms has made these groups of interest struggle to make regulation less harmful to them. An example of this is the modification of the NOM-012 of weights and dimensions of trucks. During the recent public consultancy process to modify it, there were arguments to increase the limits on weight and dimensions, as well as calls to introduce technology devices to increase efficiency. At the same time, there were arguments to limit dimensions and weight to avoid accidents. In any case, any regulation or standards such as the NOM-012 should be modified based on hard evidence.

Freight

The market of freight road transportation consists of SMEs and larger firms. In 2015, SMEs, which comprise owners with a fleet from one to one hundred trucks, accounted for 99.4% of the total firms in the sector and 72.4% of the total fleet. This implies that less than 0.6% of firms have 27.6% of the fleet—265 trucks by firm on average. In contrast, the micro firms, which comprises owners with a fleet from one to five trucks, also called *truck man* (*hombre camion*), accounted for 25.6% of the total fleet in Mexico (109.8 thousand firms with 206.4 thousand vehicles, so 1.8 trucks on average per firm, see Table 1.1.

Table 1.1. **National freight fleet by type of owner**

Type of firm	Units	Number of firms	%	Number of vehicles	%
Micro (*hombre camion*)	1 to 5	109 890	81.6	206 416	25.6
Small	6 to 30	21 389	15.9	245 066	30.4
Medium	31 to 100	2 610	1.9	132 571	16.4
Large	> 100	837	0.6	222 352	27.6
Total		**134 726**	**100**	**806 405**	**100**

Source: SCT (2015a), "Estadística Básica del Autotransporte Federal" (Basics Statistics of Federal Road Transport 2015), www.sct.gob.mx/transporte-y-medicina-preventiva/autotransporte-federal/estadistica/2015/ (accessed 9 November 2016).

The total fleet in Mexico in 2015 was about 806 405 vehicles, 85% of which are used for transporting general freight and the remaining 15% for specialised freight, such as dangerous materials, cars without rolling, funds and values, cranes, and large vehicles. However, 91% of the firms involved in transport focus on specialised freight and 9% on general freight. Around 51% of the total fleet in Mexico is categorised as driving units with an average age of 17.5 years; and 48% of the fleet is categorised as drag units with an average age of 17.1 years.

The state with the most freight operators (individuals and firms)[1] is Mexico City with 21% of the individuals and 22% of total firms, see Figure 1.1. The states with most individuals in road transport are Mexico City, Nuevo León, Jalisco, Estado de Mexico and Guanajuato, which account for 48.5% during 2015. In contrast, the states with a majority of firms are Nuevo Leon, Jalisco and Tamaulipas, which together with the Mexico City hold 48.2%. Firms have a larger participation in specialised transportation[2] compared to individuals; for instance 24.5% of the firms transported products under special conditions (5 228 of 21 337 versus 7% of the individual's share (9 299 of 135 377).

Figure 1.1. **Firms and individuals operating road transport freight by entity in 2015**

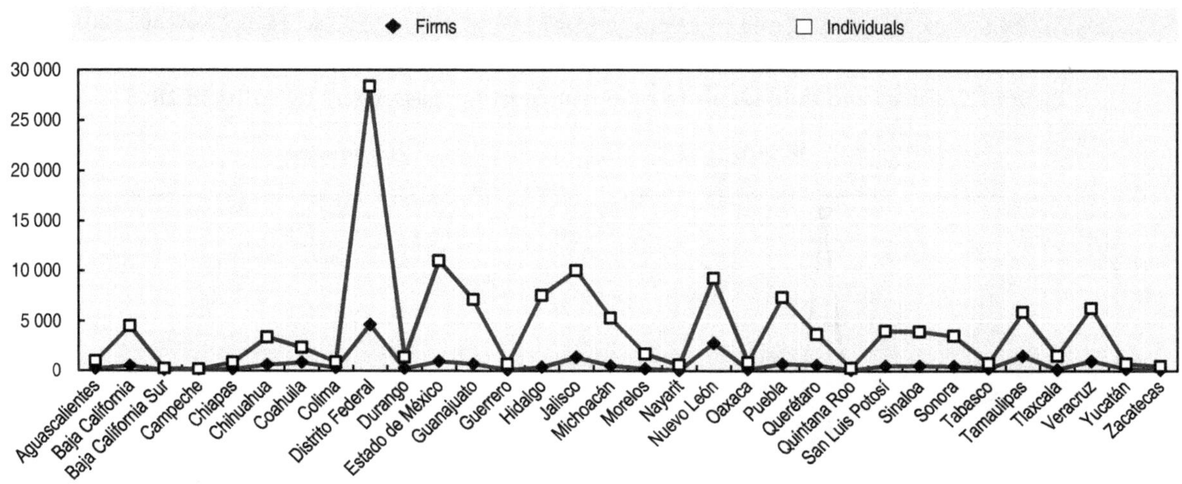

Source: SCT (2015a), "Estadística Básica del Autotransporte Federal 2015" (Basics Statistics of Federal Road Transport 2015), www.sct.gob.mx/transporte-y-medicina-preventiva/autotransporte-federal/estadistica/2015/ (accessed 9 November 2016).

Passengers

As in the case of air transport, road transport share infrastructure with passenger transportation. Thus, the road congestion and the quality of the infrastructure are affected by freight and passenger vehicles. The road transportation of passengers in Mexico meets a demand of around 3 million people with 48 287 registered vehicles in 2015—56% owned by 97 large firms which represented 3.6% of the total number of firms. On average, large firms owned 276 vehicles, see Table 1.2. In contrast, 44% of the fleet was owned by SMEs which represented 96.4% of the firms. The *truck man* had 6.4% of the fleet with an average of 1.5 vehicles *per head* and the small firms owned 14% with an average of 14 vehicles.

Approximately 61% of the total fleet is concentrated in six states: Distrito Federal, Jalisco, Guanajuato, Estado de México, Nuevo Leon and Veracruz. The most important of these is the Distrito Federal that concentrates 33% of the total, see Figure 1.2. The thirteen states with lower participation have less than 10% of the fleet— Morelos, Sonora, Aguascalientes, Quintana Roo, Baja California Sur, Yucatán, Chihuahua, Guerrero, Nayarit, Durango, Campeche, Zacatecas and Colima. Only 5% of the fleet is owned by individuals and 95% by firms and both are concentrated at 36% in the Distrito Federal, followed by Chiapas with 6%, Michoacán and Jalisco with 5% and Sinaloa and Coahuila with 4%.

Table 1.2. **National passenger fleet by type of owner**

Type	Units	Number of firms	%	Number of vehicles	%
Micro (*truck man*)	1 to 5	1 933	71.3	3 079	6.4
Small	6 to 30	475	17.5	6 765	14.0
Medium	31 to 100	207	7.6	11 614	24.1
Big	> 100	97	3.6	26 829	55.6
Total	2 712	2 712	100	48 287	100

Source: SCT (2015a), "Estadística Básica del Autotransporte Federal 2015" (Basics Statistics of Federal Road Transport 2015)., www.sct.gob.mx/transporte-y-medicina-preventiva/autotransporte-federal/estadistica/2015/ (accessed 9 November 2016).

Figure 1.2. **Firms and individuals in road transport for passengers by entity in 2015**

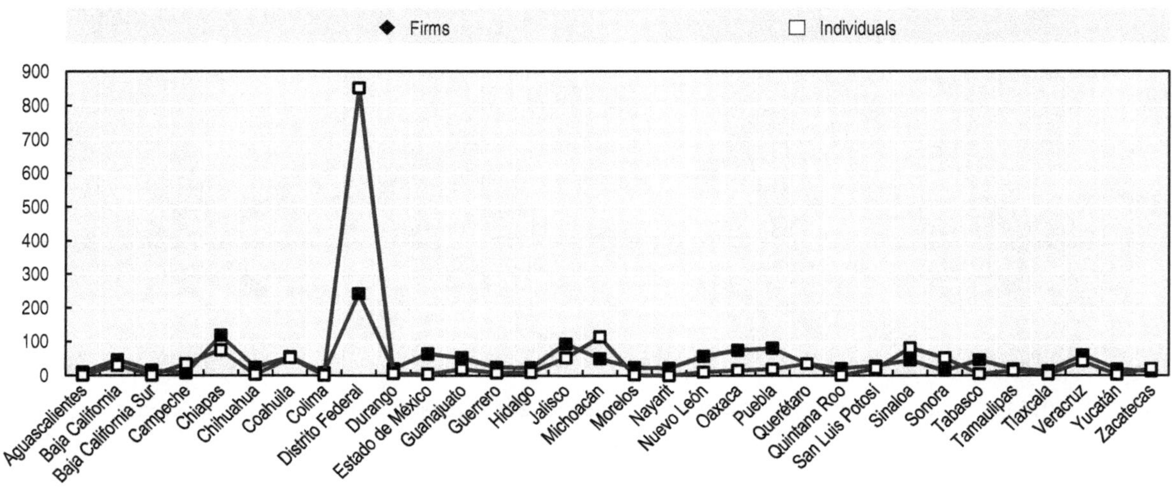

Source: SCT (2015a), "Estadística Básica del Autotransporte Federal 2015" (Basics Statistics of Federal Road Transport 2015), www.sct.gob.mx/transporte-y-medicina-preventiva/autotransporte-federal/estadistica/2015/ (accessed 9 November 2016).

Economic performance

Transport by road is the most important mode of transport in Mexico in terms of production, volume and employment – it generates approximately 2 million direct jobs.[3] In fact, it has had a steady economic growth since its deregulation, except in times of economic crises, for instance in early 2000's and 2008.

The average growth of the GDP of road transport in the period of 1995-2015 is 6.1%, the highest of all the transport modes as shown in Table 1.3. This growth pace has meant that road transported accounted for between 4.4 and 5.0% as a proportion of the GDP, in spite of the strong growth of the other modes of transport. This is possible because of the central role of the road transport for the Mexican economy.

Table 1.3. **GDP by mode of transport in Mexico, 2015**

Concept	GDP (MXN)	Share of total GDP	Average growth 1995-2015	Total growth 1995-2015
Total GDP	14 664 491.85		2.8%	78.6%
Tertiary sector	8 962 800.11	61.1%	3.1%	90.7%
Transport, mail and storage	852 321.87	5.8%	3.1%	84.0%
Air transport	30 391.34	0.2%	5.2%	189.4%
Rail transport	17 134.60	0.1%	3.9%	99.4%
Maritime transport	8 480.08	0.06%	2.1%	11.7%
Road transport	689 057.05	4.7%	6.1%	83.6%
Freight	420 099.12	2.9%	4.4%	128.1%
Passengers	268 957.93	1.8%	1.6%	40.8%

Source: National Institute of Statistics and Geography (INEGI), www.inegi.gob.mx (accessed 9 November 2016).

Freight

Freight road transport represents an important share of the value of the services sector, and the GDP as a whole, as shown in Table 1.3. While each the rest of the modes of transport represented less than 1% of the GDP of the country, freight transport by road accounted for 2.9% of the GDP of 2015. Its average growth rate from 1995 to 2015 was 4.4%, which is 1.6% higher than the total GDP of Mexico in the same year. Finally, the accumulated growth in the period studied was the fastest, with an increase of 128.1%, only after air transport.

In 2015, the total freight transported by road was 522 990 tonnes and 245.13 million of tonnes by kilometre. The average growth rate of tonnes transported by this mode was 2.2% from 1980 to 2015 (Figure 1.3). The total growth of road transport of freight measured in tonnes from 1995 to 2015 was 42.6% while the GDP growth was 128% for the same period. During that period of time, the increase in tonnes on this mode was slower than any other mode.

Figure 1.3. **Road transport freight in thousand tonnes in Mexico**

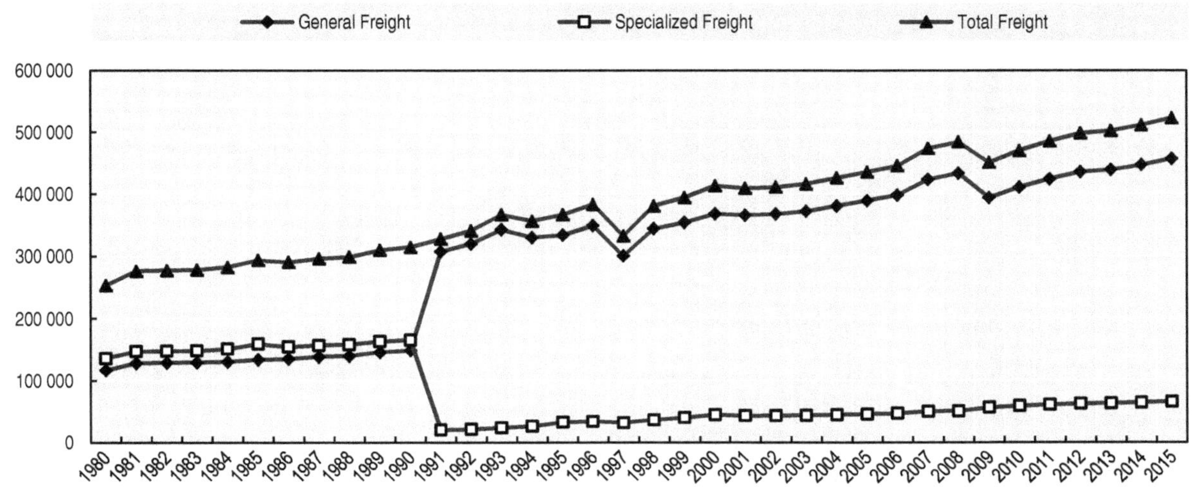

Source: SCT (2015a), "Estadística Básica del Autotransporte Federal 2015" (Basics Statistics of Federal Road Transport 2015), www.sct.gob.mx/transporte-y-medicina-preventiva/autotransporte-federal/estadistica/2015/ (accessed 9 November 2016).

Freight transport by road had two mayor falls, one in 1997 and the other in 2009 in which the tonnes transported decreased 13% and 7% respectively; in both cases after severe macroeconomic crises. Figure 1.3 also shows that road specialised freight transport dropped heavily in 1990, while the general freight service increased more or less in the same amount. This was the result of deregulation during the 90s, which eliminated some restrictions which differentiated specialised cargo from general service.[4]

Passengers

The economic value of road transport of passengers accounts for 31.6% of the sector's GDP, and 1.8% of the total of Mexican economy (Figure 1.4). The average growth of its GDP during the period of 1995-2015 was the lowest among the other modes of transport at 1.6%. Similarly, the total growth in the same period was slower than any other mode exempt maritime by 30%, with, a total growth of 40.8%.

Transport of passengers increased 1.67 times from 1980 to 2015 (Figure 1.4). Taking as a reference the period of 1995 and 2015, the average growth of passengers was approximately 1.0%. This rate however, is lower than the rate of the general and the transport subsector value added for the same period. Road transportation is the most frequent mode for passengers with almost 96.5% of the market in 2015. As in other cases the falls in growth of road transport were in 1997 and 2009 coinciding with national crisis.

Figure 1.4. **Evolution of passenger transportation in Mexico**

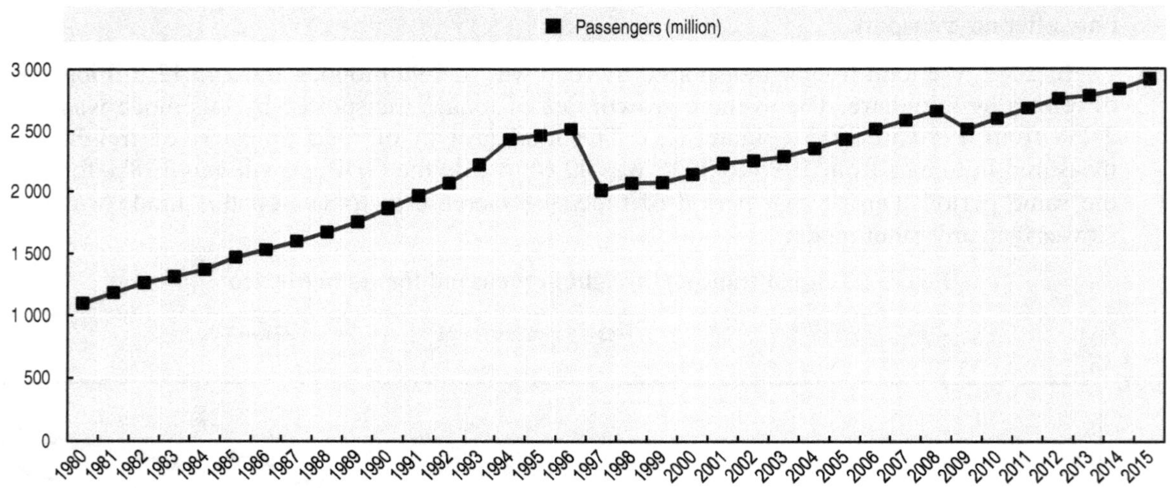

Source: SCT (2015a), "Estadística Básica del Autotransporte Federal 2015" (Basics Statistics of Federal Road Transport 2015), www.sct.gob.mx/transporte-y-medicina-preventiva/autotransporte-federal/estadistica/2015/ (accessed 9 November 2016).

International road freight transport

More than half of Mexico's international trade by value is carried by road (67% in 2015), most of it across the border with the United States. Figure 1.5 illustrates that the value of Mexican exports to the United States represent a big share of the total Mexican exports, which were 82% in 2015. In addition, over 85% of the exports to United States take place through roads, which makes this mode of transports vital for Mexican international trade. Figure 1.5 also shows the growth that international freight transport has had, reaching 48.7% during the period 2007-2015 and 54.7% specifically to the United States over the same period.

Figure 1.5. **Mexican total exports, exports to the United States, exports by road, and exports to the United States by road**

USD billion

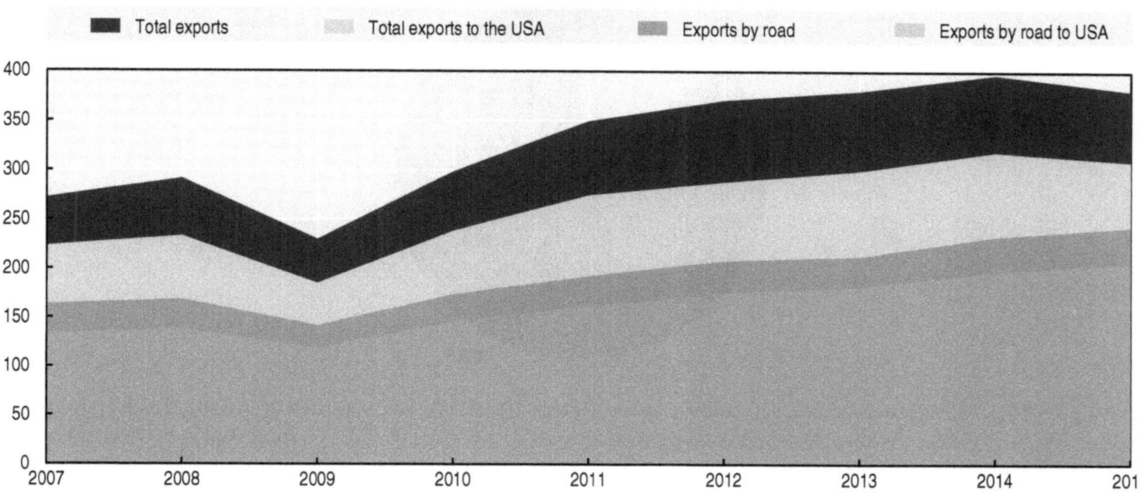

Source: Data extracted from the Economic Information Database of INEGI: www.inegi.org.mx/sistemas/bie/ (accessed 9 November 2016).

The United States is Mexico's largest trading partner, and the relationship is mutual as Mexico has been the United States' third largest trading partner from 2006 to date (Figure 1.6) and cross border traffic accounts for a large share of total road freight transport (Figure 1.7).

Figure 1.6. **Top three US trade partners**

USD billion 2015

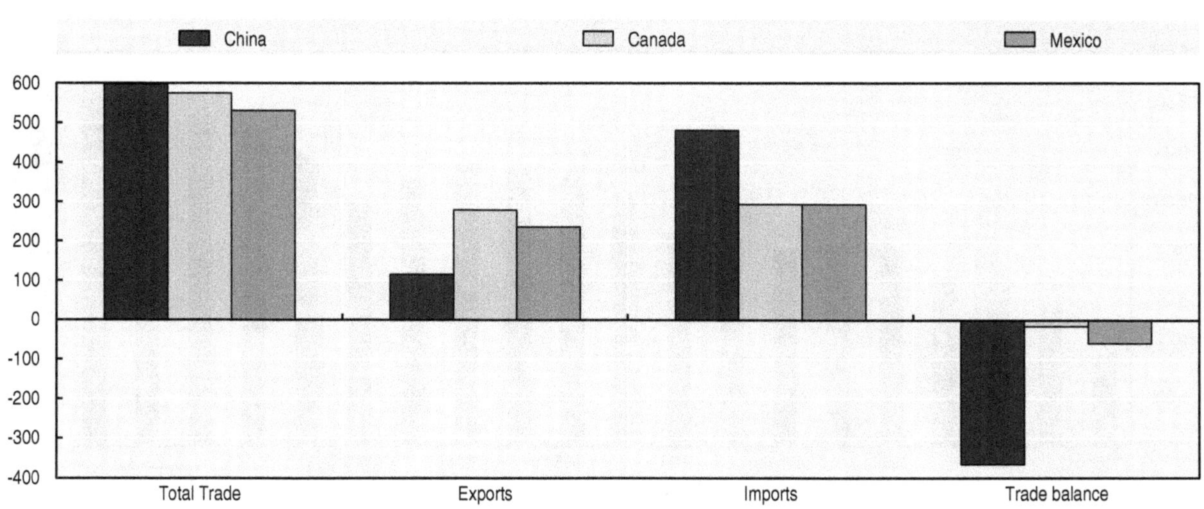

Source: U.S. Census Bureau, Foreign Trade, https://www.census.gov/foreign-trade/statistics/highlights/top/top1512yr.html (accessed 9 November 2016).

Figure 1.7. **Share of Mexico/US trade in total road freight haulage 2014**

Million tonnes

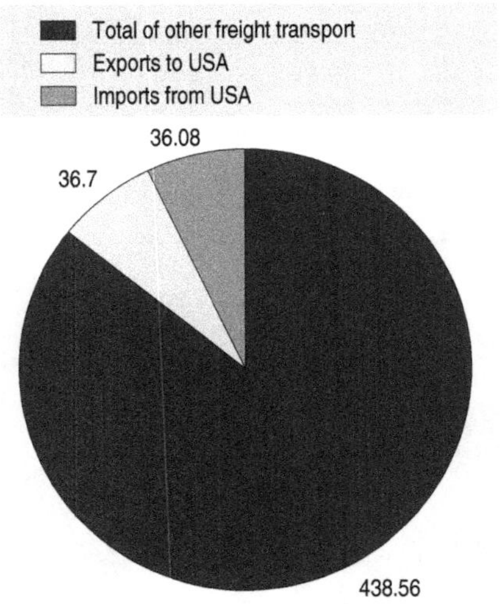

Source: SCT (2015a), "Estadística Básica del Autotransporte Federal 2015" (Basics Statistics of Federal Road Transport 2015), www.sct.gob.mx/transporte-y-medicina-preventiva/autotransporte-federal/estadistica/2015/ (accessed 9 November 2016). Statistics from IMT.

In terms of volume, the US imported from Mexico 37 106 thousand tonnes by road in 2015 (Figure 1.8). The volume of US imports from Mexico has had an average growth in the period 1996-2015 of 7.6% and a total growth of 287.8% in the same period. Moreover, US imports from Mexico (or Mexico's exports) accounted for 7.1% of the total freight volume transported by road in Mexico in 2015. Figure 1.9 shows a positive tendency, and there is still further opportunity to grow in terms of value and volume.

Figure 1.8. **US imports from Mexico and growth**

USD billion

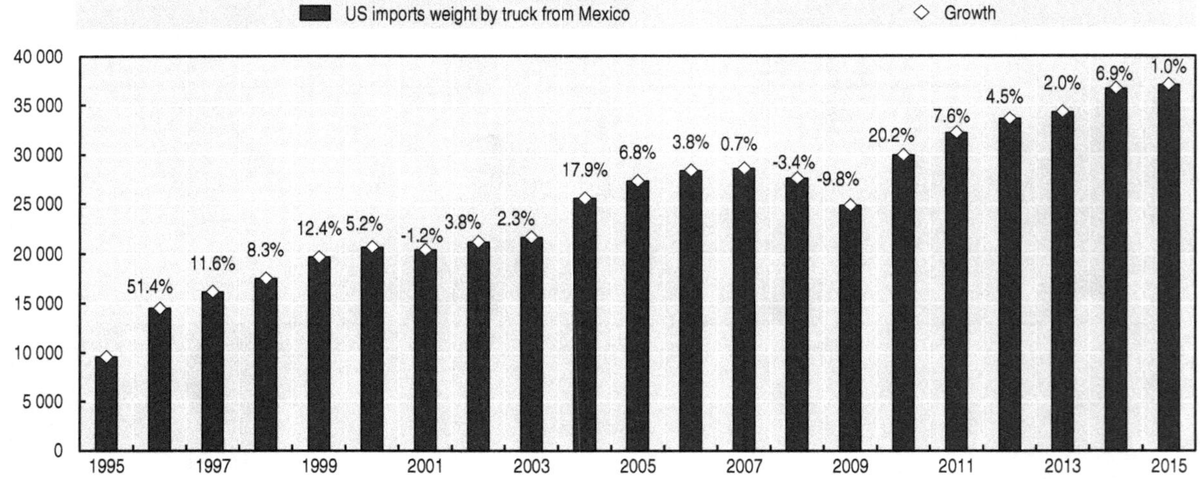

Source: U.S. Department of Transportation, Research and Innovative Technology Administration, Bureau of Transportation Statistics, TransBorder Freight Data.

Figure 1.9. **Share of the road transport of freight exported to the United States through trucks**

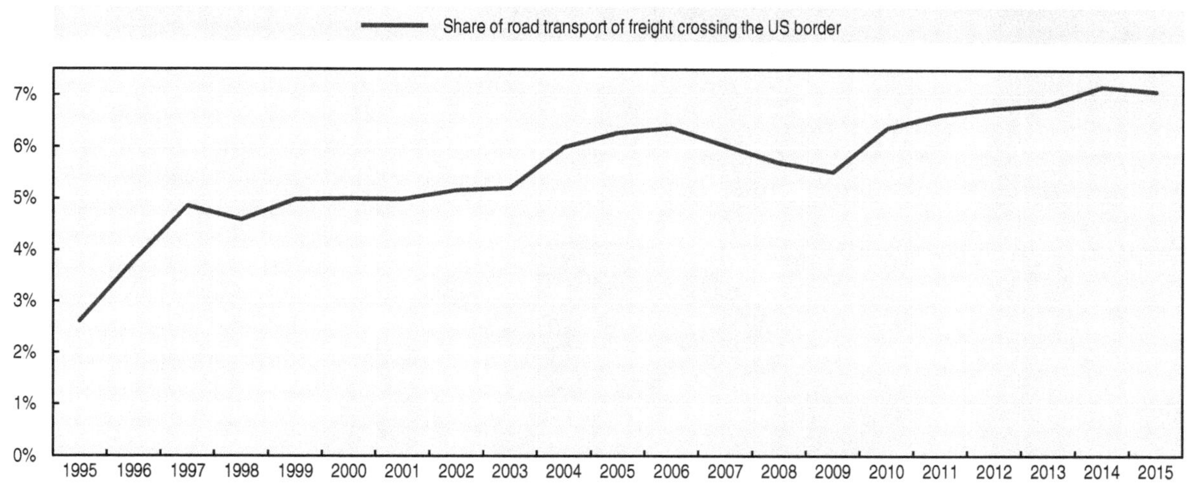

Source: US Department of Transportation, Research and Innovative Technology Administration, Bureau of Transportation Statistics, Trans-border Freight Data and Road statistics of the Ministry of Communications and Transport 2015 (SCT).

Until the US Bus Regulatory Reform Act of 1982, Mexican[5] and Canadian trucks could operate freely in the United States, provided they complied with US safety laws. The Act imposed a two-year moratorium on new authorisations for trucks registered in Canada and Mexico[6] and while the moratorium was soon lifted for Canada, the issue was not addressed with Mexico until the NAFTA negotiations in 1994. Under the Act, some Mexican trucks could receive OP-2 type registration[7] and were permitted to operate within specified commercial zones in the four U.S.-Mexico border states—Texas, California, New Mexico, and Arizona. These commercial zones generally extend from 3 to 20 miles from the border, reaching up to 75 miles. For haulage beyond a commercial zone, Mexican carriers were required to transfer loads to a U.S. truck for delivery to the final destination. Delays in delivery and added costs are associated with the transfer of goods. The Department of Transportation estimates that the requirement to off-load cargo adds USD 400 million in transportation and warehousing costs annually (Alexander and Soukup, 2010).

In 1995, the U.S. Congress passed the Interstate Commerce Commission Termination Act, which authorised the President to lift the moratorium on Mexican carrier movements beyond the commercial zones if removal was deemed consistent with the obligations of the United States under a trade agreement or with United States transportation policy. This gave the President flexibility to implement the trucking provisions under NAFTA, which entered into force on January 1, 1994. Discussions about the conditions and requirements to be imposed on Mexican trucks took several years. In 2002, rules for Mexican carries that operate in the US were published.[8] Mexican carriers must carry a certificate issued by the US transport authority (without such authorisation, Mexican trucks are limited to making deliveries to the designated commercial areas along the border); they are subject to intensive supervision in Mexico and the United States during the first 18 months after authorisation has been granted; they can only cross the border when a safety inspector is on duty; drivers have to go through alcohol and drug tests and are controlled for compliance with maximum working hours, and must be able to manage required data reporting and safety management systems; vehicles must be insured with a US registered company. Despite the restrictions, Mexico-U.S. border crossings now almost equal those between Canada and the United States (see Figure 1.10).

Figure 1.10. **NAFTA pilot programme: distribution of crossings by location as of 10 October 2014**

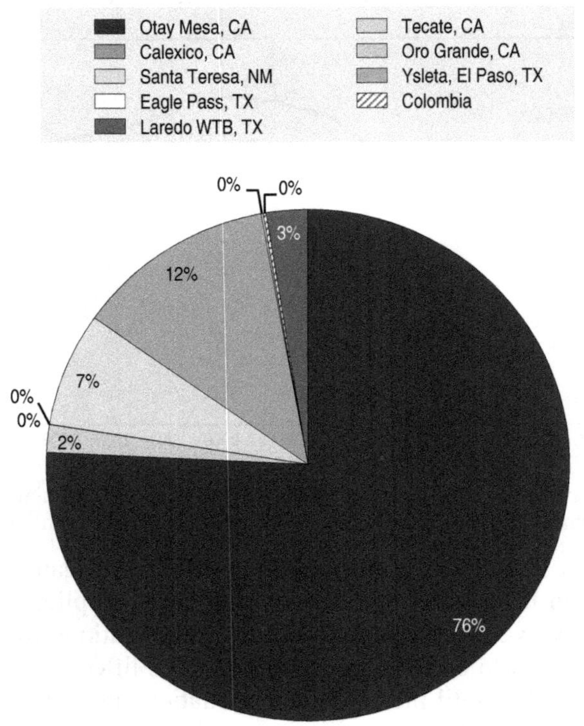

Source: US-Mexico Cross-Border Long-Haul Trucking Pilot Program Report FINAL January 2015, https://www.fmcsa.dot.gov/sites/fmcsa.dot.gov/files/docs/US-Mexico%20Cross-Border%20Long-Haul%20Trucking%20Pilot%20Program%20Report%20FINAL%20January%202015.pdf (accessed 10 November 2016).

A long-haul authorisation pilot programme began in September 2007 but was de-funded (effectively ended) by the US Congress in March 2009. Mexico continued to admit US companies registered in the trial to enter the country but imposed retaliatory tariffs (permitted under NAFTA and costing an estimated USD 2.4 billion to US exporters) on certain U.S. goods in response to the programme's termination.

A new three-year pilot programme to allow long-haul Mexican trucks into the United States began in April 2011 with the first Mexican truck crossing the border in October 2011. The Mexico-domiciled motor carriers that participated in the pilot programme were required to complete a pre-authorisation safety audit before being granted operating authorisation and were required to complete a compliance review.[9]

As of October 2014 when the pilot programme ended there were thirteen Mexico-domiciled carriers with long-haul operating authority,[10] two of these accounting for 90% of crossings, with three quarters of the crossings at Otay Mesa, the main border-crossing point near San Diego in California. Over 80% of the mileage of the Mexican trucks crossing the border is on roads in the border states, as shown in Figure 1.11. Despite fears of trucking unions in the United States that Mexican hauliers would undercut local carriers, few Mexican truck make longer journeys. Almost 90% of trips terminated in commercial zones along the border, only 4% reached non-border States. Joint ventures and sunk costs in logistics centres determine that many loads are passed to U.S. hauliers at points near the border; a pattern that might change over time with a fully open border, albeit gradually.

At the beginning of 2015 the pilot programme was replaced by an identical permanent system. The distribution of traffic and operators is evolving gradually and is currently similar to the situation in 2014.

FMCSA monitors the safety of Mexican trucks through road-side inspections. Twenty per cent of the border crossings were inspected in the three years of the pilot. The key safety indicator is "out-of-service" rates, which is the frequency of violations of standards severe enough to prevent a truck or driver from being allowed to continue a journey until the deficiency is addressed. In the United States, 20% of trucks that undergo a roadside inspection are taken out of service and about 5% of truck drivers have committed violations that prevent them from continuing their journeys. Based on 2013 data,[11] four of the Mexican carriers in the pilot had vehicle-out-of-service rates similar to that of US trucks, the remainder had much lower rates. The two Mexican carriers that accounted for most of the crossings (and 85% of the inspections) have *vehicle-out-of-service* rates of 10% and 13%.

Figure 1.11. **Sales of heavy vehicles 2009-2015 in Mexico**

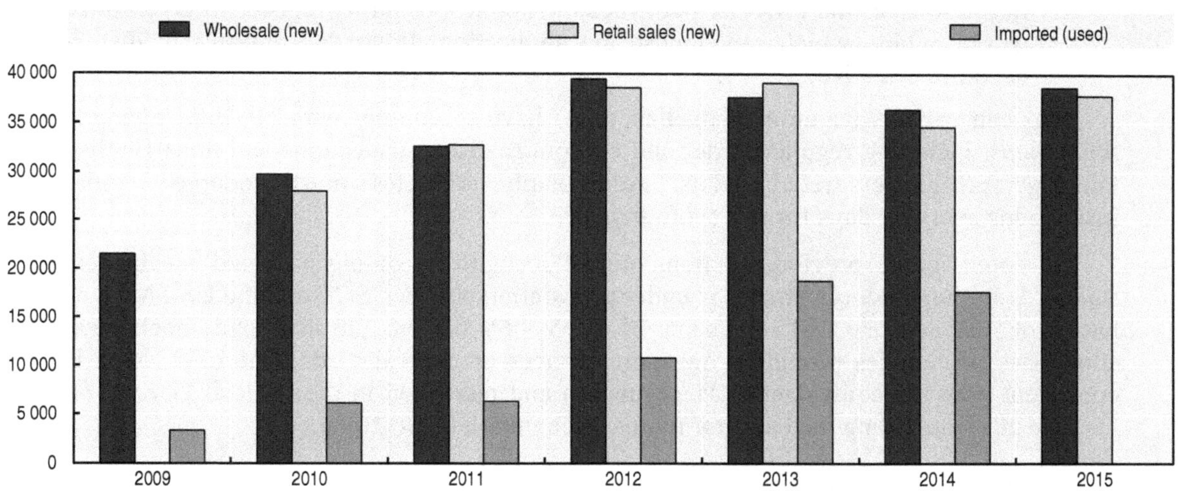

Note: No data was available for 2015 imports and 2009 retail sales at the time of writing.

Source: ANPACT (2015), "Boletín Estadístico Mensual" (Monthly Statistical Bulletin), www.anpact.com.mx/ (accessed 9 November 2016).

The *US Federal Motor Carrier Safety Administration* completed an assessment of the pilot programme for the *House and Senate Appropriations Committees* in January 2015.[12] The assessment was positive, as the statistics taken from the pilot programme confirmed that Mexican carriers have safety levels that were at least as good as US and Canadian carriers.[13] The FMCSA opened a register to receive requests from Mexican carriers for licences to operate on routes across borders on 15 January.[14] Carriers would be asked to go through an audit of their safety programmes in order to be granted this authorisation.

To facilitate cross-border transport, Mexico's DGAF and the US FMCSA are updating their 1991 *Memorandum of Understanding* on the equivalency of the Mexican Federal Driver's License (*Licencia Federal de Conductor*) and the US Commercial Driver's License, to mutually recognise procedures and results regarding issuance of licenses (Federal Register, 2011).

At present, the US Department of Transportation (DOT) is accepting applications from Mexico-domiciled motor carriers interested in conducting long-haul operations. The current process to get a long-haul operating authority and be able to transport international trade beyond the US-Mexico commercial zones the carrier consist in four phases:

1. In phase one, the applicant must submit a non-refundable fee of 300 USD and send to FMCSA the filled forms: the application for a *US DOT number*; the application for *Long-Haul Operating Authority* and the *Designation of Agents for Service of Process* and pay.
2. In phase two the FMCSA confirms that the application is complete, and conducts a Pre-Authorisation Safety Audit (PASA) to confirm that the applicant has safety management systems in place to be able to comply with Federal Motor Carrier Safety Regulations, for instance the Controlled Substances and Alcohol testing.
3. Phase three begins after complying with the PASA, when the carrier must file a proof of financial responsibility.
4. In phase four, the FMCSA publishes the application in its register to give notice to the public, which can oppose the application. If no one opposes it, then it becomes effective.

Mexican carriers (same as Canadian ones) have to comply with all U.S. laws and regulations, including regular border and random roadside inspections and meet English language proficiency requirements. Additionally, vehicles must undergo regular inspections every 90 days for at least four years.

As noted in the previous section, mutual recognition of physical and mechanical standards for heavy-duty vehicles is under preparation between SCT and the US FMCSA, based on the January 2015 revision of NOM-068 on the physical and mechanical conditions of vehicles providing transport services on federal roads. The new NOM is consistent with the equivalent DOT regulation and published in the Official Gazette on 15 June 2015 providing the basis for mutual recognition (CFR, 2011).

Production and imports of heavy vehicles

Eleven commercial vehicle manufacturers had production facilities in Mexico in 2014,[15] placing it as the 7th producer of heavy vehicles worldwide. These firms manufactured 190 978 heavy vehicles in 2015, nearly 157 000 of which were exported—87% —to the United States (INEGI, 2015). However, nationally heavy vehicle sales were just over 76 000 in the same year, which represents a 6.2% growth of wholesales and 9.3% in retail sales (Figure 1.12).

Much of the sales of heavy vehicles in Mexico are in the form of used imported vehicles, particularly from the US, due to Mexico's regulatory framework allowing the import of heavy vehicles through the NAFTA agreement. Figure 1.11 illustrates the imports of used heavy vehicles, where 63 076 units entered the Mexican territory during the period from 2009 to 2014.

The main characteristic of heavy the vehicles entering the Mexican market is their age. The vehicles imported during this timeframe have an average age of 16.1 years, and 77% of them are more than 10 years old. Only 12 vehicles imported were less than 5 years old. Figure 1.13 highlights the range of age of these units. This has a significant impact from a safety and environmental perspectives, which will be discussed in the next sections.

Figure 1.12. **Age of imported used heavy vehicles for the period 2009-2014 in Mexico**

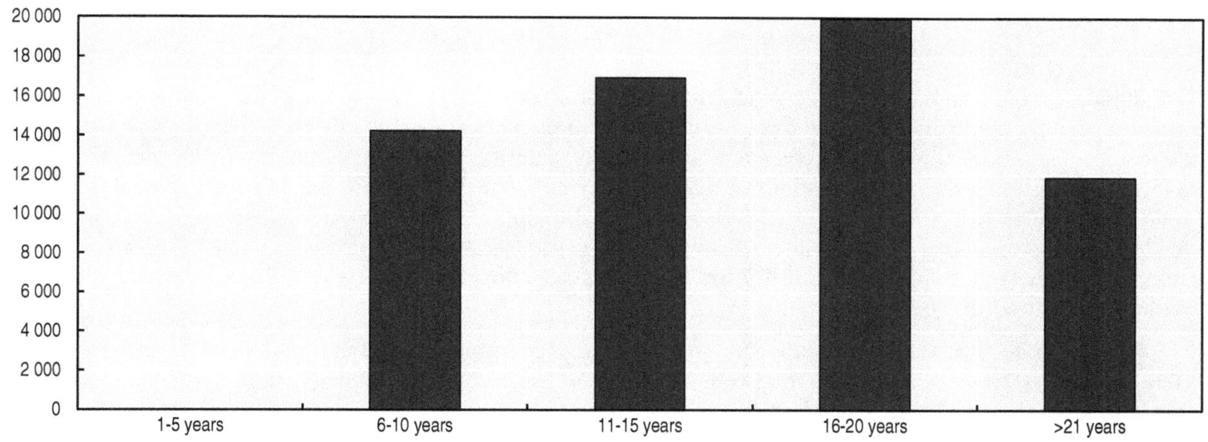

Source: ANPACT (2015), "Boletín Estadístico Mensual" (Monthly Statistical Bulletin), www.anpact.com.mx/ (accessed 9 November 2016).

In the import of used heavy vehicles from the United States, the units should comply with the physical-mechanical conditions and safety and environmental regulations that any other national vehicle does. To achieve this, the entry of units to the territory should be conditional to the minimum standards stated in the NOMs, and to a maximum age of 6 years, which is the age that the scrappage and renewal programme allows.

General regulatory framework

National context

Commercial freight transport was deregulated between 1989 and 1993,[16] when a market-oriented approach replaced the restrictive system of licencing operators as providers of public services. The deregulation was supplemented with restrictions on market entry to ensure safety standards and financial security.

Many firms entered the market after 1990 and within five years, road transport prices had dropped by 23% in real terms (see Box 1.1). Vigorous intervention by the competition authority (COFECO) following deregulation has largely eliminated behaviour which tended to be anticompetitive (Dutz, Hayri and Ibarra, 2000).

Box 1.1. **The Mexican road freight industry: the World Bank case study on competition and prices**

"Prices fall overall, but fastest in lower quality-of-service segments". Rate analysts in SCT found that between 1987 and 1994 trucking rates nationwide declined 23% in real terms. One official in SCT estimated that general cargo trucking cargo rates in 1994 on the major route between Laredo and Mexico City were about 30% lower in real terms than the prevailing rates in 1987. Another study concluded that while there is only incidental and anecdotal evidence on changes in truck tariffs, all the evidence points to reduction of the order of 25% in real terms. The substantial reduction in overall tariff levels documented in available nationwide studies is corroborated by survey results. Almost all downstream users of trucking services interviewed reported that the cost of hiring a truck had fallen in real terms since 1989.

Box 1.1. **The Mexican road freight industry: the World Bank case study on competition and prices** (*cont.*)

Estimates of the size of the decline generally ranged between 5 and 15%. More careful probing of additional exogenous factors confirms that there have been significant declines in real prices of a given service delivered, though the magnitude of the price change is difficult to quantify given the variations in the actual service provided. For instance, one shipper estimated that an additional 20% price fall for the originally available service should be attributed to the higher quality levels now available, including newer trucks, faster delivery, and more reliable shipping facilitated by more sophisticated tracking systems. Another shipper estimated that the price fall would have been even more substantial if it did not incorporate the effect of new toll roads, which he estimated added 6% to the cost of a typical trip.

Regarding rate structure, there appears to have been an important differentiation of prices to reflect differentiation of services provided to distinct classes of users. Customers who ship high value-to-weight components where timeliness and reliability of delivery are critical are willing to pay substantially more for higher quality service. For such shippers, the logistics cost generally represents less than 10% of the product price. These services are generally provided by the larger, more sophisticated carriers. These prices do not appear to have come down as much, no doubt reflecting the increased quality elements embedded in the price and the relatively less intensive competition prevalent between the larger, technologically most sophisticated trucking fleets. On the other hand, customers who ship high volume, high weight products where the logistics cost is substantial generally seek to minimise transportation costs. These lower quality services tend to be provided relatively more by the small owner-operators. These are the prices that have come down most substantially.

Source: Dutz, M., A. Hayri and P. Ibarra (2000), "Regulatory Reform, Competition, and Innovation: A Case Study of the Mexican national competition agency Road Freight Industry", *World Bank Policy Research Paper 2318*, www-wds.worldbank.org/external/default/wdscontentserver/iw3p/ib/2000/05/25/000094946_00050505302442/rendered/pdf/multi_page.pdf, p. 21.

The regulator of road transportation is the SCT, through the General Direction of Federal Road Transport (DGAF). The legal framework consists mainly of the following regulations:

- Federal Law on Roads, Bridges and Motorized Transport (*Ley Federal de Caminos, Puentes y Autotransporte Federal*, LCPAF)
- Law of General Communication Routes (*Ley General de Vías de Comunicación*, LGVC)
- Law of Public-Private Associations (*Ley de Asociaciones Público Privadas*, LAPP)
- Federal Law to Control Chemicals Precursors, Essential Chemical Products and Machines to Elaborate Capsules, Pills and Tablets (*Ley Federal para el Control de Precursores Químicos, Productos Químicos Escenciales y Máquinas para Elaborar Capsulas, Tabletas y Comprimidos*, LGCPQ).

Some of these laws are supported by specific by-laws (*reglamentos*) and NOMs. The most important NOMs are related to road transport and auxiliary services, safety, dangerous materials, package and weight and dimensions. The NOM-012-SCT-2 for instance, sets limits in dimensions and weights for freight trucks allowed to circulate in Mexican roads. A draft to amend this technical regulation was published in the official federal gazette of Mexico (DOF) on June 11, 2014 and it replaced the NOM-012-SCT-2-2008 of 13 January 2014. The modification of this NOM was prompted by allegations by some stakeholders that double-articulated trucks increase road accidents and impose more damage to the road. The most important changes of the amendment were:

1. Articulated trailers must include devices to increase safety
2. Elimination of the obligation for buses, trucks (type "C") and articulated trucks (type "R") to comply with technical requirements to be allowed to use national roads, such as security devices and pneumatic suspension
3. Reduction from 150 to 50 kilometres of the limit to connect between high-specific roads and B type roads (low-specific roads) with permission
4. Reduction of the maximum weight from 80 to 75.5 tons.

One of the most important changes in the NOM-012-SCT-2-2014 was the reduction in the connectivity permission from 150 to 50 kilometres for low specification roads. This change should be evaluated *ex post* in terms of the effects on economic performance of the transport industry, as it should be assessed whether these changes made the transport of goods by road more expensive vis-à-vis.

Supporting the NOM, the Article 8 of the by-law on Weight, Dimension, and Capacity of the Road Transport Vehicles that can circulate in Roads and Bridges with Federal Jurisdiction (RPDC) states that the SCT will monitor, verify and control that road transport vehicles, auxiliary services and private transport comply with the regulation. The verification and inspection of weight and dimensions is done in fixed verification centres or through verification units approved by the Federal Law of Measurements and Technical Standards (*Ley Federal de Metrología y Normalización*, LFMN). While the SCT has the faculty to conduct measurements in the verifications centres the Federal Police may conduct them while the trucks are circulating federal highways.

Prior to the preparation of the draft amendment of the NOM-012-SCT-2-2008 the SCT set up a panel of eight independent experts to review and assess the impact of regulation on measurement and weight in road transportation. This panel was formed by transport experts, academics and researchers, amongst others. Some of main findings and recommendations are shown in Table 1.4.

Similarly, the NOM-068 "establishes the physical and mechanical specifications of vehicles to ensure safe transit on roads and of other users of these (…)". The standard also explains the process of verification of the vehicles, and the aspects that they need to comply with in order to acquire the authorisation to circulate in federal roads. Enforcement inspections are also considered in the standard. NOM-068 was revised in 2014 and the new NOM-068-2-SCT-2014 is now consistent with the equivalent U.S. Department of Transport regulation. It entered into force on 18 May 2015 providing the basis for mutual recognition between Mexico and the United States.

Another important feature of the regulatory framework of road transport is the formality to import used trucks from the United States under the North America Free Trade Agreement (NAFTA)—which has the objective to regulate the import of used vehicles. In July 1st, 2011 the Ministry of Economy published in the official gazette, the Decree in which the import of used vehicles in Mexico is regulated (Import used Vehicles Decree (DOF, 2011). In Article 6, the decree states that vehicles cannot be imported when their circulation in the origin country is restricted or prohibited due to its characteristics or technical conditions or when the vehicle does not comply with the physical-mechanical or environment protection conditions established in relevant regulations, such as the NOM-068 and the Agreement in which the environmental conditions to import heavy vehicles are established[17]—which allows the importation of heavy vehicles with engines produced from 2004 onwards, among others.

Table 1.4. **Main expert panel findings and recommendations about NOM-012 on weight and dimensions**

Findings	Recommendations
There is no evidence that accidents in road transport are related to the double trailers.	• Maintain the limits of 66.5 tonnes for fulles (double trailers) and exceptionally allow 75.5 tonnes under the condition of compliance with technical requirements and speed limits • Develop statistics about the sector for at least three years. • Driver's permits should be valid for two years except in the cases of fulles that transport dangerous material, in which case it should last for one year. • Promote the use of new technology in trailers to guarantee safety. • The SCT should promote rail transport, mainly for dangerous materials and prohibit transport via road. • The truck fleet has to be renewed in order to improve performance, but financial help should be provided.
There is no specific regulation concerning workdays in road transport. There is a draft NOM regarding fatigue for drivers but it is still in draft form.	• Explore with the Ministry of Labour and Social Prevision (STPS) the possibility to establish regulation on maximum working hours for drivers. • Regulate time schedules.
The general Direction of Road Transport is not a strong regulator.	• Enhance the regulator and make it more independent from the federal government.
There is a lack of information about the vehicle fleet in the country. The SCT is about to change the license plates of all trucks.	• Link the license plate with the truck.
Training of drivers is not a standard practice.	• Set up training programmes.
Connectivity is not adequate.	• Roads have to be reclassified in order to develop a current map of truck permission through roads and establish schedule circulations flows.

Source: Responses by the Ministry of Communications and Transport (SCT) to the OECD questionnaire.

The Decree has been updated four times, and is in force until December 2016. The National Association of Producers of Motor Coaches and Trucks (ANPACT) has raised concerns on this decree, arguing that it results in older trucks on the road, with a reduced mechanical quality, thus decreasing safety in roads.

There are gaps in the regulation of heavy road freight transport, most notably in the absence of driving and rest time regulation to avoid fatigue. A number of regulations are currently under amendment providing opportunities to improve the regulation and efficiency of the sector. This opportunity area will be explained further in the *Safety* section.

Federal regulations apply to federal highways and vehicles using federal highways. State regulations apply on state roads and to vehicles using only state roads. Regulations vary between states although Federal regulations generally function as a model for State laws. A deep revision of state regulation would be object of a specific study due to its size and variation among the country.

International framework: recognition of technical inspections

Standardised requirements to which the components of road vehicles should conform are established by the UNECE "Agreement Concerning the Adoption of Uniform Technical Prescriptions for Wheeled Vehicles, Equipment and Parts…"[18] issued on 20 March 1958. Over the years the agreement has had 134 regulations annexed to it, with two additional regulations entering into force in the middle of 2015. The agreement provides equal safety and environmental requirements in the 51 Contracting Parties to the 1958 Agreement, including 41 UNECE countries, as well as the European Union, Japan, Australia, South Africa, New Zealand, the Republic of Korea, Malaysia, Thailand, Tunisia and Egypt.

The UNECE "Agreement concerning the Establishing of Global Technical Regulations for Wheeled Vehicles, Equipment and Parts…",[19] issued on 13 November 1998, and the Agreement concerning the Adoption of Uniform Conditions for Periodical Technical Inspections of Wheeled Vehicles and the Reciprocal Recognition of such Inspections, issued on 13 November 1997, provide governments with a legal framework for adoption of global technical regulations and for carrying out technical inspections of vehicles in use, and for the reciprocal recognition of the certificates of such inspections.

European Union

In the European Union the minimum common rules for periodical technical inspections of vehicles are set out in Directive 2014/45/EU (previously 2009/40/EC) on periodic roadworthiness tests for motor vehicles and their trailers. The rules for the technical roadside inspection of the roadworthiness of commercial vehicles are established in the Directive 2014/47/EU (repeals 2000/30/EC). At the time of writing the previous directives are in force because the directives of the EU have to be transposed in the national law and this takes time. The new directives came into force on 20 May 2014 and transposition has to happen before 20 June 2018.

The directives require that passenger cars and light commercial vehicles (M1 and N1 type vehicles) will be tested four years after their first registration date, and every two years thereafter. M1-category vehicles used as taxis or ambulances; buses and coaches (M2, M3); heavier commercial vehicles (N2, N3); and heavy trailers (O3, O4) must be checked one year after their first registration date and subsequently each year. Member states may choose to conduct additional roadworthiness tests, and in practice many member countries apply more stringent schedules. Additionally, between periodic inspections, roadside checks can be carried out for commercial vehicles.

Directive 2014/45/EU also sets the minimum technical requirements for testing centres equipment and skill levels for the inspectors who carry out the tests. The testing itself is required to consider impact on the environment as well as safety aspects of the vehicles. Defects are assessed in accordance with common rules and severity ratings.

United States and Canada

The United States and Canada are countries that do not recognise the standards of the 1958 UNECE Agreement. This means that the agreement-compliant vehicles are not authorised for import, sale or use on the territories of those countries. In order for a vehicle to be compliant for use in the US and Canada, it has to be tested to prove it meets domestic regulation. The United States and Canada have signed the 1998 Agreement, but there are no provisions in place for mutual recognition or approvals.

Federal Motor Vehicle Safety Standards (FMVSS) regulate technical characteristics of road vehicles in the United States. Currently the US does not recognise UNECE standards for vehicles on its territory. Ways to narrow the regulatory differences between US and EU are being sought as part of the Transatlantic Trade and Investment Partnership (TTIP) negotiations.

In Canada the Motor Vehicle Safety Standards (MVSS) are similar to the standards of the United States. Canada works closely with the US to align its standards. Contrary to the US, Canada also accepts parts of the UNECE main standards as allowable alternatives (14 articles of 17). It is expected that Canada could recognise all UNECE standards under the Comprehensive Economic and Trade Agreement (CETA) in negotiation between Canada and the European Union. This would come into effect in 2016 at the earliest.

Also to facilitate cross-border transport, mutual recognition of physical and mechanical standards for heavy-duty vehicles is under preparation between SCT and the US FMCSA. This will be based on the new NOM-068-STC-2-2014 on physical and mechanical conditions of vehicles providing transport services on federal roads, published in January 2015.

Safety

Working hours and conditions: regulation of driving time

Fatigue is a factor in a significant proportion of road crashes. Almost all OECD countries therefore regulate driving hours and rest times for commercial drivers with specific legislation. The exceptions are Mexico and Korea, where only general labour regulations apply. In Mexico, drivers are required to keep a log of driving times, but there are no legal national limits on continuous driving times. Under the Federal Law of Labour, Article 257, drivers can be hired by the hour, by kilometre or by trip. Guidelines have been issued (for instance, by the Mexican Institute of Transport) recommending drive-time is kept to 8 hours a day (or night) as is the case for standard labour conditions, but this is not an enforceable limit. The National Advisory Committee for Surface Transport Norms (*Comite Consultivo Nacional de Normalización del Transporte Terrestre*) established a sub-committee in December 2014 to analyse the issue with a view to issuing a NOM on driving and rest times. In this context, Mexico should complete this effort and set it as priority next regulatory step.

Therefore, it is strongly recommended that regulation of fatigue and hours of service be given priority in the regulatory agenda. It will make control of driving times possible, with assured benefits for road safety, although it will not solve all problems related to fatigue, or drug abuse to cope with fatigue. Long waiting times at borders and ports, for example, contribute to fatigue but may escape regulation through legislation on services hours. Issues with the effectiveness of hours of service regulations are common to all jurisdictions, but regulations are the essential starting point for managing fatigue. Regulations usually distinguish between non-driving working time, for example completing paper work and waiting at depots, terminals and borders and true rest time.

European Union regulations

In the European Union the maximum daily and fortnightly driving times and minimum rest periods for drivers of road haulage and passenger transport vehicles is set out in regulation (EC) No 561/2006. The regulation applies to national and international passenger transport and road haulage operations. The aim of the regulation is to establish common conditions for competition in road haulage and passenger carriage markets to avoid distortion of competition, whilst safeguarding road safety and reasonable working conditions for drivers.

Regulation (EC) No. 561/2006 establishes a maximum daily driving time of 9 hours, which can be extended twice per week to 10 hours, a daily rest period of at least 11 hours, and breaks of at least 45 minutes after 4.5 hours of driving.

Table 1.5. **List of national exceptions in regulation on safety in transport in the European Union**

	Austria	**Belgium**	**Bulgaria**	**Croatia**	**Cyprus**	**Czech Republic**	**Denmark**	**Estonia**	**France**	**Germany**	**Hungary**	**Ireland**	**Italy**	**Latvia**	**Lithuania**	**Luxembourg**	**Malta**	**Netherlands**	**Poland**	**Portugal**	**Romania**	**Slovakia**	**Slovenia**	**Spain**	**Sweden**	**United Kingdom**
13.1 a: non-competing public authorities	x	x		x	x	x	x		x	x	x	x		x	x			x	x		x	x	x	x		xg
13.1 b: agricultural etc. own activity < 100 km	x	x	x	x	x	x	x	xj	xp	x	x	x		x	x			x	x	x	x	x	xm	xa	x	xh
13.1 c: agricultural/forestry tractors < 100 km	x	x	x	x	x	x	x	x	x	x	x	x		x	x	x			x	x	x	x	xm	x	x	x
13.1 d: <7.5 tonnes universal services < 50 km		x	x	x	x	x	x		x	x	x	x	x	x	x	x		x	x	x	x	x	x	x		xi
13.1 d: <7.5 tons for driver's use for work < 50 km	xz	x		x	x	x	x	x	x	x	x	x		x	x	x		x	x	x	x	x	x	x	x	x
13.1 e: operating on islands < 2300 square km				x	x	x	x		xq	x		x					x		x	x				xb	x	x
13.1 f: <7.5 t< 50 km gas/electricity				x	x	x	x	x	x	x	x	x			x	x			x	x		x	x	x		x
13.1 g: instruction/examination dr.license/CPC		x		x		x	x	x		x		x	xw	x	x	xy		x	x	x		x	x	x	x	x
13.1 h: sewerage/flood protection/water etc.	xu	x	x	x	x	x	x	x	xr	x	x	x	x	x	x	xk		x	x	x	x	x	x		x	x
13.1 i: non-comm.pass.transp. Betw. 10-17 seats	x	x		x	x	x	x	xc	xs	x	x	x		x	x				x	x		x			x	x
13.1 j: circus/funfair	x	x	x	x	x	x	x	x	x	x	x	x	x	x	x	x		x	x	x		x	x	xd	x	x
13.1 k: mobile projects for education	x	x		x	x	x	x		x	x	x	x		x	x			x	x	x	x	x	x	x		x
13.1 l: milk/animal feed from/to farms	xn	x		x	x	x	x	xk	xt	x	x	x	x	xk	xk	x		x	x	x		x	x	xe	x	x
13.1 m: transporting money/valuables	xn	x	x	x	x	x	x		x	x	x	xv		x	x			x	x	x	x	x	x	x		
13.1 n: animal waste or carcasses		x		x	x	x	x	x	x	xo	x	x		x	x			x	x	x	x	x	x		x	x
13.1 o: hub facilities	x	x	x	x	x	x	x		x	x	x	x		x	x			x	x	x		x	x	x		x
13.1 p: live animals farms -> markets v.v. < 50 km	x	x		x	x	x	x	x	x	x	x	x		x	x			x	x	x	x	x	x	x	x	x

Table 1.5. **List of national exceptions in regulation on safety in transport in the European Union** (*cont.*)

Note: "x" states an exception. The letter besides the x refers to the following:

a: additional restriction: agriculture etc. own activity within a range < 50 km.
b: additional restriction: operating on islands < 1500 square km
h: A vehicle which is being used by a fishery undertaking does not fall within the description specified unless the vehicle is being used: (a) to carry live fish, or (b) to carry a catch of fish from the place of landing to a place where it is to be processed
j: within a radius of 50 km of the place where the vehicle is usually based, including towns within this area
k: as of 1/01/2008 Estonia, Latvia and Lithuania will mutually apply the exception from Articles 5 to 9 to vehicles used for milk collection from farms etc., only in cases where the service radius does not exceed 100 km
m: within a radius of up to 50 km
n: derogation concerns only obligatory breaks (Article 7 of the Regulation); Articles 5,6,8 and 9 remain applicable for these two types of vehicles
u: vehicles used by municipal highways departments and driven by regional or municipal employees are fully exempt; vehicles used by highways departments for winter maintenance purposes are exempt from Article 7 on breaks, unless the vehicle is covered by the previous exception; drivers of vehicles used by competent authorities for the disposal of domestic waste are exempt only from Article 7 on breaks; drivers of other vehicles under this para are exempt provided that driving is not their main activity
r: for door-to-door household refuse collection and disposal, only within a radius of 100 km
s: not for the transport of children
t: within a radius of up to 150 km of the base of the undertaking
q: additional restriction: operating on islands < 400 square km
w: it refers only to the obligation of equipping and using tachograph
y: exception only for the (learning) driver, instructor must respect Regulation (EC) No 561/20006
z: drivers of vehicles under this para are exempt provided that driving is not their main activity

Source: European Commission (2014), "Report from the Commission to the European Parliament and the Council on the implementation in 2011-2012 of Regulation (EC) No 561/2006 on the harmonisation of certain social legislation relating to road transport and of Directive 2002/15/EC on the organisation of the working time of persons performing mobile road transport activities", Brussels, http://eur-lex.europa.eu/legal-content/en/txt/pdf/?uri=celex:52014sc0342&from=en (accessed 21 November 2016).

Article 13 (1) of the regulation provides exceptions from application of provisions on driving times, breaks and rest periods based on differences between existing national regulations, when the European rules were first introduced. The member states are free to choose which exceptions apply on their territory. A summary of the national exceptions is provided in Table 1.5 above. These exceptions are covered by national legislation, for example, in the UK in the Transport Act 1968, in Germany in the crew Regulation (*Fahrpersonalverordnung*), and in Latvia Cabinet Regulation No.279.

Box 1.2. **AETR Agreement**

Nineteen European countries outside the EU are signatories to the AETR (European Agreement concerning the Work of Crews of Vehicles engaged in International Road Transport, 1970). For transport journeys to or through their territories the AETR rules apply. The AETR rules apply to the whole journey, including the parts of the journey that are done in any EU country. The AETR agreement has been amended to recognise the digital tachograph, in line with European Union regulation (EC) No 561/2006 from 2010 that makes digital tachographs standard in the Union. Albania, Andorra, Armenia, Azerbaijan, Belarus, Bosnia and Herzegovina, Kazakhstan, Liechtenstein, Macedonia, Monaco, Montenegro, Moldova, Russia, San Marino, Serbia, Turkey, Turkmenistan, Ukraine and Uzbekistan

Source: United Nations (2006), "European Agreement concerning the Work of Crews of Vehicles Engaged in International Road Transport "(AETR).

Article 14 of regulation (EC) No. 561/2006 allows the European Union member states to grant exceptions in urgent cases to the application of driving times. These are granted on *per-case* basis by the countries and usually relate to extreme weather conditions. The enforcement of the driving time regulation is based on the records of tachographs fitted to every vehicle.

Some countries outside of the EU have aligned at least part of their regulation signing the AETR Agreement. Box 1.2. further explains the agreement.

United States Hours of Service Regulations

In the United States, *Hours of Service Regulations* regulate the driving time for the drivers, differentiated for the goods-carrying and passenger-carrying services (see Box 1.3). The maximum driving times are limited to 11 or 14 hours for goods-carrying drivers, and 10 or 15 hours for passenger-carrying drivers, depending on the length of the rest period. Drivers are required to record driving time in a logbook or using an electronic on-board recorder, which is similar to the digital tachograph in Europe. The driver is obliged to retain on board a log for the previous seven consecutive days for roadside inspection.

Box 1.3. **US DoT driving time requirements**

FMCSA regulations on Hours of Service require drivers of heavy vehicles to maintain a DoT log book, which is a daily calendar divided into half-hour increments for logging the point-to-point driving record of the driver. The Hours of Service Rules include the following stipulations:

- Drivers may drive 11 hours, following 10 hours off-duty.
- Drivers may not drive beyond the 14th hour after coming-on duty, following 10 hours off-duty.
- Drivers may not drive after 60/70 hours on-duty in 7/8 consecutive days.
- A driver may restart a 7/8 consecutive day period after taking 34 or more consecutive hours off-duty.

Source: FMCSA Regulations, Part 395, "Maximum driving time for property-carrying vehicles", www.fmcsa.dot.gov/regulations/title49/section/395.3 (accessed 21 November 2016).

The regulations adopted in North America, Europe and elsewhere have been able to provide the necessary flexibility to account for the constraints of *just-in-time* delivery and routine disruption to service schedules. Adopting regulations that correspond or are aligned in many respects to US FMCSA *Hours of Service Regulations* might be considered because of the benefits in simplifying compliance for drivers crossing the border and to fuel international road transport. Whatever system is preferred, regulatory priority should be given to putting hours of service regulations into practice.

New vehicles and imported used vehicles

Standards applicable to road vehicles with first registration in Mexico are provided under the Federal Law on Standards and Measurement (DOF, 2012a), with SCT responsible of the issued standards for vehicles under the Law on Roads, Bridges and

Motor Transport.[20] Mechanical and safety standards for motor vehicles are set under NOM-068 last revised in 2014. Safety standards for trailers and methods of testing are set by NOM-035.[21] However, environmental standards are set in the NOM-045-SEMARNAT-2016 (DOF, 2012b) and the Agreement to disclose the environmental conditions to import used vehicles equipped with a diesel engine and gross vehicular weight greater than 3 857 kg.[22]

The Law on Roads, Bridges and Motor Transport, revised on 2014, regulates the "construction, operation, exploitation, conservation and maintenance of roads and bridges (...)" and the federal transport services that operate within them. According to the law, SCT can issue standards for roads, bridges and vehicles and monitor, verify and inspect their compliance.

NOM-068 establishes the physical and mechanical conditions of the vehicles to guarantee their safe transit in federal roads, and the safety of others circulating in them. It represent the baseline of the tools and systems (and their conditions), required for the vehicles, to circulate. Similarly, NOM-035 states the minimum safety and operational measures for new or used trailers, semi-trailers and converters. Both standards apply both to manufacturers and importers, and to all the vehicles and trailers, semi-trailers and converters used inside of the Mexican territory.

A large number of imported second hand vehicles enter the Mexican fleet each year. In August 2014 ANPACT reported a figure of 5 imported used vehicles for every new truck sold.[23] This makes the enforcement of regulation on environmental and safety standards for these vehicles paramount. Imported second hand vehicles are likely to be equipped to lower standards than new domestic vehicles in terms of safety and emissions control technology.

Trade in second hand vehicles is subject to provisions of NAFTA but trade agreements generally follow the GATTs rules and allow for controls to be imposed achieving non-economic objectives through:

- Taxes, including "green tariffs" or "eco-tariffs"
- Minimum mechanical and technical standards
- Minimum environmental standards.

Some countries require emissions inspections with second-hand vehicles that fail tests not allowed into the country. Another option is for imported second hand vehicles to be required to meet specified environmental standards (e.g. Euro III or US EPA, 2004). A bill to this effect has been prepared by the Transport Committee of the Senate IN Mexico and is awaiting passage.[24] This is a positive development.

Safety standards for trailers, NOM-035

As well as the large number of old vehicles on the road there are a large number of old, used and reconditioned trailers, some that clearly do not meet the standards set out in NOM-035. In the case of Mexico, non-standard and unsafe dollies (tow bars) are a particular problem. NOM-035 requires trailers to be fitted with an identification plate confirming compliance with the norm. In the United States and many other countries a second plate with a serial or VIN number has to be attached to the dolly.

In this context, Mexico should consider amending NOM-035 to include the obligation to attach a plate confirming conformity with safety standards to dollies (tow bars) in order to facilitate inspections and enforcement of the regulation.

It is vital that the physical-mechanical, environmental and safety regulations in force, and the ones yet to come, apply to both imported and national vehicles through the Mexican territory, and this can only be implemented with a wide enforcement programme of compliance.

Enforcement

Enforcement of compliance with heavy-duty vehicle licensing and operating regulations is undertaken by the police and a team of 400 SCT inspectors. They undertake road-side checks and visits to company premises. Companies are sampled according to size and date of last visit. Supervisions to companies that register accidents are conducted as well.

Commercial vehicles present a significant risk to other road users because of their size and weight. They typically travel long distances with heavy cargo. Without well-established maintenance programmes, these vehicles can quickly develop safety faults. The quality of vehicle fleet maintenance varies with operators in Mexico, ranging from among the best in the OECD to among the worst. Compulsory road-side inspections are essential to maintaining standards and the safety of the road environment. The system implemented in the European Union is explained in Box 1.4. Countries with enhanced road safety policy-making have dedicated teams of police officers for inspecting commercial vehicles. In New Zealand, for example, the police's *Commercial Vehicle Investigation Unit* has 110 dedicated staff, including vehicle mechanics (Cliff, 2014). In Mexico this would translate into a dedicated force of between 750 and 3 000 officers depending on whether relative GDP or population is employed as basis for comparison—a measure based on the number of vehicles on the road would be also valid. It is acknowledged that Mexico's police forces are short of resources in all areas. The *Federal Police* force is better resourced and more effective than state and municipal forces but relatively small—municipal forces however, cannot inspect federal duties. Nevertheless, road safety enforcement should be among the priority areas for reinforcement.

Box 1.4. **Roadworthiness testing in the European Union**

Each Member State tests for the roadworthiness of vehicles circulating on its roads. The European Union has agreed minimum standards of testing for all vehicles to meet, and vehicles passing these tests are allowed to circulate on any Member State's roads. Tests are administered annually in garages registered for carrying out inspections, reinforced by roadside testing. Heavy vehicles over 3.5 tons gross laden weight are tested from the first year onwards, smaller vehicles from the fourth year onward. The standards are set out in Directive 2009/40/EC on roadworthiness tests for motor vehicles and their trailers.

Brakes are checked on 88 specific points, most of them concerning signs of excessive wear and including testing of performance/efficiency against design specifications. Seven other categories of equipment are tested including: steering; lights; axles, wheels, tyres and suspension; chassis and chassis attachments; seat belts; speedometers, tachographs and speed limiters; and noise. Vehicles failing tests must be repaired before they can resume duty.

Source: Directive 2009/40/EC, http://eur-lex.europa.eu/legal-content/en/txt/html/?uri=celex:32009l0040&from=en.

Elevated levels of cargo theft and carriage of illegal drugs make road-side checks more hazardous for the enforcement services. Shifting responsibility for inspections of vehicles, loads and drivers from the police to a dedicated unit with powers limited to enforcement of road safety might facilitate enforcement by insulating inspectors from responsibility for controlling contraband.

When road-side inspections are organised as a targeted campaign and a sufficient rate of checking is in place, coupled with sufficient penalties, inspections can be effective in deterring most infractions, including drink-driving offences, poor vehicle maintenance, overloading, driving without a license or insurance.

In Mexico, seventy road-side weighing stations have been installed nationally to control for overloading of heavy goods vehicles. This is about the same as the number of inspection weigh-stations as in the US state of California[25] (a state with a third of Mexico's population). Budget constraints mean they are not able to operate 24 hours a day, 7 days a week. A pilot automated weighing station is being tested in Queretaro, equipped with automatic number plate recognition. And 14 corridors have been designated to be equipped with automatic stations over time.

In the United States, many states now use electronic bypass systems with automatic vehicle identification (PrePass, NORPASS, Drivewyze etc.). The system stores safety and compliance records for each registered vehicle. Roadside transponders monitor equipped vehicles on the approach to weigh-stations. Safety and compliance records determine how often trucks from the same company are pulled in. Compliant vehicles will be permitted to pass by without a check 95% of the time. It is recommended that this kind of compliant operator system is incorporated in Mexico's automatic weigh-station programme.

It should be noted that weigh stations need to be maintained in good working order to be effective. Past investments in control technologies – weighing stations, speed control cameras – have sometimes been ineffective because of poor maintenance.

Enforcement is most effective when the haulage company, as well as the driver, consignors and all relevant parties are subject to sanctions. Mexico has enacted chain of responsibility legislation in 2016 to sanction that everyone in the supply chain has an obligation to ensure that breaches of road transport laws do not occur, and if a party's actions, inactions or demands contribute to an offence, they can be held legally accountable.[26] Chain of responsibility legislation in other OECD countries covers mandatory driving time and rest limits, respect of speed limits, safe operation and loading of vehicles, vehicle maintenance and driver fitness for work.[27] Some jurisdictions have provided powers for inspection of the accounts of companies shipping and receiving freight to verify compliance with loading limits. For example, in New South Wales the Roads and Maritime Services Authority levies multimillion dollar fines on companies found to have shipped or received tonnages (for example of grain) that significantly exceed the legal capacity of the haulage services contracted. Within limits, Roads and Maritime Authorised Officers can enter premises without consent and without a warrant for both monitoring, and investigation purposes. This has proved highly cost effective in enforcing maximum loading limits. Such extensions of powers under chain of responsibility legislation should be considered in Mexico. Currently Mexican tax authorities can investigate company accounts after SCT notifies them of a non-compliant operator, more proactive powers might be awarded to SCT inspectors.

Complex behavioural infractions such as speeding will require specific deterrence efforts, with fixed automatic speed cameras and mobile speed enforcement units. Although automatic speed cameras have been installed along federal highways it is understood that most are currently not used. This should be reversed, and be complemented with mobile speed control patrols dosed at sufficient intensity to bring compliance with speed limits to acceptable levels (targeting all road users as a priority for overall road safety policy). The enforcement of federal traffic regulations, however, is an exclusive faculty of the Federal Police. In many jurisdictions (France for example) police are equipped to take payment of fines at the roadside, with IT systems linked to a central database.

Road safety policy co-ordination

Mexico has one of the poorest road safety records in OECD countries in terms of killed and seriously injured per head of population and per vehicle (light duty vehicles included). Heavy goods vehicles are involved in a relatively small proportion of crashes but the mass of heavy vehicles means that the consequences of crashes involving them are disproportionately serious. International experience underlines that co-ordinated leadership is required to make major improvements in road safety outcomes (ITF, 2008). A range of institutions are responsible for managing road safety in Mexico, many showing strong performance in specific areas, given the resources available, but co-ordination appears inadequate. For example, detailed statistics on deaths and injuries are collected by IMT for federal roads but data is not collated centrally for crashes on state roads.

In most areas (speed, alcohol, infrastructure, etc.) increased funding for road safety investment and management appears needed. In the area of crash reporting, for example, investment in addressing under-reporting and improving crash reports in the police service would be warranted (starting with crashes involving heavy vehicles) as a basis for developing more effective interventions and enforcement strategies.

Designation of a lead co-ordinating agency in the higher levels of government to develop strategy for reducing the number of killed and seriously injured on the roads is likely to be needed to achieve significant improvement. The role of such a lead agency is not to replace existing agencies and centres of expertise, but to focus attention in government, and consult with stakeholders and the public on the introduction of new safety interventions, to achieve support and understanding of the value of enhanced enforcement. A lead agency is also important for co-ordinating interventions between stakeholders to achieve a systematic approach to safety, and for working at the highest levels of government to ensure the resources available are commensurate with the targets set. Parallels exist in the area of security, where in the late 1990s the Ministry of the Interior led a 'National Security Protocol' that resulted in the rate of crimes affecting the sector falling. New initiatives of this sort for security and for road safety would be beneficial.

Environmental protection

In Mexico, Heavy-duty diesel vehicle emissions standard (NOM-044 of SEMARNAT), establishes the maximum permissible limits of emissions of hydrocarbons, non-methane hydrocarbons, carbon monoxide, nitrogen oxides, non-methane hydrocarbons plus oxides of nitrogen, particulate matter and smoke opacity from the exhaust of new engines that use diesel as fuel and that will be used for the propulsion of motor vehicles with a gross vehicle weight greater than 3 857 kilograms; and from the exhaust of new units with a gross vehicle weight of more than 3 857 kilograms equipped with this type of engines. The Ministry of Environment and Natural Resources

(SEMARNAT) through the Federal Procurement of Environment Protection (PROFEPA) is the authority competent for the enforcement of NOM-044. This standard is of mandatory observance for manufacturers, importers and assemblers of new diesel engines. In order to import or commercialize the mentioned engines and units in the Mexican territory, they have to obtain a Certificate of compliance with the NOM, issued by PROFEPA.

NOM-044 is currently under revision (see Box 1.5). Coupled with increasing availability of ultra-low sulphur diesel, there is an opportunity for early adoption of cleaner vehicles and accelerated turnover of the existing fleet. The new regulation would significantly lower limits on emissions of particulate matter (PM) and nitrogen oxides (NOx) from trucks and buses, and requires that new heavy-duty diesel vehicles sold in Mexico be equipped with advanced emissions control devices and on-board diagnostic systems. These additions to NOM-044 would bring Mexico's regulatory framework into alignment with the international heavy-duty vehicle market, matching the most progressive standards worldwide. The *International Council for Clean Transportation* estimates that over the period 2018 to 2037, the tighter standards would result in a net benefit to Mexico of USD 123 billion (MXN 1.6 trillion), taking into account the value to society of 55 000 avoided early deaths from air pollution, and the reduced climate impact from lower emissions of black carbon.[28]

Box 1.5. **Mexican, United States and European Union air pollutant emissions standards**

Mexico is updating its heavy-duty diesel vehicle emissions standards in 2015 to be equivalent to the latest standards in force in the United States at the Federal level and in the European Union. On 1 December 2014, COMARNAT, the national regulatory committee of the Ministry for Environment and Natural Resources (SEMARNAT) approved the update to existing emissions standards regulating particulate matter (PM), nitrogen oxides (NOx), hydrocarbons (HC) and carbon monoxide (CO) from heavy-duty diesel engines and vehicles, including trucks, buses and large pickups and vans. The modification to NOM-044-SEMARNAT-2006 was published on 17 December 2014 for a 60 day consultation period. Following this COMARNAT is to approve the regulation.

The new standards will require new heavy-duty diesel vehicles sold after 1 January 2018 to meet emissions standards equivalent to those in the United States (EPA, 2010) and European Union (Euro VI). The proposal to fully align with the prevailing US and European standards in 2018 will require new vehicles to be equipped with diesel particulate filters, advanced NOx after treatment, full on-board diagnostic systems and fail safe devices which ensure correct operation of emissions control systems (see Annex A1.1).

Source: Elaboration by the OECD Secretariat with information from www.cofemermir.gob.mx, www.semarnat.gob.mx, and www.dof.gob.mx

The current regulation in Mexico provides manufacturers with two compliance pathways, modelled on the US Environmental Protection Agency and the European Union standards, incorporating outdated versions of those standards that imply different compliance costs. The current proposal would update NOM 044 to EPA 2010 and Euro VI standards with full on-board diagnostics systems by January 2018. The options are functionally equivalent, require the same emissions-control and diagnostics technologies, and will result in the same compliance costs. Manufacturers will have little problem meeting the new standards, which they meet already in other North American markets. Vehicle owners should benefit despite any (moderate) increase in price as engines designed to meet the more stringent PM and NOx limits are also more fuel-efficient than those on the Mexican market at present. Harmonisation of standards across North America also removes a potential barrier to cross-border long-haul freight transport (see Box 1.5).

The emissions-control technologies required to meet the updated standards depend on ultra-low-sulphur diesel fuel (ULSD). More than 30% of the diesel fuel sold in Mexico already meets ultra-low sulphur limits, including fuel supplied to Mexico City, Monterrey, and Guadalajara, and the share of ULSD will continue to grow. Nevertheless, to promote adoption of the new limits, there may be a case for introducing temporary fiscal incentives and there may be opportunities to introduce incentives for early adoption or phase-in of the vehicle standards.

The fuel quality standard enacted by the Energy Regulatory Commission (NOM-EM-005-CRE-2015) establishes the specification of quality to be met by petroleum fuels in each stage of the production and supply chain in the Mexican territory. NOM-EM-005 requires nation-wide availability of ultra-low sulphur diesel by 1 Jul 2018. At the same time, energy sector reform will open Mexico to new retail gas stations in January 2016 and new importers of gasoline and diesel (starting January 2017 or before). The standard requires nation-wide availability of ultralow sulphur diesel, with an accelerated phase for the three largest cities and identified major freight routes and low sulphur gasoline (average 30 ppm / maximum 80 ppm) from December 2015. More than half of the current diesel supply is ultra-low sulphur. There thus appears to be no reason to delay implementation of the new vehicle standards.

Heavy duty standards on fuel economy have begun to be developed by the Commission for the Efficient Use of Energy (*Comisión Nacional para el Uso Eficiente de la Energía*, CONUEE) to mitigate emissions of CO_2 and cut fuel bills, with interest from U.S.—based manufacturers for harmonisation with U.S. fuel economy standards. It is recommended that work on these standards resumes once NOM-044 is finally issued.[29]

Scrappage and renewal incentives

The average age of heavy goods vehicles in Mexico was 17.5 years in 2015 (see Table 1.6 and Figure 1.13). This compares to 7 years in Canada,[30] 12 years in the EU (see Figure 1.14) and 15 years for heavy rigid trucks and 11 years for articulated trucks in Australia.[31] In Mexico, whilst an age limit exists for public buses, there is no limit for trucks. For heavy trucks, 36% of the fleet is over 21 years old and 23 228 units are over 40 years old. These old vehicles are technically poorly equipped in terms of safety and emissions, compounded by the deterioration in performance that inevitably affects old vehicles. Removing the oldest vehicles from circulation and replacing them with new or recent second hand vehicles could improve safety and pollution significantly, although older vehicles tend to be driven far fewer kilometres than newer vehicles.

The government has introduced incentives to scrap old vehicles since 2003, which was updated in March 2015,[32] raising the levels of offering up to MXN 250 000, which is thought to be the critical level for the subsidy (see Table 1.7). This was the result of a negotiation between the Ministry of Economy, SCT, SEMARNAT and the Ministry of Finance. The specific incentives consist of a credit equivalent to the smallest quantity between the price in which the old vehicle is being purchased, the 15% of the price of the new vehicle, or the following prices:

- Truck-tractors of five-wheel type: MXN 250 000
- Single-unit trucks of three axis with gross vehicle weight of at least 14 500 kg: MXN 160 000
- Single-unit trucks of two axis with gross vehicle weight of at least 11 794 kg: MXN 107 000
- Integral buses with capacity of more than thirty installed seats; MXN 250 000
- Conventional buses with capacity of more than thirty installed seats: MXN 145 000
- Comprehensive platform or chassis for integral buses with more than thirty installed seats: MXN 150 000
- Comprehensive platform or chassis for conventional buses with more than thirty installed seats: MXN 87 000.

Table 1.6. **Heavy vehicle fleet in Mexico in 2015**

Age (years)	Trucks	Busses
0-5	82 276	14 455
6-10	77 580	13 846
11-15	60 195	18 982
16-20	42 736	8 578
21-25	43 765	10 060
26-30	26 151	2 632
31-35	32 372	2 551
36-40	26 487	2 232
41-45	14 428	1 161
46-50	5 737	121
> 50	3 063	0
Fleet	414 790	74 618
Average age	17.5	14.5
Vehicles over 21 years old	152 003	18 757

Source: SCT (2015a), "Estadística Básica del Autotransporte Federal 2015" (Basic Statistics of Federal Road Transport 2015), www.sct.gob.mx/fileadmin/direccionesgrales/dgaf/est_basica/est_basica_2015/estadistica_basica_del_autotransporte_federal_2015.pdf (accessed 9 November 2016).

Figure 1.13. **Heavy vehicle fleet in Mexico in 2015**

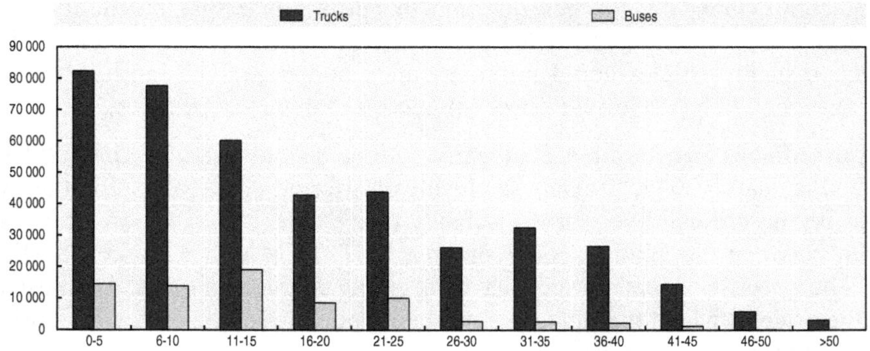

Source: SCT (2015a), "Estadística Básica del Autotransporte Federal 2015" (Basic Statistics of Federal Road Transport 2015), www.sct.gob.mx/fileadmin/direccionesgrales/dgaf/est_basica/est_basica_2015/estadistica_basica_del_autotransporte_federal_2015.pdf (accessed 9 November 2016).

Figure 1.14. **Average age of vehicles in the European Union**

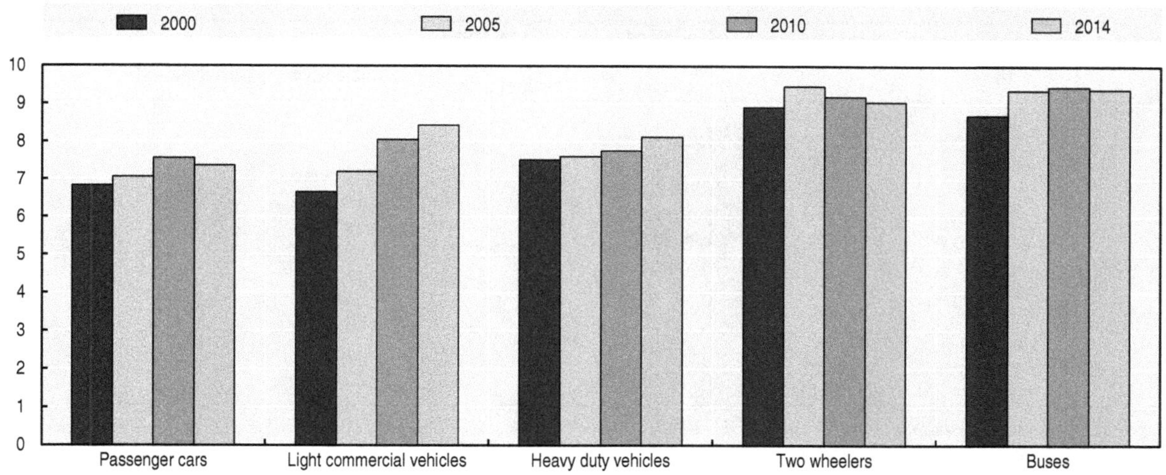

Source: Elaborated by the OECD Secretariat with data from the European Environment Agency using EU TREMOVE data, www.eea.europa.eu/data-and-maps/indicators/average-age-of-the-vehicle-fleet/average-age-of-the-vehicle.

Table 1.7. **HDV scrapping programmes in Mexico and in other countries**

Country	Programme name	No. of subsidised vehicles	Conditions / eligibility of vehicles	Time frame for application	Premium per vehicle (EUR)	Further information	Source
Chile	Change your truck (Cambia tu camion)	500	Trade in vehicles: Older than 24 years. New purchased vehicles: Better fuel efficiency than the old vehicle.	07.09.2009 – 07.10.2009	7 400 – 18 500	Total programme expense: 6.2 M Euros. CO2 mitigation 120 000 T/year	Zarchy, 2009
China	Old-Swap-New		Vehicles traded in: 10 to 15 years old.	01.06.2009 – 31.05.2010	1 200 – 2 000		Scrapmonster2011; Pengfei, 2011
Colombia	Vehicle renovation (Renovación Vehicular)	4 000			20 500 (average)	Total programme expense: 82 Mio. Euros	Ministro de Transporte, 2011
	PND 2010-14	5 000 /year		2010-14		Participation via reverse auctions Higher premiums if HDV emit less emissions	Ministro de Transporte, 2011
Japan	Vehicle replacement programme	Up to 690 000 vehicles in total	Trade in vehicles: older than 12 years New purchased vehicles: comply with new 2005 standards	01.04.2009 – 31.03.2010	7 300 (up to 8t) 16 440 (<12t)	Total programme expenses: 3.4 billion)	JAMA, Kim, 2009
	Non replacement programme		New purchased vehicles: Comply with 2015 fuel efficiency Standards 10% Nox and PM emissions compared to 2005 standards		3 650 (up to 8t) 8 220 (<12t)		

Table 1.7. **HDV scrapping programmes in Mexico and in other countries** (*cont.*)

Country	Programme name	No. of subsidised vehicles	Conditions / eligibility of vehicles	Time frame for application	Premium per vehicle (EUR)	Further information	Source
Mexico	Programme to replace and renovate vehicles (Esquema de Sustitución y Renovación Vehicular)	21 214 (between 2004 and 2012)	Vehicles traded in: Older than 10 years. New vehicles purchased: Maximum age 6 years.	2003-2015	15% of the value of the "new" HDV		SCT, 2012
	Renovation programme (Programa de renovación)	46 800 (between 2004 and Feb. 2012)				Total programme expense 1.4 billion pesos	NAFIN, 2012

Source: GIZ Mexico based on data from ITDP 2012, SEPSA 2014 and TSTES 2013, for GIZ, SCT and SEMARNAT http://transport-namas.org/projects/t-nama-countries-iki/mexico/.

The keys to ensuring such schemes are cost effective is to target the worst vehicles, guarantee they are taken out of service and destroyed, avoid creating opportunities for abandoned vehicles being repaired to be eligible for a scrapping bonus and, where incentives are provided for renewal rather than just scrapping, ensuring replacement of only vehicles that meet high safety and environmental standards qualify.[33] The current programme complies with some of these good practices, as it requires the old vehicle (older than 10 years) to be destroyed as part of the payment for the new unit; the owner must provide proof of ownership of the destroyable unit, proof of its operation on transport services, permit, car plates and physical-mechanical and environmental verifications, at least from 1 January 2014 to the scrapping date.[34]

Additional features of the programme are the possibility to provide two vehicles for scrapping and acquire a new one, with the focus of the benefit on the sector of the *truck man*, from whom half of the destroyed vehicles must come from. The unit to be acquired must be new or up to 6 years old.

Cost-effectiveness tends to decline as the size of the programme increases but in Mexico the large number of very old vehicles suggests the public resources available for such a scheme is more likely to be the limiting factor. In this line, the programme is to be in force for the period of 2015-17 and it has a ceiling of up to 6 thousand vehicles to destroy for each calendar year, which according to STC[35] is 83% higher than in the last 10 years.

More generally a government sponsored scheme provides credit for heavy-duty vehicle renewals for qualifying owners. A financial plan is underway to be launched by the National Development Banking Institution[36] to provide liquidity for the *truck man* to have access to the programme. An Investment Plan for Mexico was requested to complement the facility with loans from the World Bank. Clean Technology Funds, administered by the World Bank, which carry a zero interest rate in principle, and offer a way of expanding the scheme tied explicitly to high standard vehicles.[37] However, if disbursement is channelled through commercial banks that take fees, the attractiveness of this source of finance might be limited.

Figure 1.15. **Vehicles destroyed 2004-2015**

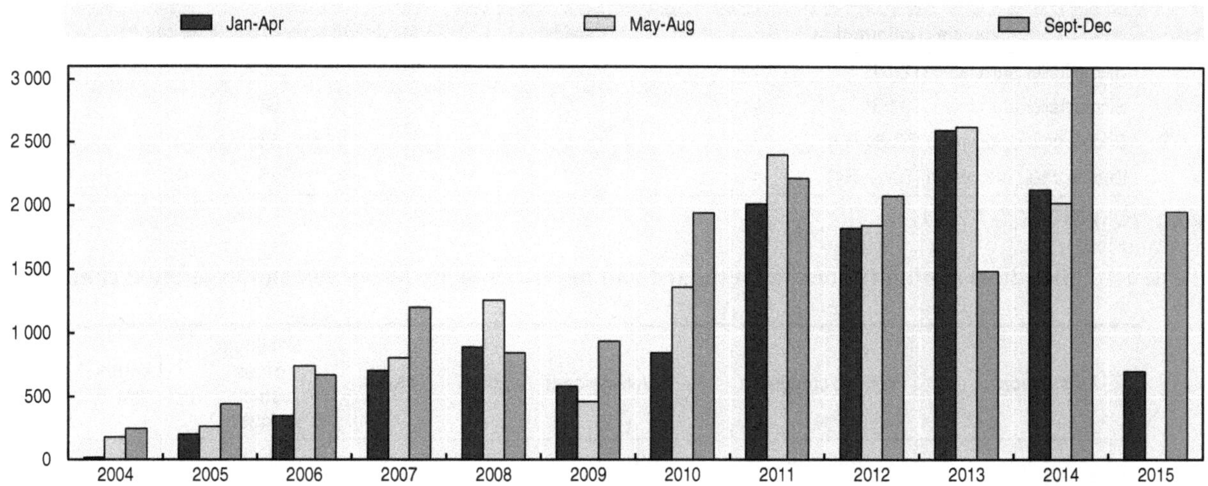

1. Figures from July to December 2015 are under the new decree.

Source: ANPACT.

Weights and dimensions

All OECD countries set maximum weights and dimensions for heavy goods vehicles in order to ensure compatibility with the design of bridges, tunnels, road carriageways and junction layouts. Most jurisdictions provide for a standard articulated vehicle of around 16 to 21 metres in length and 36 to 48 tons gross laden vehicle weight authorised for use on the primary road network, be it state or federal roads. In Europe this has been extended to an international standard for 16.5 metre 40 tonne trucks guaranteed access to primary roads in all of the countries of the European Union. Standard truck-trailer combinations are similarly authorised for use across the network in most jurisdictions.

Longer, heavier vehicles are authorised for use on specified parts of the road network in most countries. In some federal systems standards for these vehicles are set at state level. In such cases there is often a degree of harmonisation nationally, as for example in Australia (see Table 1.8), which has nationally accepted standards for vehicles pulling two or three trailers on designated parts of the road network. Even longer and heavier road trains are authorised for use on parts of the road network, including unsurfaced roads. "B-doubles", 68.5 tonne vehicles with two trailers, have become a standard workhorse vehicle and are authorised for use on parts of the urban road networks in many cities.

Table 1.8. **Harmonised Australian standards for long, heavy vehicles**

Vehicle configuration	Axles	Maximum gross vehicle weight (t)	Maximum length (m)
B-double (tractor and two 'B-coupled' trailers)	9	68.5	26
B-double (tractor and two 'B-coupled' trailers)	12	91	36.5
Double road train (tractor and two "A-coupled" trailers)	11	85.5	36.5
Triple road train (tractor and three "A-coupled" trailers)	16	125	53.5

Source: ITF (2011), "Car Fleet Renewal Schemes: Environmental and Safety Impacts and Sustainability", International Transport Forum, OECD, www.itf-oecd.org/sites/default/files/docs/11fleet.pdf.

Table 1.9. **Mexican standards for heavy vehicles**

Vehicle configuration	Axles	Maximum gross vehicle weight (t)
Single trailer articulated (T2-S1)	3	30
Single trailer articulated (T3-S3	6	54
Double trailer articulated (T2-S1-R2)	5	53
Double trailer articulated (T3-S2-R4)	9	76

Source: NOM-012-SCT-2-2014.

Table 1.10. **Standard configurations for standard and higher capacity heavy vehicles in selected countries**

Jurisdiction	Vehicle category	Vehicle configuration	Axles	Maximum gross vehicle weight (t)	Length (m)
USA national road network	Standard	Articulated tractor-trailer	5	36.3	19
	Standard	B double	5	36.3	22
	Standard	Articulated tractor-trailer	6	41.9	19
US Western States	Higher capacity (standard in some states)	"Rocky Mountain" Double	9	57	31
Canada national road network	Standard	Articulated tractor-trailer	5	39.5	22
	Standard	Articulated tractor-trailer	6	46.5	22
Canadian Western Provinces	Higher capacity (standard in some states)	B double	8	62.5	20
	Higher capacity (standard in some states)	B double	9	62.5	38
South Africa	Standard	Articulated tractor-trailer	5	43.5	15
	Standard	Articulated tractor-trailer	6	49.3	18
	Higher capacity	B double	8	56	22
Brazil	Standard	B double	7	57	20
EU trunk road network	Standard	Articulated tractor-trailer	5	40	16.5
	Standard	B double	5	40	18.75
Netherlands motorways	Higher capacity	B double "European Modular Vehicle"	7	60	25.2
Denmark	Standard	Articulated tractor-trailer	6	48	16.5
	Higher capacity	B double "European Modular Vehicle"	8	60	25.2
Sweden	Standard	B double	8	60	25.2

Source: ITF (2008), Aurell, J., T. Wadman and V. Trucks, "Vehicle combinations based on the modular concept", Report No. 1/2007, Committee 54: Vehicles and Transports, Sweden, www.modularsystem.eu/download/facts_and_figures/20080522att02.pdf.

The United States has national standards for use of a designated national road network (about four times the length of the interstate highway system) defined in maximum weights per axle (9.1t for a single axle, 14.5t for a tandem axle), maximum trailer lengths and a maximum gross vehicle weight of 36.3 tonnes. Typical vehicles are 19 to 22 metres long. Longer, heavier vehicles are permitted on the trunk roads of some western States. These limits and typical vehicles configurations are summarised in Table 1.10 for the United States and a selection of other countries. Maximum vehicle standards for Central American countries estimated by the Inter-American Development Bank are summarised in Table 1.11.

Mexico's limits for the weight and dimensions of commercial vehicles (Table 1.9) are set out in NOM-012 that applies to vehicles using federal roads.[38] Revisions published on 14 November 2014 came into force in mid-January 2015. Maximum weights are determined according to axle and wheel configurations. The largest single trailer articulated truck weight is 54t. The largest double trailer vehicle (known as a 'full' in Mexico) is limited to 75.5 tons (66.5t plus an allowance of 1.5t per drive axle and 1.0t per standard axle). The 2014 revision to the standard reduced this maximum limit for double articulated truck from 80 tons, by cutting the allowance per standard axle from 1.5 to 1.0t.

Table 1.11. **Maximum permitted weights for heavy trucks in Central America**

Vehicle type	Element	Regional	CR	SV	GT	HN	NI	PA	DO
C2	Front axle	5.0	5.0	5.0	5.0	5.0	5.0	4.0	9.0
	Tractor axle	10.0	10.0	10.0	10.0	8.0	9.0	10.0	9.0
	Total	15.0	16.0	15.0	15.5	-	-	-	-
C3	Front axle	5.0	5.0	5.0	5.0	5.0	5.0	5.5	9.0
	Tractor axle	16.5	15.0	16.5	16.5	16.0	16.0	16.4	14.5
	Total	21.5	21.0	21.5	22.0	-	-	-	-
C4	Front axle	5.0	5.0	5.0	5.0	5.0	5.0	5.5	9.0
	Tractor axle	20.0	23.0	20.0	20.0	20.0	20.0	22.0	-
	Total	25.0	29.0	25.0	25.0	-	-	-	-
T2-S1	Front axle	5.0	5.0	5.0	5.0	5.0	5.0	5.5	9.0
	Tractor axle	9.0	10.0	9.0	9.0	8.0	9.0	10.0	9.0
	Trailing axle	9.0	10.0	9.0	9.0	8.0	9.0	10.0	9.0
	Total	23.0	26.0	23.0	23.0	-	-	-	19.5
T2-S2	Front axle	5.0	5.0	5.0	5.0	5.0	5.0	5.5	9.0
	Tractor axle	9.0	10.0	9.0	9.0	8.0	9.0	10.0	9.0
	Trailing axle	16.0	16.5	16.0	16.0	16.0	16.0	16.4	14.5
	Total	30.0	32.5	30.0	30.0	-	-	-	27.3
T2-S3	Front axle	5.0	5.0	5.0	5.0	5.0	5.0	5.5	9.0
	Tractor axle	9.0	10.0	9.0	9.0	8.0	9.0	10.0	9.0
	Trailing axle	20.0	23.0	20.0	20.0	20.0	20.0	22.0	
	Total	34.0	39.0	34.0	34.0	-	-	-	30.1
T3-S1	Front axle	5.0	5.0	5.0	5.0	5.0	5.0	5.5	9.0
	Tractor axle	16.0	16.5	16.0	16.0	16.0	16.0	16.4	14.5
	Trailing axle	9.0	10.0	9.0	9.0	8.0	9.0	10.0	14.5
	Total	30.0	32.5	30.0	30.0	-	-	-	30.1
T3-S2	Front axle	5.0	5.0	5.0	5.0	5.0	5.0	5.5	9.0
	Tractor axle	16.0	16.5	16.0	16.0	16.0	16.0	16.4	14.5
	Trailing axle	16.0	16.5	16.0	16.0	16.0	16.0	16.4	14.5
	Total	37.0	39.0	37.0	37.0	-	-	-	30.1
T3-S3	Front axle	5.0	5.0	5.0	5.0	5.0	5.0	5.5	9.0
	Tractor axle	16.0	16.5	16.0	16.0	16.0	1.0	16.4	14.5
	Trailing axle	20.0	23.0	20.0	20.0	20.0	20.0	22.0	-
	Total	41.0	45.5	41.0	41.0	-	-	-	-
B-double		No	Yes	No	Yes	-	-	Yes	No

CR: Costa Rica; SV: El Salvador; GT; Guatemala; HN: Honduras: NI: Nicaragua; PA; Paraguay; DO: Dominican Republic.

Source: Elaborated by the OECD Secretariat with data from IDB (2013), "Trucking Services in Belize, Central America, and the Dominican Republic: Performance Analysis and Policy Recommendations".

NOM-012 was recently updated in Mexico (see section *General Regulatory Framework*) and the SCT indicated that it foresees the inclusion of the NOM-012-SCT-2-2014 in the National Normalization Program of 2017 to review its contents. Changes to truck weight and dimension limits tend to be controversial in all jurisdictions. Similar arguments over the advantages and disadvantages of raising limits for standard vehicles arise in the US, Europe and Australia even though the limits currently in force in these jurisdictions range from 36 to 91 tonnes.

At stake with higher limits, on the positive side, are improved productivity and potentially fewer vehicles on the road. Higher productivity translates into lower logistics costs, which drives economic growth and translates directly into higher profitability for own-account operators. In the case of general hauliers, the benefit of higher productivity will be passed on to customers through competition. Larger loads in principle result in fewer journeys and a contribution to containing emissions and road congestion (ITF, 2011).

Those opposing higher limits note there will be a rebound effect. Larger loads mean lower unit costs, and lower prices which will stimulate more trade and transport. This effect is, however, only expected to offset 10% of the reduction in truck-kilometres driven achieved with higher productivity vehicles. Operators of smaller trucks may see larger vehicles as a threat to business. Rail companies also generally see higher weight limits as a threat to business, but the impact depends very much on the nature of the rail market nationally. In Europe, for example, the impact of moving from a 40t to a 60t limit might have little effect on rail freight in Germany but could wipe-out the deep sea container business in the UK railways because of the relatively short haul lengths in the UK. In Sweden introduction of 60 tonne trucks was beneficial to the competitiveness of the railways, providing for enhanced feeder services in the timber hauling business (ITF, 2011).

Heavier vehicles require adequate safety regulation. In general, higher capacity vehicles behave as well or better than standard vehicles in tests of braking, stability and manoeuvrability as they are designed to high standards (ITF, 2011). Heavier vehicles also need to be configured to respect design standards for the strength of roadways and bridges. As with safety, heavier vehicles can perform as well as or better than standard vehicles when well designed (ITF, 2011). *Pneumatic suspension* is for example superior to *leaf suspension* in terms of road wear, other things being equal (see next subsection on EU standards). Axle lengths determine the dynamic impact on bridges, but gross vehicle weight is ultimately a limiting factor in relation to bridge design.

Weights and dimensions regulation in the European Union

European Union Directive 96/53/EC of 25 July 1996 (with amendments in Directive 2002/7/EC) sets standard maximum dimensions for vehicles in national and international road traffic and weights for vehicles used in international traffic within the EU. The EU member states are free to set different maximum authorised weights for domestic journeys. The aim of Directive 96/53/EC is to ensure that there are no obstacles to international use of standard commercial road freight and passenger vehicles in the European Union. The requirements of the directive are transposed into the national legislation of member states. A list of maximum permissible weights and dimensions for European countries is available from the ITF website www.internationaltransportforum.org/IntOrg/road/dimensions.html.

In the European Union air suspension is defined as a suspension system in which at least 75 % of the spring effect is carried by a pneumatic device. Regulation No 1230/2012 defines the characteristics of an air suspension system and sets conditions of equivalence between mechanical and air suspension. According to Directive 96/53/EC, maximum allowed weights depend on a list of factors, including spacing between the axles, the number of tyres on each axle and the type of suspension fitted. Vehicles equipped with air suspension are permitted higher weights than those without. For example, for a vehicle with 4 axles the maximum allowed weight of a truck with a semi-trailer is 36 tonnes; but under certain conditions if the driving axle is fitted with twin tyres and air suspension or equivalent the limit is raised to 38 tonnes.

Elements to consider when assessing changes in regulation in weight and dimensions for road transport

Determining the benefits and costs of higher (or lower) weight limits with any precision requires testing of the specific vehicles in question and modelling of their impacts on infrastructure under prevailing national conditions. The Mexican Transport Institute is well equipped to undertake the physical testing, with state-of-the-art road-wear testing machinery and facilities for testing braking, stability and handling performance of trucks. SCT is establishing a group of experts to report on the compatibility of higher maximum weight limits with the Mexican road environment with a view to guiding future changes to standards. Such a study is, however, unlikely to be able to arbitrate between different sections of the trucking industry over the perceived advantages and disadvantages of higher weight limits. After receiving the recommendations from the Experts' Panel, a Follow-up and Evaluation Group was formed with experts, business chambers, industry organisations and government officials.

SCT is required to undertake two evaluations of the 2014 amendments to NOM-012. The implementing arrangements specified in Article 13 of the norm require SCT to undertake studies to evaluate the effectiveness of the norm within three years of it entering into force, in preparation for the next programmed 5-yearly revision. In the immediate term, the Federal Commission for Better Regulation (COFEMER) has asked SCT to undertake an *ex post* assessment of the amendments.

COFEMER's *ex post* regulatory impact assessment is a "voluntary" regulatory quality tool that aims to improve regulation (Comisión Federal de Mejora Regulatoria, 2013). Under the process COFEMER selects which norms should be reviewed and issues a request to the ministry responsible requiring an *ex post* assessment, within 30 working days of the date of entry into force of the norm. For NOM-012, the assessment must be submitted at the end of February 2016. After submission, COFEMER either accepts and publishes the assessment or reverts to the Ministry requesting more information. On 27 May 2016, the Mexican Institute of Transport submitted a report of accidents by request of the General Direction of Federal Transport so as to be integrated to the *ex post* impact evaluation of the NOM-012. Afterwards on 19 July 2016, COFEMER sent to the SCT a report of *ex post* evaluation. COFEMER outlines the objectives of *ex post* assessment as:

- To check achievement of the objectives
- To verify improvements brought about
- To identify opportunities for further improvement.

The procedure requires collection of data to verify theoretical assumptions on the basis of experience but allows for a broad range of modelling techniques to be used to assess impacts. It starts with identification of the problem addressed by the regulation and identification of the objectives of the norm and includes identification of potential alternative measures.

The introduction to NOM-012-2-2014 specifies the following criteria for setting new weight limits:

- Preservation of infrastructure
- Environmental protection
- Promoting productivity
- Promoting the safety of all road users.

It stresses the objective of the 2013-18 National Development Plan to accelerate economic growth and the duty placed on SCT to reduce the costs of economic activity through the way in which it develops and manages infrastructure. It also stresses the 2013-18 Transport and Communications Sector Program and its focus on delivering an effective logistics and transport services that are efficient, safe and increase the competitiveness and productivity of economic activities. The introduction to the norm notes that "attention to diverse themes" is required, hinting that trade-offs may need to be made between productivity and the other criteria but not making this explicit.

The objectives are thus clearly stated and the problem addressed is identified as follows: To improve levels of safety and reduce damage to infrastructure it is necessary to set maximum limits to weights and dimensions for commercial vehicles in accordance with the physical and technical characteristics of the infrastructure.

Impact assessment of the amendments to NOM-012 can be undertaken in two respects: overall achievement – objective 1 and 3 of the COFEMER *ex post* assessment procedure; improvement brought about by the amendments made – objective 2.

Starting with this narrower, second task, the main change to the norm in the 2014 amendment is removal of the weight allowance for pneumatic suspension. This reduced the maximum capacity for the largest trucks from 80 to 75.5 tons. Assessment of the impacts will require both empirical data and modelling. Such exercises have been undertaken in a number of countries for weight increases. Mexico may be unique in reducing statutory weight limits but the same methodology applies. Three relevant examples from other OECD countries of assessment of the impact of changes in regulations on maximum truck weights and dimensions are:

- McKinnon (2004) The Economic and Environmental Benefits of Increasing the Maximum Truck Weight: the British Experience, a research paper reviewing basement of increasing the limit from 41 to 44 tonnes
- Rijksaterstaat (2011) Longer and Heavier Vehicles in Practice: Economic, Logistical and Social Effects, the Ministry of Infrastructure and Environment's evaluation of the impact of licensing 60 tonne combination vehicles in a system where the standard maximum weight is 40 tonnes
- Risksolutions (2014) Evaluation of the Longer Semi-Trailer Trial: Annual Report 2013, a report for the UK Department for Transport reviewing the impact of using trailers up to 2.05m longer than the standard 13.6m units.

Box 1.6. **Procedure used to forecast the impact of weight increase in the United Kingdom**

1. Estimates were obtained from the UK Department for Transport's Continuing Survey of Road Goods Transport (CSRGT)[1] of the distances travelled by 38, 40 and 41 tonne vehicles with weight-constrained loads and the total tonne-kms moved over these distances.
2. Maximum payload weight (MPW) ratios were calculated. These were expressed as the ratios of the MPWs that could be carried on 38 tonne 5 axle vehicles (24 tonnes), 40 tonne 5 axle vehicles and 41 tonne 6 axle vehicles (26 tonnes) to the maximum carrying capacity of the 44 tonne 6 axle vehicle (29 tonnes).
3. The vehicle-kms travelled with weight-constrained loads were multiplied by the MPW ratios to estimate the potential gross saving in laden vehicle-kms.
4. The gross saving in laden vehicle-kms was converted into a gross saving in total vehicle-kms by allowing for empty running. It was assumed that the average empty running figure for 38, 40 and 41tonne vehicles (28%) would also apply to the new 44 tonne vehicles.
5. High, medium and low migration factors were applied to the gross savings in vehicle-kms in recognition of the fact that some loads would reach volume, scheduling or other constraints at a MPW of less than 29 tonnes. Separate migration factors were used for 38 and 40/41 tonne vehicles. These factors were chosen subjectively though in consultation with a group of industry specialists and road freight operators.
6. Allowance was made for traffic generation by applying the Government's National Road Traffic Forecast elasticity value of 0.1 to the estimated saving in road haulage costs per tonne-km from increasing MPWs from 24 to 29 tonnes (for 38 tonne vehicles) and 26 to 29 tonnes (for 40/41 tonne vehicles). The traffic generation factors were applied to road freight tonne-kms carried by vehicles carrying weight-constrained loads.
7. Allowance was made for three levels of modal diversion: high—19% of tonne-kms transfer to road, medium—10% transfer and low 5% shift (based on a studies for the Department of Transport).
8. The average load factor for new 44tonne vehicles (on laden trips) was estimated with reference to the current load factors of the 38, 40 and 41tonne vehicles derived from CSRGT data. These were, respectively, 63%, 72% and 82%. On this basis, it was assumed that the 44 tonne truck would have an average load factor of 70%.
9. The net savings in vehicle-kms were calculated for each of the levels of load migration and modal diversion.
10. The net savings in vehicle-kms were translated into transport cost savings. This was done using an average vehicle operation cost value of GBP 0.65 per vehicle-km obtained from the Motor Transport cost tables.
11. Environmental cost savings were derived using monetary valuations of air pollution, climate change, noise disturbance and traffic accidents provided by AEA Technology. The environmental estimates for rail freight were based on the use of the new, cleaner Class 66 locomotives. Average environmental externalities were valued at 0.87 pence per tonne-km for road and 0.28 pence per tonne-km for rail.

1. https://www.gov.uk/government/statistics/continuing-survey-of-road-goods-transport-gb-respondents-section; https://www.gov.uk/government/collections/road-freight-domestic-and-international-statistics.

Source: McKinnon (2004), "The economic and environmental benefits of increasing the maximum track weight: the British experience", *Transport Research*, Part D, Elsivier; Department for Transport, UK (2012), "Road freight: domestic and international statistics", retrieved from: https://www.gov.uk/government/collections/road-freight-domestic-and-international-statistics.

The impact on productivity, despite being a complicated enough process (see Box 1.6), is the simplest part of the overall assessment. Productivity will be reduced for the users of the largest double articulated trailers and their clients. These vehicles are operated typically by large retail companies, who either hired them from haulage firms or have their own-account transport operators. Data on how many vehicles this concerns and average load factors for them are not readily publicly available. It should be possible to obtain such data from industry sources and through surveys, but as the analysis described in McKinnon illustrates, a full assessment requires separate identification of the proportions of loads subject to a weight or volume constraint. To be accurate, assessment should also aim to sample overloading under the 80 and 76 tonne limits as well as the impact on average load factors.

For hauls where trucks are typically fully loaded, the impact of a reduction in weight on the number of extra vehicles that need to be used is simply proportionate. Where loads vary, the calculation is not so straightforward and there may be no substitute for interviews and sampling by survey. Back-haul load factors need also to be taken into account. Data on load factors is again not currently publicly available. The National Observatory for Transport and Logistics to be established by SCT and in preparation by the Mexican Transport Institute could be charged with assembling the necessary data for impact assessments under NOM-012.

Generally truck fleets can be expected to adapt to a change in weight limit, but in Mexico's current case there may be little impact in this respect as the configuration of the large double articulated truck remains unchanged in terms of axles, wheels and dimensions. Manufacturers are unlikely to begin to market customised 76 tonne designs, not least because of the possibility that the 80 tonne limit is reinstated after the next five-year review.

Environmental impacts depend in large part on the number of vehicle-kilometres driven, as calculated in relation to productivity. The maximum weight limit reduction will therefore probably have a negative effect on the environment. Emissions may also be affected by the change in effort required to accelerate with a fully loaded vehicle, 5% lighter under the amended regulation. This will depend on the motor used in each truck configuration. On-road emissions testing is probably the only way to establish if there is a significant difference; test-bed emissions and on-road emissions in real driving condition can differ greatly. CO_2 emissions can be readily calculated from fuel purchase records but there is no substitute for on-road sampling of NOx and particulate emissions.

Safety impacts are likely to be too small to model or monitor. The trucks affected by the weight change were designed to operate safely at the higher weight limit. A reduction in mass carried reduces the kinetic energy involved in any crash, but a 5% change to a heavy load will be of only marginal relevance to the damage done in terms of life lost or injury. Other factors are much more important: overloading; condition of the vehicle in terms of maintenance of breaks, lights, etc.; conformity with design standards, especially trailers; age of vehicle; use of advance safety technologies. Behavioural factors are also much more important than the change in maximum authorised weight: speeding; fatigue; driving under the influence of drugs and alcohol. Monitoring might be able to reveal changes over time but standard of monitoring and reporting of crash causation are currently poor, inconsistent and far from systematic in Mexico. It is difficult to foresee advances in crash reporting sufficient to provide a basis for monitoring the impact of a maximum weight change in the time frame, even for a five-year review of the norm.

Pavement wear may benefit from a reduction in maximum loads. The incidence of overloading and poor maintenance of suspension may be more important, however, and data collected to date is probably insufficient to provide a baseline. An approximation of the impact on road wear can be modelled, with the results of accelerated road wear testing machines. Such tests have been carried out in Mexico by IMT and could be repeated and improved to assess the change to NOM-012. It should be kept in mind that the largest vehicles are not necessarily the most aggressive towards infrastructure, but the reduction in weight can be expected to have a small benefit for road wear – albeit offset by the increase in truck-kilometres driven. Evaluation for the 1 year *ex post* assessment will have to rely on modelling as the time-scale needed for detecting marginal infrastructure wear through direct monitoring is much longer.

Removal of the incentive to fit pneumatic suspension is potentially problematic. Pneumatic suspension reduces road wear, as reflected in the European Union's regulations and in the revised NOM-012 itself in relation to commercial passenger vehicles (Article 6.1.1.1.1). It would be unwanted if manufacturers phased out pneumatic suspension in trucks for the Mexican market, not least because pneumatic systems make it much easier to install automatic weigh-in-motion equipment, part of the package for advanced compliance monitoring systems of the sort already deployed in Australia, to improve enforcement of safety and operating regulations and reduce the cost of enforcement. The value of pneumatic suspension to preserving infrastructure is questioned by the Mexican authorities, and would merit a testing programme to validate suppression of the incentive in NOM-012, or provide the basis for design of a new incentive element in the norm at whatever overall weight limit is retained.

Bridge integrity is unlikely to be affected by the change in NOM-012 as 80 tonne double articulated trucks were found to be acceptable under the bridge formula applied for infrastructure compliance in Mexico. The assessment will be verified by the expert group for the 3-year review of the NOM. Compliance with operation on designated routes – federal highways – is little affected as 76 and 80 tonne trucks are similarly incompatible with surfaces and bridges on roads under State jurisdiction built to lower design standards.

It should be stressed that in undertaking impact assessments, specific costs will have to be established for Mexican conditions. Whilst the methodologies developed elsewhere, for example as described by McKinnon (2004) can be applied to the extent that data available in Mexico permits, cost factors should be transferred with care. McKinnon provides the example of infrastructure costs developed in the US where strengthening the design of roadways to carry larger vehicles produces large unit costs for the assessments undertaken in the US. These figures were not transferable to the United Kingdom as no strengthening of roadways was needed to accommodate the change from 41 to 44 tonnes. Similarly in Mexico, switching between 80 and 76 tons will not require design changes.

Professional qualifications

Conditions for entry to the profession of truck driving are regulated in all OECD countries. Regulations usually impose tests of financial capacity and familiarity with safety and operating regulations for the sector, as a condition for awarding of a licence to operate haulage services. Markets have developed to provide insurance bonds to provide the necessary financial guarantees at low cost for owner-drivers in most countries. Certification requirements in Mexico are minimal. The National Chamber for Road Freight Transport, CANACAR (*Cámara Nacional del Autotransporte de Carga*), provides training on tax and regulatory issues for members, focusing on assisting small enterprises and the National Confederation of Mexican Carriers, CONATRAM (*Confederación Nacional de Transportistas Mexicanos*) also provides guidance. Government may wish to support these efforts and work with organisations representing owner-operators such as the Mexican Alliance Carriers Organization (*Alianza Mexicana de Organización de Transportistas*) to improve standards and prepare for the introduction of stricter professional standards. The NOM-012-SCT-2-2014 establishes a specific licence for double articulated vehicles, since March 2016 the SCT is granting these licences. They include specific training, and additional requirements.

Recommendations

Enforcement of safety regulations

The resources available for enforcement should be increased. The number of SCT inspectors for roadside checking of heavy goods vehicles needs to be substantially increased. A modernisation of the equipment must be carried out, as well as an improvement of the organisation for the inspectors. Police resources for vehicle inspections also need to be increased and consideration given to establishing a dedicated unit charged only with enforcement of heavy vehicle regulations.

Driving and rest time regulation

The regulation in preparation to regulate hours of service should be completed and adopted as a matter of priority. Until now, there is only a project proposal of a NOM regarding the risks associated to fatigue, whose process to be released has not finished.

In the European Union there is a maximum driving time of 9 hours that can be extended to 10 hours twice a week. In the United States, driving times vary between 10 and 15 hours, depending on whether the driver is carrying passengers of freight and on the length of the resting period.

Safety and security

Resources should be allocated to ensuring existing weigh-stations are maintained in operating condition and operated 24/7. Many of the 70 existing stations are reportedly out of commission or manned only intermittently. In fact, according to the dynamics of the sector (cargo transported, fleet, kilometres of road, etc.) the checking points should be increased substantially to enforce regulation based on risk assessments.

A pilot programme introducing automatic weighing stations is welcome. It is recommended that a compliant operator system is incorporated in this programme.

It is recommended to establish a lead agency with focus on road safety at the highest levels of government.

Standards for vehicles at first registration

Regulations for the design and testing of trailers, NOM-035, should be amended to include the obligation to attach a plate confirming conformity with safety standards to dollies (tow bars) as is the requirement in the United States in order to facilitate inspections and enforcement of the regulation.

Environment

Emissions standards should be introduced in the regulation for imported second hand vehicles. For instance, the proposed heavy-duty vehicle emissions standards, adopting EPA 2010 and Euro VI limits, are welcome and should be adopted as a matter of priority and the implementation of NOM-EM-005 for fuel quality, requiring nationwide availability of ultra-low sulphur diesel by 2018 should be prioritised.

Weights and dimensions

The maintenance of the expert group to examine optimal weight and dimension limits for trucks in relation to infrastructure and safety is welcome. It should be supported with the resources necessary to deliver its report by 2018 as provided for by NOM-012-SCT and as a basis for revision of the limits in 2020. The evaluation of the expert team must be based on evidence, and statistics production has to be enhanced.

The value of pneumatic suspension to preserving infrastructure merits a testing programme to establish the potential value of reintroducing an incentive element under NOM-012, whatever maximum overall weight limit applies. This could be part of the *ex ante* assessment of the norm required in 2016.

Notes

1. Mexican law distinguishes at least two types of legal entities to undertake economic activities: individuals and firms, both with different legal and fiscal obligations.

2. Dangerous materials, cars without rolling, funds and values, drag cranes, rescue and drag cranes and large vehicles.

3. Basics Statistics of the Road Transport (*Estadística Básica del Autotransporte Federa*)l. 2015, SCT, www.sct.gob.mx/transporte-y-medicina-preventiva/transporte-ferroviario-y-multimodal/anuarios-dgtfm-edicion-digital/ (accessed 9 November 2016).

4. IMT-SCT (1992), Assessment of the status of freight in Mexico 1990-1991: Movements road, IMT and SCT (*Evaluación de la situación del transporte de carga en México 1990-1991: Movimientos por carretera*).

5. Freight trucks residing in Mexico would request authorization to operate in the US to the former US Interstate Commerce Commission (Mendoza and Diaz, 2003)

6. Authorisations granted before 1982 were respected (Mendoza and Diaz, 2003).

7. Freight trucks residing in Mexico but owned by US registered companies, Mexican trucks carrying goods exempt from tariffs, and Mexican trucks and pick-ups that cross the United States territory for delivery in Canada (Mendoza and Diaz, 2003).

8. See U.S.-Mexico Cross-Border Trucking Pilot Program, US FMCSA, www.fmcsa.dot.gov/international-programs/mexico-cross-border-trucking-pilot-programme and Status of Mexican Trucks in the US, John Fritelli, Congressional Research Service, January.

9. http://digitalcommons.ilr.cornell.edu/cgi/viewcontent.cgi?article=2230&context=key_workplace.

10. FMCSA, www.fmcsa.dot.gov/sites/fmcsa.dot.gov/files/docs/MX-Trucking-Pilot-Program-Report.pdf.

11. Status of Mexican Trucks in the United States, John Fritelli, Congressional Research Service, January 2014, http://digitalcommons.ilr.cornell.edu/cgi/viewcontent.cgi?article=2230&context=key_workplace.

12. United States-Mexico Cross-Border Long-Haul Trucking Pilot Program Report to Congress, www.fmcsa.dot.gov/sites/fmcsa.dot.gov/files/docs/MX-Trucking-Pilot-Program-Report.pdf.

13. http://eleconomista.com.mx/industrias/2015/01/09/eu-abre-su-frontera-camioneros-mexicanos.

14. Federal Register /Vol. 80, No. 10 /Thursday, January 15, 2015 /Notices, Acceptance of Applications for Mexican-Domiciled Long-Haul Operations, www.gpo.gov/fdsys/pkg/FR-2015-01-15/pdf/2015-00555.pdf.

15. Secretaría de Economía (2014), Monografía de la Industria Automotriz.

16. Law of Roads, Bridges and Federal Motor Carrier, 1993 (*Ley de Caminos, Puentes y Autotransporte Federal*).

17. Agreement to disclose the environmental conditions to import used vehicles equipped with a diesel engine and gross vehicular weight greater than 3 857 kgs., 2011 (*Acuerdo por el que se dan a conocer las condiciones ambientales a que se sujetará la importación de vehículos usados equipados con motor a diésel y con peso bruto vehicular mayor a 3 857 kilogramos*).

18. Agreement Concerning the Adoption of Uniform Technical Prescriptions for Wheeled Vehicles, Equipment and Parts which can be fitted and/or be used on Wheeled Vehicles and the Conditions for Reciprocal Recognition of Approvals Granted on the Basis of these Prescriptions.

19. Agreement concerning the Establishing of Global Technical Regulations for Wheeled Vehicles, Equipment and Parts which can be fitted and/or be used on Wheeled Vehicles.

20. *Ley de Caminos, Puentes y Autotransporte Federal*, 1993, revised June 2014.

21. www.sct.gob.mx/fileadmin/_migrated/content_uploads/64_nom-035-sct-2-2010.pdf.

22. Agreement that notifies the environmental conditions that the imports of used vehicles with diesel motor and weight higher than 3 857 kg will be subjected to, 2011 (*Acuerdo por el que se dan a conocer las condiciones ambientales a que se sujetará la importación de vehículos usado equipados con motor a diésel y con peso bruto vehicular mayor a 3 857 kilogramos, 2011*).

23. http://mexicoautomotivesummit.com/highlights.html.

24. www.senado.gob.mx/sgsp/gaceta/63/1/2016-04-28-1/assets/documentos/dict_com_y_transp_35_39_y_50_lcpaf.pdf.

25. There are 65 weigh-stations for road-side inspections in California, www.coopsareopen.com/california-weigh-stations.html. The law requires trucks passing open stations to pull in and check loads. Stations close access ramps when they are fully occupied to prevent long delays.

26. Criteria of the Shared Responsibility in the provision of the service protected by the Waybill or Proof that Protects the Transport of Goods, 2016 (*Criterios de Aplicación de la Corresponsabilidad en la prestación del servicio que ampara la Carta de Porte o Comprobante que Ampara el Transporte de Mercancías*), http://dof.gob.mx/nota_detalle.php?codigo=5439315&fecha=31/05/2016.

27. A useful checklist of responsibilities under Australia's National Heavy Vehicle Law is provided here: https://www.nhvr.gov.au/law-policies/heavy-vehicle-national-law-and-regulations.

28. ICCT, www.theicct.org/revising-mexicos-nom-044-standards-considerations-decision-making.

29. NOM-EM-005 is an emergency standard. The Energy Regulatory Commission is yet to publish a final standard.

30. Canadian Vehicle Survey 2005, Resources Canada, http://oee.nrcan.gc.ca/Publications/statistics/cvs05/pdf/cvs05.pdf.

31. Annual vehicle census, Australian Bureau of Statistics, www.ausstats.abs.gov.au/ausstats/subscriber.nsf/0/f19b5d476fa8a3a6ca257d240011e088/$file/93090_31%20jan%202014.pdf.

32. Decree that promotes the renovation of the vehicular park of motor road, 2015 (*decreto por el que se fomenta la renovación del parque vehicular del autotransporte*), www.dof.gob.mx/nota_detalle.php?codigo=5386771&fecha=26/03/2015.

33. Car Fleet Renewal Schemes: Environmental and Safety Impacts and Sustainability, International Transport Forum, OECD 2011.

34. www.sct.gob.mx/despliega-noticias/article/conferencia-de-prensa-programa-del-gobierno-federal-para-la-renovacion-de-vehiculos-de-carga-y-1/.

35. Official press statement, www.sct.gob.mx/uploads/media/se_actualiza_el_programa_de_renovaci%c3%93n_de_veh%c3%8dculos_de_carga_y_de_pasaje.pdf.

36. Nacional Financiera.

37. More information on Clean Technology Funds for Mexico can be found on: https://www-cif.climateinvestmentfunds.org/country/mexico/mexico-ctf-programming.

38. NOM-012-SCT-2-2014, "About the maximum weight and dimensions that the motor vehicles are authorised to circulate in the general communication roads of federal jurisdiction" (*Sobre el peso y dimensiones máximas con los que pueden circular los vehículos de autotransporte que transitan en las vías generales de comunicación de jurisdicción federal*).

References

Alexander, K. and B. Soukup (2010), "Obama's First Trade War: The US-Mexico Cross-Border Trucking Dispute and the Implications of Strategic Cross-Sector Retaliation on U.S. Compliance Under NAFTA", *Berkeley Journal of International Law*, Vol. 28/2, pp. 313-342, http://scholarship.law.berkeley.edu/cgi/viewcontent.cgi?article=1383&context=bjil (accessed 21 November 2016).

Aurell, J., T. Wadman and V. Trucks (2007), "Vehicle combinations based on the modular concept", Report No. 1/2007, Committee 54: Vehicles and Transports, Sweden, www.modularsystem.eu/download/facts_and_figures/20080522att02.pdf.

Australian Bureau of Statistics (2014), "Motor Vehicle Census", www.ausstats.abs.gov.au/ausstats/subscriber.nsf/0/f19b5d476fa8a3a6ca257d240011e088/$file/93090_31%20jan%202014.pdf.

Blumberg, K., F. Posada and J. Miller (2014), "Revising Mexico's NOM 044 Standards: Considerations for Decision-making", *International Council on Clean Transportation Working Papers*, ICCT, www.theicct.org/sites/default/files/publications/icct_nom-044_proposal_20140530.pdf (accessed on 16 November 2016).

Camara de Disputados (1993), "Ley de Caminos, Puentes y Autotransporte Federal" (Law of Roads, Bridges and Federal Autotransports), revised June 2014, www.diputados.gob.mx/LeyesBiblio/ref/lcpaf.htm.

Canadian Vehicle Survey (2005), Resources Canada, http://oee.nrcan.gc.ca/Publications/statistics/cvs05/pdf/cvs05.pdf.

CFR (2011), CFR Title 49 Transportation Parts 300 to 399, revised 1 October 2011, https://www.fmcsa.dot.gov/regulations/title49/b/5/3 (accessed 23 November 2016).

Clean Technology Funds for Mexico (2016), https://www-cif.climateinvestmentfunds.org/country/mexico/mexico-ctf-programming (accessed 15 November 2016).

Cliff, D. (2014), "Effective Enforcement Policies", prepared for an expert meeting on Halving the Number of Road Deaths in Korea, ITF.

Comisión Federal de Mejora Regulatoria (2013), "La MIR ex post" (*Ex post* RIA), www.cofemer.gob.mx/documentos/mirexpost.pdf (accessed 15 November 2016).

Comisiones Unidas de Comunicaciones y Transportes y de Estudios Legislativos Segunda (2016), "Dictamen de las Comisiones Unidas de Comunicaciones y Transportes y de Estudios Legislativos Segunda Respecto de la Minuta con Proyecto de Decreto por el que se reforman y adicionan los Artículos 35, 39 y 50 de la Ley de Caminos, Puentes y Autotransporte Federal, 12 de abril 2016", (Opinion of the Commissions on Transport and Legislative Studies Second Concerning the Draft with a Decree which amends and adds Articles 35, 39 and 50 of the Law on Roads, Bridges and Autotransporte Federal, 12 April), www.senado.gob.mx/sgsp/gaceta/63/1/2016-

04-28-1/assets/documentos/dict_com_y_transp_35_39_y_50_lcpaf.pdf (accessed 22 November 2016).

Coops are Open (2012), "Total Weigh Stations & Truck Scales in California", www.coopsareopen.com/california-weigh-stations.html (accessed November 2016).

Del Mazo, A. (2016), "Criterios de Aplicación de la Corresponsabilidad en la prestación del servicio que ampara la Carta de Porte o Comprobante que Ampara el Transporte de Mercancías" (Criteria for Application of Stewardship in the provision of the service that covers the Letter of Carry or Proof that Protects the Transport of Goods), Federal Official Gazette, http://dof.gob.mx/nota_detalle.php?codigo=5439315&fecha=31/05/2016 (accessed November 2016).

Department for Transport, United Kingdom (2012), "Road freight: domestic and international statistics", https://www.gov.uk/government/collections/road-freight-domestic-and-international-statistics.

Department of Transportation (2015), "Acceptance of Applications for Mexican-Domiciled Long-Haul Operations", *Federal Register*, Vol. 80/10, p. 2179. www.gpo.gov/fdsys/pkg/FR-2015-01-15/pdf/2015-00555.pdf (accessed 21 November 2016).

Dieselnet (n.d), "United States Heavy-Duty Onroad Engines", https://www.dieselnet.com/standards/us/hd.php (accessed 22 November 2016).

Dieselnet (n.d.), "European Union Heavy-Duty Truck and Bus Engines", https://www.dieselnet.com/standards/eu/hd.php (accessed 22 November 2016).

DOF (2016), "Norma Oficial Mexicana NOM-EM-005 Especificaciones de calidad de los petrolíferos" (National Standard on Oil Quality Specifications), April, www.dof.gob.mx/normasOficiales/5985/cre2a11_C/cre2a11_C.html.

DOF (2015a), "Decreto por el que se prorroga el diverso por el que se regula la importación definitiva de vehículos usados (Decree that extends the regulation of definitive importation of used vehicles), *Federal Official Gazette*, 31 December, http://dof.gob.mx/nota_detalle.php?codigo=5421975&fecha=31/12/2015.

DOF (2015b), "Decreto por el que se fomenta la renovación del parque vehicular del autotransporte" (Decree promoting the renewal of the vehicle fleet of motor vehicles), *Federal Official Gazette*, 26 March, www.dof.gob.mx/nota_detalle.php?codigo=5386771&fecha=26/03/2015.

DOF (2014a), Norma Oficial Mexicana NOM-012-SCT-2-2014 Sobre el peso y dimensiones máximas con los que pueden circular los vehículos de autotransporte que transitan en las vías generales de comunicación de jurisdicción federal (National Standard on the maximum weight and dimensions with which the vehicles of motor transport may circulate in the general roads of federal jurisdiction), revised November 2014.

DOF (2014b), Norma Oficial Mexicana NOM-068-SCT-2-2014 Transporte terrestre-Servicio de autotransporte federal de pasaje, turismo, carga, sus servicios auxiliares y transporte privado-Condiciones físico-mecánica y de seguridad para la operación en vías generales de comunicación de jurisdicción federal. (National Standard for Road Transport, Federal Autotransport Service of fees, tourism, freight, its auxiliary services and private transport. Physical-Mechanical Conditions and Safety for the

Operation in Federal Roads), December, 2014, www.dof.gob.mx/normasoficiales/5578/sct2a11_c/sct2a11_c.html.

DOF (2012a), "Ley Federal sobre Metrología y Normalización" (Federal Law on Metrology and Standardization), revised November 2012, http://dof.gob.mx/nota_detalle.php?codigo=5279501&fecha=28/11/2012.

DOF (2012b), Proyecto de Modificación a la Norma Oficial Mexicana NOM-045-SEMARNAT-2006, Protección ambiental. Vehículos en circulación que usan diesel como combustible. Límites máximos permisibles de opacidad, procedimiento de prueba y características técnicas del equipo de medición (Project to modify the Mexican Legal Standard NOM-045-SEMARNAT-2006, Environmental protection. Vehicles in circulation using diesel as fuel. Maximum allowed capacity limits, test procedures and technical features of the measurement equipment), *Federal Official Gazzette*, 23 November 2012, www.dof.gob.mx/normasoficiales/4963/semarnat11_c/semarnat11_c.html (accessed 23 November 2016).

DOF (2011), Decreto por el que se regula la importación definitiva de vehículos usados (Decree thats regulates definitive imports of used vehicles), *Federal Official Gazzette*, 1 July, http://dof.gob.mx/nota_detalle.php?codigo=5198960&fecha=01/07/2011 (accessed 23 November 2016).

DOF (2010), Norma Oficial Mexicana NOM-035-SCT-2-2010 Remolques y semirremolques-Especificaciones de seguridad y métodos de prueba (National Standard on Trailers and Semitrailers' safety specifications and test methods), September, www.sct.gob.mx/fileadmin/_migrated/content_uploads/64_NOM-035-SCT-2-2010.pdf.

DOF (2006), Norma Oficial Mexicana NOM-044-SEMARNAT-2006, Que establece los límites máximos permisibles de emisión de hidrocarburos totales, hidrocarburos no metano, monóxido de carbono, óxidos de nitrógeno, partículas y opacidad de humo provenientes del escape de motores nuevos que usan diesel como combustible y que se utilizarán para la propulsión de vehículos automotores nuevos con peso bruto vehicular mayor de 3 857 kilogramos, así como para unidades nuevas con peso bruto vehicular mayor a 3 857 kilogramos equipadas con este tipo de motores (National Standard that establishes the maximum allowable limits for total hydrocarbons emission, non-methane hydrocarbons, carbon monoxide, nitrogen oxides, particulates and smoke opacity from the exhaust of new engines using diesel fuel and which will be used for the propulsion of motor vehicles that weigh more tan 3 857 kg and new units that weigh more than 3 857 kg.), October, http://dof.gob.mx/nota_detalle.php?codigo=4934189&fecha=12/10/2006.

Dutz, M., A. Hayri and P. Ibarra (2000), "Regulatory Reform, Competition, and Innovation: A Case Study of the Mexican national competition agency Road Freight Industry", *World Bank Policy Research Paper 2318*, www-wds.worldbank.org/external/default/wdscontentserver/iw3p/ib/2000/05/25/000094946_00050505302442/rendered/pdf/multi_page.pdf.

El Economista (2015), "EU abre su frontera a camioneros mexicanos" (The US opens its border to Mexican trucks), http://eleconomista.com.mx/industrias/2015/01/09/eu-abre-su-frontera-camioneros-mexicanos.

Elvira, J. and B. Ferrari (2011), "Acuerdo por el que se dan a conocer las condiciones ambientales a que se sujetará la importación de vehículos usados equipados con motor a diésel y con peso bruto vehicular mayor a 3 857 kilogramos", *Federal Official Gazette*, 20 April 2011, Mexico City.

European Environment Agency (2010), "Average age of road vehicles", www.eea.europa.eu/data-and-maps/figures/average-age-of-road-vehicles (accessed 21 November 2016).

European Parliament (2014), "Directive 2014/45/EU on periodic roadworthiness tests for motor vehicles and their trailers and repealing Directive 2009/40/EC", *Official Journal of the European Union*, pp. 51-128.

European Parliament and Council (2006), "Regulation (EC) No. 561/2006 of The European Parliament and of The Council of 15 March 2006 on the harmonisation of certain social legislation relating to road transport and amending Council Regulations (EEC) No 3821/85 and (EC) No 2135/98 and repealing Council Regulation (EEC) No 3820/85, http://data.europa.eu/eli/reg/2006/561/2015-03-02.

European Union (2009), "Directive 2009/40/EC on roadworthiness tests for motor vehicles and their trailers" (Recast) (Text with EEA relevance), *Official Journal of the European Union*? http://eur-lex.europa.eu/legal-content/en/txt/html/?uri=celex:32009l0040&from=en (accessed 21 November 2016).

Federal Register (2011), "Pilot Project on NAFTA Trucking Provisions: Commercial Driver's License Memorandum of Understanding with the Government of Mexico, Federal Motor Carrier Safety Administration, Department of Transportation. Vol. 76/197, 6 October 2011, https://www.gpo.gov/fdsys/pkg/FR-2011-10-12/pdf/2011-26442.pdf (accessed 23 November 2016).

Fritelli, J. (2014), Status of Mexican Trucks in the United States, Frequently Asked Questions, Congressional Research Service, Washington, D.C., http://digitalcommons.ilr.cornell.edu/cgi/viewcontent.cgi?article=2230&context=key_workplace (accessed on 16 November 2016).

GIZ Mexico based on data from ITDP 2012, SEPSA 2014 and TSTES 2013, for GIZ, SCT and SEMARNAT, http://transport-namas.org/projects/t-nama-countries-iki/mexico/ (accessed on 16 November 2016).

IDB (2013), "Trucking Services in Belize, Central America, and the Dominican Republic: Performance Analysis and Policy Recommendations", *Technical Note*, No. IDB-TN-511, www19.iadb.org/intal/intalcdi/PE/2013/11626.pdf (accessed 16 November 2016).

IMT-SCT (1992), "Evaluación de la situación del transporte de carga en México 1990-1991: Movimientos por carretera" (Evaluation of the situation of the freight transport in Mexico 1990-1991: Movements by highway), Instituto Mexicano del Transporte (IMT) y Secretaría de Comunicaciones y Transportes (SCT).

INEGI (2015), "Encuesta Mensual de la Industria Manufacturera" (EMIM), (Monthly survey on the Manufacturing Industry), database, January, www.inegi.org.mx.

ITF (2016), "Effective Enforcement Policies", in *Halving the Number of Road Deaths in Korea: Lessons from other Countries*, *International Transport Forum Policy Papers*, No. 23, OECD Publishing, Paris, http://dx.doi.org/10.1787/5jlwvz85537c-en.

ITF (2013), Transport Statistics database, www.itf-oecd.org/search/statistics-and-data?f%255B0%255D=field_publication_type%3A648 (accessed 16 November 2016).

ITF (2011), "Car Fleet Renewal Schemes: Environmental and Safety Impacts and Sustainability", International Transport Forum, OECD, www.itf-oecd.org/sites/default/files/docs/11fleet.pdf.

ITF (2008), *Towards Zero: Ambitious Road Safety Targets and the Safe System Approach*, OECD Publishing, Paris, http://dx.doi.org/10.1787/9789282101964-en.

Legifrance (2016), "Article L441-6", last modified 6 August 2015, www.legifrance.gouv.fr/affichcodearticle.do?cidtexte=legitext000005634379&idarticle=legiarti000019294314 (accessed on 16 November 2016).

Macías et al. (2013), "Policy Handbook for the Regulation of Imported Second-Hand Vehicles", *GFEI Working Paper*, No. 7, www.globalfueleconomy.org/publications/Pages/WorkingPapers.aspx.

McKinnon, A.C. (2004), "The economic and environmental benefits of increasing the maximum track weight: the British experience", *Transport Research*, Part D, Elsivier.

Mendoza, E. and E. Diaz (2003), "Obstaculos al comercio en el TLCAN: el caso del transporte de carga. Revista de Comercio Exterior" (Barriers for trade in NAFTA: the freight transportation case), Vol. 53, December, pp. 1112-1120.

Mexico Automotive Summit (2016), "Highlights from Mexico Automotive Summit 2016", www.mexicoautomotivesummit.com/highlights/.

National Heavy Vehicle Regulator (2016), "Checklist of responsibilities under Australia's National Heavy Vehicle Law", https://www.nhvr.gov.au/law-policies/heavy-vehicle-national-law-and-regulations (accessed 15 November 2016).

Rijksaterstaat (2011), "Longer and Heavier Vehicles in Practice: Economic, Logistical and Social Effects", Ministerie can Infrastructuur en Milieu.

Risksolutions (2014), "Evaluation of the Longer Semi-Trailer Trial: Annual Report 2013", Report for the UK Department for Transport, June.

Sanderson, T. (2012), "Mexico cross-border trucking program remains stalled", Transplace 3PL CEO Blog, http://blog.transplace.com/lists/categories/category.aspx?categoryid=19&name=mexico-cross-border-trucking.

SCT (2015a), Conferencia de prensa "Programa del Gobierno Federal para la Renovación de Vehículos de Carga y Pasaje" (Press conference: "Federal Government Program on the Renovation of Freight and Passengers Vehicles), www.sct.gob.mx/despliega-noticias/article/conferencia-de-prensa-programa-del-gobierno-federal-para-la-renovacion-de-vehiculos-de-carga-y-1/ (accessed on 16 November 2016).

SCT (2015b), "Official press statement", www.sct.gob.mx/despliega-noticias/article/se-actualiza-el-programa-de-renovacion-de-vehiculos-de-carga-y-de-pasaje-del-gobierno-federal/.

Secretaría de Economía (2014), "Monografía de la Industria Automotriz, 2014" (Automotive Industry Monograph, 2014).

STC (2015a), "Estadistica Basica del Autotransporte Federal 2015" (Basic Statistics of Federal Road Transport 2015), www.sct.gob.mx/transporte-y-medicina-preventiva/autotransporte-federal/estadistica/2015/ (accessed 9 November 2016).

STC (2013a), "Programa de Inversiones en Infraestructura de Transporte y Comunicaciones 2013-2018", (Investment Programme on Transport Infrastructure and Communications 2013-18), www.ferroistmo.com.mx/programa_de_inversiones_sct_2013-2018.pdf (accessed 2 December 2016).

STC (2013b), "Anuario de Información Estadística 2013" (Statistic Yearbook 2013), www.sct.gob.mx/fileadmin/DireccionesGrales/DGP/estadistica/Anuarios/Anuario-2013.pdf (accessed 19 May 2016).

TransportPolicynet (n.d.), "Mexico: Heavy-duty: Emissions", http://transportpolicy.net/index.php?title=Mexico:_Heavy-duty:_Emissions.

U.S. Census Bureau (2015), "Foreign Trade. Top Trading Partners", December, https://www.census.gov/foreign-trade/statistics/highlights/top/top1512yr.html (accessed 22 November 2016).

U.S. Department of Transport (2015), "United States-Mexico Cross-Border Long-Haul Trucking Pilot Program Report to Congress", www.fmcsa.dot.gov/sites/fmcsa.dot.gov/files/docs/MX-Trucking-Pilot-Program-Report.pdf.

U.S. Department of Transportation (2015), "Research and Innovative Technology Administration, Bureau of Transportation Statistics, TransBorder Freight Data", http://transborder.bts.gov/programs/international/transborder/TBDR_QA.html (accessed on May 23, 2016).

U.S. FMCSA (2015), "U.S.-Mexico Cross-Border Trucking Pilot Program", www.fmcsa.dot.gov/international-programs/mexico-cross-border-trucking-pilot-program (accessed 22 November 2016).

U.S. Government Publishing Office (2016), Federal Motor Carrier Safety Administration (FMCSA) Regulations, Part 395.3 "Maximum driving time for property-carrying vehicles", Hours of Service, www.ecfr.gov/cgi-bin/retrieveecfr?gp=1&ty=html&h=l&mc=true&=part&n=pt49.5.395 (accessed 16 November 2016).

United Nations (2006), "European Agreement concerning the Work of Crews of Vehicles Engaged in International Road Transport (AETR)", https://www.unece.org/fileadmin/dam/trans/doc/2010/sc1/ece-trans-sc1-2010-aetr-en.pdf.

Annex A1.1

US, EU and Mexican standards and their progressive tightening over time

Table 1.A1. **US EPA and California emission standards for heavy-duty CI engines (g/bhp hr)**

Year	CO	HCa	HCa+NOx	NOx	PM	
					General	Urban bus
1974	40	-	16	-	-	
1979	25	1.5	10	-	-	
1985	15.5	1.3	-	10.7	-	
1987	15.5	1.3	-	10.7d	0.60f	
1988	15.5	1.3b	-	10.7d	0.60	
1990	15.5	1.3b	-	6.0	0.60	
1991	15.5	1.3c	-	5.0	0.25	0.25g
1993	15.5	1.3c	-	5.0	0.25	0.10
1994	15.5	1.3c	-	5.0	0.10	0.07
1996	15.5	1.3c	-	5.0e	0.10	0.05h
1998	15.5	1.3	-	4.0	0.10	0.05h
2004j	15.5	-	2.4i	-	0.10	0.05h
2007	15.5	0.14k	-	0.20k	0.01	
2010	15.5	0.14	-	0.20	0.01	
2015	15.5	0.14	-	0.02l	0.01	

Non-methane hydrocarbons (NMHC) for 2004 and later standards.

For methanol-fuelled engines, the standard is for total hydrocarbon equivalent (THCE).

California: NMHC = 1.2 g/bhp·hr, in addition to the THC limit.

California: NOx = 6.0 g/bhp·hr.

California: Urban bus NOx = 4.0 g/bhp·hr.

California only, no federal PM limit.

California standard 0.10 g/bhp·hr.

In-use PM standard 0.07 g/bhp·hr.

Alternative standard: NMHC+NOx = 2.5 g/bhp·hr and NMHC = 0.5 g/bhp·hr.

Under the 1998 Consent Decrees, several manufacturers supplied 2004 compliant engines from October 2002.

NOx and NMHC standards were phased-in on a percent-of-sales basis: 50% in 2007-2009 and 100% in 2010. Most manufacturers certified their 2007-2009 engines to a NOx limit of about 1.2 g/bhp·hr, based on a fleet average calculation.

Optional. Manufacturers may choose to certify engines to the California Optional Low NOx Standards of 0.10, 0.05 or 0.02 g/bhp·hr.

Source: ICCT.

Table 1.A2. **EU emission standards for heavy-duty diesel engines: steady state testing**

Stage	Date	Test	CO	HC	NOx	PM	PN	Smoke
			g/kWh				1/kWh	1/m
Euro I	1992, ≤ 85 kW	ECE R-49	4.5	1.1	8.0	0.612		
	1992, > 85 kW		4.5	1.1	8.0	0.36		
Euro II	1996.10		4.0	1.1	7.0	0.25		
	1998.10		4.0	1.1	7.0	0.15		
Euro III	1999.10 EEV only	ESC & ELR	1.5	0.25	2.0	0.02		0.15
	2000.10		2.1	0.66	5.0	0.10a		0.8
Euro IV	2005.10		1.5	0.46	3.5	0.02		0.5
Euro V	2008.10		1.5	0.46	2.0	0.02		0.5
Euro VI	2013.01	WHSC	1.5	0.13	0.40	0.01	8.0×1 011	

a - PM = 0.13 g/kWh for engines < 0.75 dm^3 swept volume per cylinder and a rated power speed > 3000 min^{-1}.

PN = Particulate number (note, US EPA regulations do not include a value for number of particulates emitted).

Source: Dieselnet, https://www.dieselnet.com/standards/eu/hd.php.

Table 1.A3. **EU emission standards for heavy-duty diesel and gas engines: transient testing**

Stage	Date	Test	CO	NMHC	CH4a	NOx	PMb	PNe
			g/kWh					1/kWh
Euro III	1999.10 EEV only	ETC	3.0	0.40	0.65	2.0	0.02	
	2000.10		5.45	0.78	1.6	5.0	0.16c	
Euro IV	2005.10		4.0	0.55	1.1	3.5	0.03	
Euro V	2008.10		4.0	0.55	1.1	2.0	0.03	
Euro VI	2013.01	WHTC	4.0	0.16d	0.5	0.46	0.01	6.0×1011

a - For gas engines only (Euro III-V: NG only; Euro VI: NG + LPG)

b - Not applicable for gas fuelled engines at the Euro III-IV stages

c - PM = 0.21 g/kWh for engines < 0.75 dm^3 swept volume per cylinder and a rated power speed > 3000 min^{-1}

d - THC for diesel engines

e - For diesel engines; PN limit for positive ignition engines TBD

Source: Dieselnet, https://www.dieselnet.com/standards/us/hd.php.

Table 1.A4. **Mexican maximum permissible emissions standards for new heavy-duty vehicles**

Year	Compliance equivalent
1993	US EPA 1991
1994	US EPA 1994
1998	US EPA 1998
2006-08	US EPA 1998 or Euro III
2008-2015	US EPA 2004 or Euro IV
2015-17 (Proposal)	US EPA 2004 or Euro IV
Beginning 1 January 2018 (Proposal)	US EPA 2010 or Euro VI

Source: TransportPolicynet, http://transportpolicy.net/index.php?title=mexico:_heavy-duty:_emissions.

Chapter 2

Regulation of rail transport in Mexico

Rail services represent the main transportation mode for a number of sectors in Mexico, in particular the automotive industry in relation to international production linkages with the United States. The current regulatory framework grants exclusivity rights in the provision of rail freight transport services through concessions, and concessionaires need to negotiate about compensations for interconnection services and access rights. Prices for freight, passenger and auxiliary services are set freely, and the rail network was privatised so as to promote competition. However, a number of shippers have claimed that railway rates are too high. The rail system has important challenges: to develop capacity to collect and analyse the data needed to form judgements on issues of competition; to establish timelines for the development of analytical capacity for determining conditions for the use of trackage rights; to enhance efforts to gather and report available information to assess performance and evaluate possible public policy changes.

Overview of rail freight transport in Mexico

Market organisation

Mexico's two main freight rail companies mainly operate large block trains over long distances. The advantages of rail over other transport modes are large scale and scope economies in the network and the existence of a decreasing average cost on the line. This decreasing average cost also creates the problem of a natural monopoly on the railroad with many concomitant troubles on interconnection. Other disadvantages are low flexibility, time schedules and the need of expensive infrastructure such as railroads and terminals.

In Mexico, there are seven rail concessions with the bulk of traffic carried by two principal groups. The first is the mining company Grupo Mexico through its subsidiary *Infrastructura y Transportes Mexico* (ITM). ITM owns two concessions, Ferromex and Ferrosur. The second is Kansas City Southern Mexico (KCSM). Mexico's railways are integrated with the US and Canadian railways, running on the same gauge and operating to similar industry standards. Trains cross the borders of the three countries and US railway companies are shareholders in Mexico's two main rail concessions: Ferromex (Union Pacific 26% shareholding); and KCSM (owned by Kansas City Southern).

In terms of total transport volumes carried by rail within the Mexican territory, 46% of total tons were carried on the Ferromex network in 2015, corresponding to 58% of total ton-kms. KCSM carried 33% of total tons and ton-kms. Ferrosur carried 15% of total tons and 8% of total ton-kms (see Table 2.1). However, Ferrosur was taken over by Ferromex's parent company at the beginning of 2015 — Figure 2.1 shows the total volumes of cargo carried by rail by corridor. In the same year containerised cargo represented 9% of total traffic in ton-kms, this is shown in Figure 2.2.

Table 2.1. **Mexico's rail concessions, 2015**

Firm	Kilometres of lines	Locomotives	Freight cars	Tons (thousand)	T-KM (millions)
Kansas City Southern de México (KCSM)	4 283	424	904 178	39 995	27 819.6
Ferrocarril Mexicano (Ferromex)	7 164	608	850 683	51 312	45 704.4
Ferrosur	1 479	161	261 011	17 585	8 346.2
Línea Coahuila Durango	974	22	46 346	3 890	958.7
Ferrocarril y Terminal del Valle de México	297	31	26 114	2 346	86.3
Compañía de Ferrocarriles Chiapas-Mayab	1 550	31	8 156	545	479.7
Ferrocarril del Istmo de Tehuantepec	219	-	-	-	-
Administradora de la vía corta Tijuana- Tecate	71	3	2 702	185	6.3

Note: Ferromex and Ferrosur merged at the beginning of 2012.

Source: General Direction of Rail and Multimodal Development (DGDFM), former General Direction of Rail and Multimodal Transport (DGTFM).

Figure 2.1. **Volume of rail freight by route, 2012**

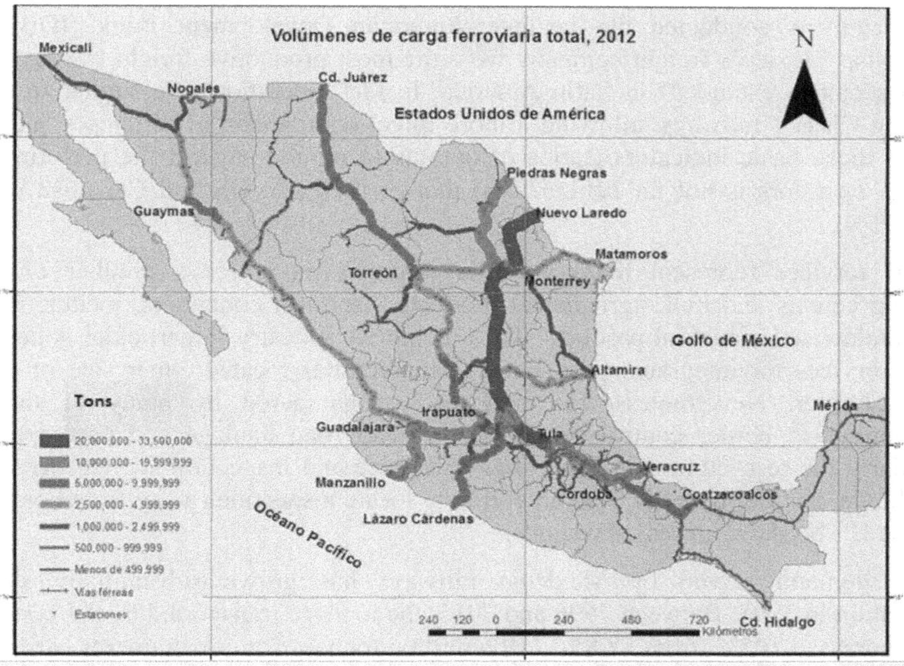

Source: IMT (2014), "Diagnostico del Sistema Ferroviario de Carga Mexicana al año 2013" (Diagnosis of the Mexican Freigh Railway System), prepared for the Texas A&M Transportation Institute (*Instituto Mexicano del Transporte* – IMT).

Figure 2.2. **Containerised rail freight by route, 2012**

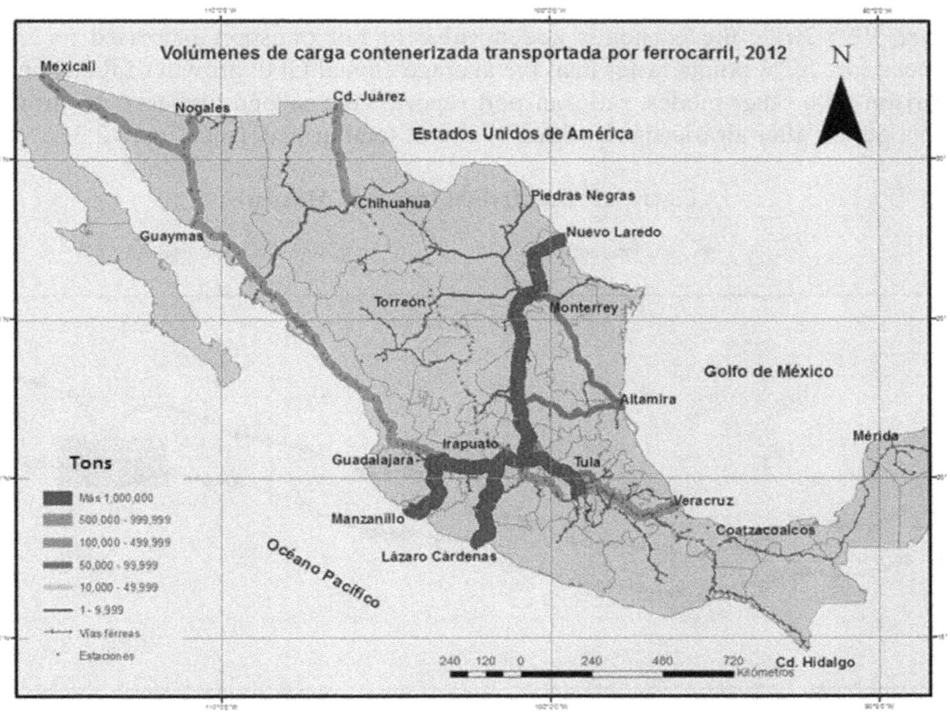

Source: IMT (2014), "Diagnostico del Sistema Ferroviario de Carga Mexicana al año 2013", (Diagnosis of the Mexican Freigh Railway System), prepared for the Texas A&M Transportation Institute (*Instituto Mexicano del Transporte* – IMT).

Economic performance of freight transport

An analysis conducted by the Inter-American Development Bank (IDB, 2013) showed that Mexico's freight company were the most productive freight railways (if the mining sector is excluded) in Latin America. In fact, operations are similar to US and Canadian Class 1 railways, allowing a more direct comparison of efficiency indicators. Most of those basic indicators (ratios of outputs to inputs) suggest the performance of Mexican operators is not far behind from that of the main US and Canadian railways (ITF, 2014).

Rail services represent the main transportation mode for a number of sectors including cereals and bulk agricultural products, deep sea containers, metals, minerals and containerised industrial products. The automotive industry in particular is dependent on rail services for integrated production from facilities located either side of the US-Mexico border. Nevertheless, rail services are hampered by many of the same shortcomings in border control services that affect road haulage and port operations, particularly the restriction of many border clearance and inspection services to standard office hours. But rail benefits from an ability to locate inspections away from borders and cross the US border with sealed wagons.

The demand served by Mexico's railways has grown substantially since its privatisation in 1995. Between 1996 and 2015, the tonnage transported by the system as a whole increased 103%, from 58.8 to 119.6 million tonnes. Tonne-kilometres carried grew by 100%, from 41.7 to 83.4 billon of tonnes-km.[1] The rail share of inland surface fright transport (road and rail) grew from 18.8% of the total in 1995, to 25.4% in 2015 (SCT). Figure 2.3 shows the trends for the rail freight system since 1983. Railway has experienced a recovery after the financial crisis of 2008, similar to other railway sectors in other parts of the world.

Over 1995-2015, the economic added value of rail transport increased on average 3.9% per year, 1.1% points faster than the average annual GDP growth of the country. In comparison with other modes, rail transport reported the second highest total growth on the same period after air transport, with a 99.4% of total growth (see Figure 2.3).

Figure 2.3. **Rail freight traffic in Mexico**

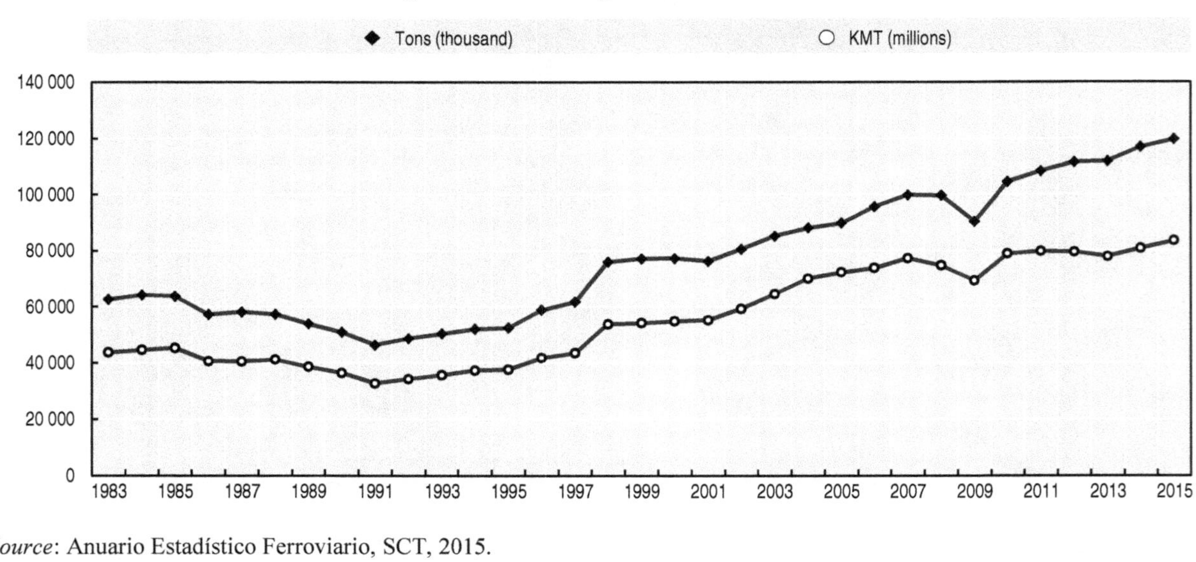

Source: Anuario Estadístico Ferroviario, SCT, 2015.

Table 2.2. **GDP by mode of transport, 2015**

Concept	GDP (MXN)	Share of total GDP	Average growth 1995-2015	Total growth 1995-2015
Total GDP	14 664 491.85		2.8%	78.6%
Tertiary sector	8 962 800.11	61.1%	3.1%	90.7%
Transport, mail and storage	852 321.87	5.8%	3.1%	84.0%
Air transport	30 391.34	0.21%	5.2%	189.4%
Rail transport	17 134.60	0.12%	3.9%	99.4%
Maritime transport	8 480.08	0.06%	2.1%	11.7%
Road transport	689 057.05	4.7%	6.1%	83.6%
Freight	420 099.12	2.9%	4.4%	128.1%
Passengers	268 957.93	1.8%	1.6%	40.8%

Source: National Institute of Statistics and Geography (INEGI).

The relative position of the GDP of freight transport by rail in comparison with other modes has been more or less static since 1995. In 1995, total production of freight transport by rail was about 8.7% of total freight (including maritime, road, rail and air). In 2015, the proportion freight carried by rail was 12.8%, representing an increase of 47.7% of the total transport pie.

On the other hand, Mexican trade with the United States via rail more than tripled from USD 20.4 billion in 1999 to USD 72 billion in 2015, recovering from a 2009 recession level of USD 34.6 billion (see Figure 2.4).

Figure 2.4. **US trade with Mexico by top rail ports**

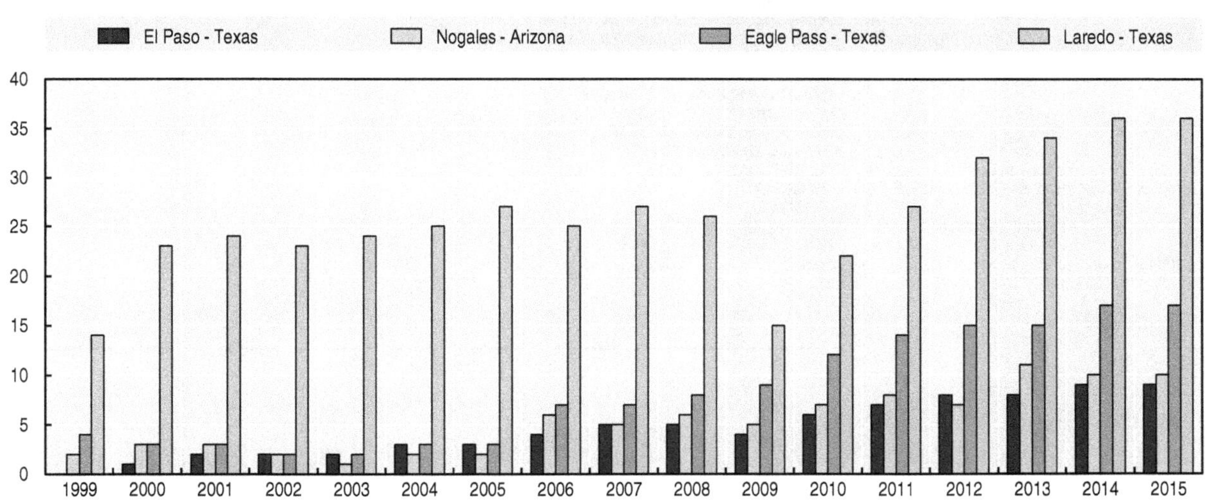

Note: USD billions.

Source: Bureau of Transportations Statistics, http://transborder.bts.gov/programs/international/transborder/TBDR_QA.html (accessed 3 August 2016).

Productivity has shown a marked increase since railway reform in Mexico. Four main productivity indicators are generally used to analyse the performance of railway companies for benchmarking comparisons with other railways. Table 2.3 summarises performance against these four indicators for Mexican railways in 1996, under FNM management, and in 2006 and 2012 under concession management. Efficiency improvements can be observed. For instance, increases in the productivity of locomotives and freight cars surpass 50%. Labour productivity has improved by 6 times as a result of the changes in operational practices, better management and the capital investments made. Forty five per cent more ton-km is carried with each litre of fuel consumed.

Table 2.3. **Performance evolution of the Mexican railway system 1996-2012**

Indicator	1996	2006	2012
Tonne-kms per locomotive (million)	26.9	59.8	59.9
Tonne-kms per freight car (million)	1.56	2.30	2.71
Tonne-kms per employee (million)	0.81	5.43	5.33
Tonne-kms per litre of fuel	80	107	116

Source: IMT (2014), "Diagnostico del Sistema Ferroviario de Carga Mexicana al año 2013", (Diagnosis of the Mexican Freigh Railway System), prepared for the Texas A&M Transportation Institute (*Instituto Mexicano del Transporte* – IMT).

Figure 2.5 shows that Mexican railways head the field under locomotive productivity benchmarking analysis amongst a set of Latin American railway companies. Ferromex and KCSM, the largest Mexican railways, have the highest locomotive productivity among the 23 non-mine railways of Latin America by a clear margin.

Figure 2.5. **Locomotive productivity of Latin American railways**

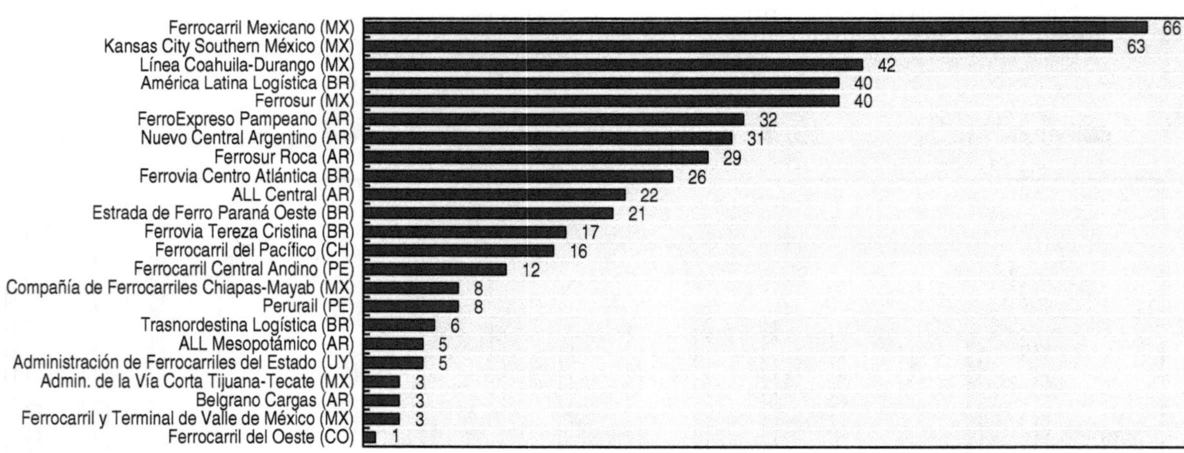

Note: Million t-km per fleet locomotive.

Source: IDB (2013), "Información Estadística sobre los Sistemas Ferroviarios Latinoamericanos" (Statistical Information on Latinamerican Railway Systems), Observatorio Regional de Carga y Logística (Freight Transport and Logistics Regional Observatory), http://logisticsportal.iadb.org/.

General regulatory framework

In Mexico, the SCT is the regulator of railway transport. The General Direction of Rail and Multimodal Transport (DGTFM) used to fulfil this role, until the Regulatory Agency for Rail Transport (*Agencia Reguladora del Transporte Ferroviario*, ARTF) was created on January 26, 2015. Currently, the counterpart on rail affairs (non-regulatory) in the side of the SCT is the General Direction of Rail and Multimodal Development (*Dirección General de Desarrollo Ferroviario y Multimodal, DGDFM*) According to the SCT website, the ARTF held its first work meeting on August 18, 2016—which corresponds with the creation date of the agency. The main legal framework for railway transport in Mexico consists of:

- Law of Rail Service *(Ley Reglamentaria del Servicio Ferroviario*, LRSF)
- Law of General Communication Routes (*Ley de Vías Generales de Comunicación*, LVGC)
- General Law of National Properties (*Ley General de Bienes Nacionales*, LGBN)
- General Law to Manage and Prevent Residuals (*Ley General para la Prevención y Gestión Integral de Residuos*, LGPGR)
- Additional laws and regulations falling under the jurisdiction of other ministries:[2]
  - By-law of the Railway System (Reglamento del Sistema Ferroviario)
  - Decree that creates the Regulatory Agency of the Rail Transport, as a deconcentrated body of the SCT (*Decreto por el que se crea la Agencia Reguladora del Transporte Ferroviario, como un órgano desconcentrado de la Secretaría de Comunicaciones y Transportes*).

Most of these laws have specific rules based on generic frameworks, such as on Mexican Official Standards (NOMS), concessions, permissions and other legal guidelines.

According to Article 7 of the LRSF, concessionaires can build, exploit, construct and operate the network and provide transport services. Also, depending on the concession, they can be allowed to provide additional services and infrastructure, such as freight terminals, passenger terminals, liquid bulk transport and supply centres for operating equipment. These additional, auxiliary services cannot only be provided by concessionaires, but also by permit holders: enterprises of individuals provided with a permit under Article 17 of the LRSF. Concessions and permissions are granted for 50 years and they can be extended for another 50 years provided that concessionaires and permit holders comply with all relevant regulations. The SCT can also grant permits with different duration for the construction of railway access points and smaller constructions.

Pricing mechanism

Prices for freight, passenger and auxiliary services are set freely (Art. 46 of LRSF), but need to incorporate contributions for interconnection between terminals, and the right to access and use infrastructure of other concessionaires (Art. 35 of the LRSF).[3]

Prices have to be set based on non-discriminatory basis with the only obligation to submit them to the DGDFM (former DGTFM)—Art 46 of LRSF. If the SCT or another party considers that the prices do hamper fair competition, they can request an opinion from the Federal Economic Competition Commission (COFECE) about the market conditions; during this period, the SCT will temporally fix tariffs of services (Art.47 of LRSF). Prices of freight services are usually set per product in a two-part tariff scheme with a fixed price plus a variable price.

The SCT can control prices on site to verify that these are being applied on a non-discriminatory basis. In addition, the SCT can ask for a random sample of invoices to concession and permission holders.

Concessionaires need to negotiate about compensations for interconnection services and access rights, but if they do not achieve an agreement after 90 days of negotiations, the SCT can establish compensations and conditions of such services and rights (Art. 35 of LRSF).

Concessions

Rail service and infrastructure administration concessions give exclusivity rights in the provision of freight transport services to the concessionaires for 30 years, with the exception of dragging and access rights established in the same document, and those freely agreed by the concessionaire.

In these concessions, one clause (*Condición 1.5)* states that concessionaires will be subject to new legislation, regulation and administrative requirements, in case the current legal provisions and administrative conditions were repealed or modified. Due to this clause, the concessionaires could lose the exclusivity over the railroads granted by the concession.

ARTF reform

The Decree that created the ARTF implied a relevant change in how public policy is made in the rail industry. With the new arrangement industry promotion will be separated from regulation, which was a conflict on matters of institutional role clarity. In Table 2.4 the distribution of faculties on regulation and industry promotion is depicted.

Table 2.4. **Railway industry regulation and promotion attributions**

Article 6: Attributions on rail service	
Ministry of Communications and Transport (Before the reform)	**Ministry of Communications and Transport** (After the reform)
	I. Plan, design and conduct the policies and programmes, as well as regulate the development of the railway system.
	II. Grant concessions and permits, as well as verifying their compliance and resolve issues of modification and termination.
	Regulatory Agency of Rail Transport
I. Plan, design and conduct the policies and programmes, as well as regulate the development of the railway system.	III. Technical regulation of railways and infrastructure interconnection.
II. Give concessions and permits, verify their compliance and resolve issues of modification and termination.	IV. Basis of tariffs regulation
III. Technical regulation of railways	V. Integrate the registry of permits and concessions.
IV. Basis of tariffs regulation	VI. Recommendation and co-operation on Public Security and related matters.
V. Sanctions	VII. Promote the expansion and use of the rail network.
VI. Integrate the registry of permits and concessions.	VIII. Register the maximum freight tariffs.
	IX. Rail industry statistics
	X. Short-rail valuations.
	XI. Sanctions
	XII. International forums participation and research conduction
	XIII. Request of information to licensees.

Source: Own elaboration based on the Law of Railway Services. This table was presented in the study "Redefining a National Transport Regulator in Mexico" prepared by the OECD for the Ministry of Economy in 2015.

The creation of the ARTF and DGDFM was designed to focus on topics as connection to logistic centers and stimulate investments on the rail network based on technical analysis. Additionally, the reform looks for institutional strengthening to achieve goals of investment, safety, crossing rights controversies, etc.

Issues over the market design

In 1937, Mexico's principal railway was nationalised and by the 1980s it was consolidated with several other Mexican railways to create the *Ferrocarriles Nacionales de Mexico SA* (FNM). By the 1990s, FNM required increasing subsidies and its infrastructure was deteriorating. According to Gomez-Ibañez and de Rus (2006), by 1994 only 40% of the 26 000 km network was in good condition and from 1990 to 1996 subsidies to FNM were on average 400 million MXN per year. Thus, under public administration, investment to maintain the railroads was not optimal, the network was not enlarged from the original size and thefts and accidents were common.

In 1995, the Federal Government took the decision to restructure entirely the rail industry. The railways were privatised via leasing three major and several short rail lines. The federal government retained ownership of the track, with the winning bidders for the concessions (leases) paying the government both a large initial lease payment, and an annual fee based on the concessionaire's profits. The three main leases were granted for 50 years renewable to 99 years, with exclusive rights to operate trains granted to the concessionaires for the first 30 years. Concessions elsewhere in the world usually grant exclusive rights for the entire concession period; Mexico's legislation provides additional flexibility to the government to assess the success of the regulatory framework in the run-up to the 30 year mark. Granting exclusive rights does not preclude the operation of trains across the networks of competing concessions, but does require agreement of terms between concession holders for running such services or, on sections of the network where trackage rights are imposed, it requires government to set terms and conditions.

Rail reforms have had far-reaching impacts for the government, taxpayer and railway companies alike. Rail transport has moved from requiring a large annual subsidy to becoming a net contributor to the federal treasury since the restructuration of the sector. Subsidies have stopped and companies began to pay for the leasing of the concessions and fees based on profits, and began paying taxes. According to the operating firms, financial statements and interviews with rail operators, the major railways have become profitable, generating a return for their investors, and resulting in the concessionaires investing in track and non-track capital.

Comparing freight tariffs before and after the reforms (Figure 2.6), a decline in tariff levels in Mexico can be seen. In such Figure, the line for FNM shows the evolution of freight tariffs between 1970 and 1990, and they have been adjusted to incorporate 70% of the losses incurred by the company. Prior to deregulation of the United States and Canadian railways in 1981, tariffs in the three countries were similar, and for some years Mexico's were lower than in the US. With deregulation, the efficiency of the US and Canadian railways began to improve rapidly and tariffs fell quickly as the graph shows.

Figure 2.6. **Tariffs in the North American Railways**

Constant USD 2012 cents*

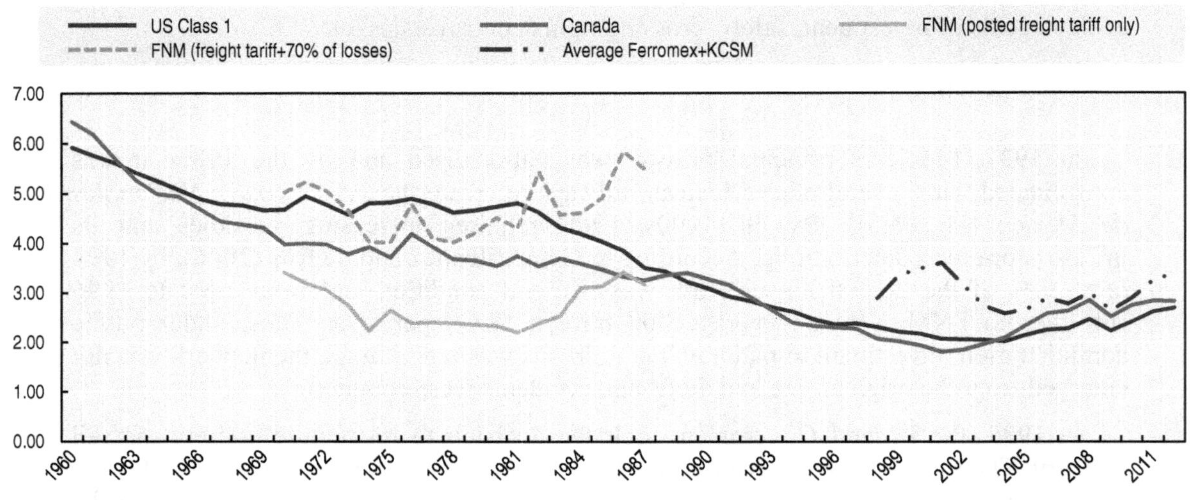

* These data are based on average actual revenues per tonne-km. The data for the United States and Canada are based on the Statistics of Class I Railroads for the US and Regulatory Association of Canada publications for Canada. Data for FNM are from FNM sources developed during the concession process by Lou Thompson (World Bank Railway Advisor at the time). Data for the concessions comes from data furnished by the concessions and published in the AAR handbook.

Source: ITF (2014), "Freight Railway Development in Mexico", *International Transport Forum Policy Papers*, No. 1, OECD Publishing, Paris, http://dx.doi.org/10.1787/5jlwvzjd60kb-en.

In contrast, the 1980s saw steeply rising tariffs and by the end of the decade they were double rates elsewhere in North America. Following deregulation in Mexico there were initially some quite large fluctuations in tariffs, before and after the year 2000, likely to be a result of ongoing adjustments following restructuring. Since 2005, convergence in average tariff levels and trends among North American railways seems to appear. Nevertheless, tariffs in Mexico have stayed at higher levels than those in the United States and Canada.

On the other hand, traffic has doubled and many shippers report that service levels have improved. Since 2005 the difference between average tariffs in Mexico and the other North American railways has been small. In view of differences in the commodity types carried, ownership of freight wagons, traffic density, scale of operations and so on, the gap in tariffs is low.

Average tariffs charged by Mexico's main railway operators compare favourably with railways elsewhere in Latin America (Figure 2.7). The figures compiled by the Inter-American Development Bank make some adjustment for commodity mix carried, removing dedicated mine railways from the comparison. Nevertheless, none of the other railways carry high value products like automobiles, auto parts and consumer electronics to anything like the extent of the Mexican railways.

Figure 2.7. **Average tariff of different railways in Latin America 2011-12**

USD cents per ton-km

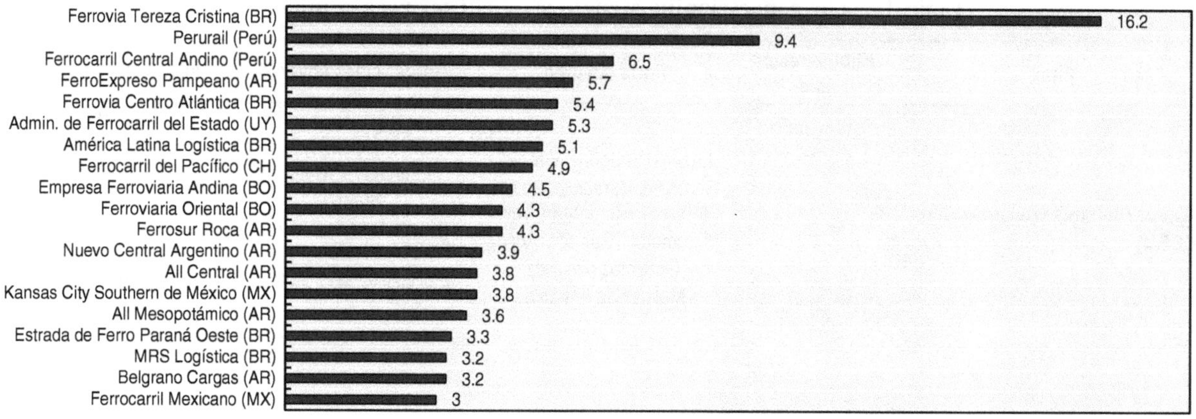

Source: IDB (2013), "Información Estadística sobre los Sistemas Ferroviarios Latinoamericanos" (Statistical Information on Latinamerican Railway Systems), Observatorio Regional de Carga y Logística (Freight Transport and Logistics Regional Observatory), http://logisticsportal.iadb.org/.

The concession system adopted was adapted to Mexican geography and freight markets, in which the system was split into three large, regionally distinct companies, and a shared terminal railway in the Mexico City metropolitan region. There are also a number of smaller companies, mostly short lines, with very low traffic levels (Table 2.5). The approach relied on competitive forces, not only on stiff competition with other modes of transport (principally road transport), but on competition between railways operating on separate lines. This was intended to yield three types of competition:

- Direct competition, with alternative routes to key locations (e.g. Monterrey) by two principal competing concessions
- Side-by-side (parallel) competition, for example by Ferromex and KCSM from the US border to Mexico City, or by Ferromex from the port of Manzanillo versus KCSM from the port of Lazaro Cardenas to Queretaro (and to Mexico City); plus
- Alternative sources of competition, for example by KCSM from the port of Lazaro Cardenas versus Ferrosur (now part of Ferromex) from the port of Veracruz, both to Mexico City.

The 1995 reform also mandated the granting of trackage or haulage rights (where one railway operates over the tracks of another and pays a fee for doing so) in specific markets where traffic was high enough to support two operators. Just over 2 000 kms of trackage rights were identified of which the most important—the main lines running north and west from Queretaro, 200 km NW of Mexico City—amounted to 929 kms. The route length subject to trackage rights amounted to 12% of the total system.

Overall, the system design relied for effective competition on intermodal direct competition in key locations, parallel and source competition, supplemented by trackage rights in specific situations. The structure included the creation of a joint terminal concession in the Mexico City region that provided competitively-neutral access to all operators into the large Mexico City market. Each of the three freight operators owned 25% of the company with a fourth 25% share remaining with government, in order to provide for access by the planned commuter passenger operators. The joint terminal company appears to have been fully satisfactory in allowing neutral access at a reasonable cost for all three main operators, and in supporting operation of at least one commuter operator.

Table 2.5. **The concessioning structure of rail services in industry**

Firm	Kilometres of line	Ports covered	Border cities covered	Inland cities covered
Kansas City Southern de México (KCSM)	4 283	Lázaro Cárdenas (Pacific) Santa Fe, Veracruz (Gulf of Mexico) with right-of-way Matamoros (Gulf of Mexico) Guaymas (Pacific) Manzanillo (Pacific)	Matamoros (United States) Nuevo Laredo (United States) Mexicali (United States)	Mexico City Hermosillo Guadalajara Irapuato Silao Puebla Monterrey Torreón Chihuahua
Ferrocarril Mexicano (Ferromex)[1]	8 643	Altamira (Gulf of Mexico) Guaymas Topolobampo Mazatlán Tampico (Gulf of Mexico) Manzanillo Coatzacoalcos (Gulf of Mexico) Veracruz (Gulf of Mexico)	Piedras Negras (United States) Mexicali (United States) Nogales (United States) Ojinaga (United States) El Paso (United States) Ciudad Juárez (United States)	Puebla Mexico City Querétaro Irapuato Tepic Guadalajara Chihuahua Los Mochis Culiacán Hermosillo Saltillo Monterrey Torreón Aguascalientes Colima
Línea Coahuila Durango	974	-	-	Sabinas Barroterán Ciudad Frontera Escalón Torreón Felipe Pescador Durango
Ferrocarril y Terminal del Valle de México	297	-	-	-
Compañía de Ferrocarriles Chiapas-Mayab[2]	1 550	Villahermosa (Gulf of Mexico) Coatzacoalcos (Gulf of Mexico) Progreso (Gulf of Mexico) Puerto Madero (Pacific) Salina Cruz (Pacific)	-	-Campeche Mérida Izamal Escárcega Ixtepec Arriaga Tonalá
Ferrocarril del Istmo de Tehuantepec	219	Salina Cruz (Pacific)		
Administradora de la vía corta Tijuana- Tecate	71	-	Tijuana Tecate	-

1. Including the lines of Ferrosur, due to its merge.

2. Currently, the Federal Government through the SCT is following a legal procedure to rescue the Compañía de Ferrocarriles Chiapas-Mayab due to the withdrawal of the service by the original concessioner. For more information on this topic consult the *Resolución que contiene la Declaratoria de rescate de la Concesión otorgada en favor de Compañía de Ferrocarriles Chiapas-Mayab, S.A. de C.V.* published on the DOF on May 4th. 2016.

Source: Ministry of Communications and Transport of Mexico.

While the restructuring and reform of 1995 brought economic growth in the sector and a decrease in tariffs, the impact on competition should be further assessed by SCT and the competition commission. Meanwhile, some issues remain, which are discussed next.

Trackage rights

The 1995 law includes provision for trackage rights to enable one rail carrier to run trains from its system onto the tracks of another carrier. The 1995 reforms included a set of mandatory trackage rights designated by the government and a provision for the railways to voluntarily negotiate additional rights among themselves. No trackage rights were implemented for over a decade, however, until outstanding rights claims between Ferromex and Kansas City Southern Mexico (KCSM) were settled to pave the way for approval of the acquisition of Ferrosur by Grupo Mexico, owner of Ferromex, in 2011.[4] However, no voluntary trackage rights were agreed to, frustrating some shippers who were expecting earlier and greater railway to railway competition via trackage rights.

Interline rates

Some shippers have observed that rates per ton-kilometre are much higher for shipments that move via an interline service (originating on one railway then transferring to another for final movement to destination), than for services on a single carrier. There are many reasons why interline rates may be justifiably higher than single carrier rates, not least because connecting movements may be short, implying higher unit costs.

One main reason is the costs of interchange—marshalling wagons, changing crews and locomotives, amongst others—that a single line rate avoids. It is also common that the single line rate is over a better route than the interchange route; even if the interline rate looks shorter it may involve worse track conditions or curves and gradients through mountainous terrain. Most importantly, railroads price on a contribution basis; if the single line rate contributes more to the originating railway than an interline move for which it receives only part of the revenue, then it will prefer the single line rate. Decisions are not taken in a vacuum and for every single line rate that a railway wants to protect, there is likely to be another single line rate that another railway wants to protect, in order to ensure the overall viability of the network. For these reasons the US STB and Canadian regulator do not generally intervene in interline rate decisions.

There appears to be no documented evidence of any systematic interline "premium" in Mexico, rather specific instances that might merit examination by the new regulatory agency (see section *Regulatory capacity*). Waybill data would need to be collected for the analysis required to identify any cases of potential over charging. Currently, no data is available to perform the above mentioned analysis.

Rail rates

In Mexico, according to LRSF, tariffs for freight, passengers and auxiliary services are set freely, but need to incorporate contributions for interconnection between terminals, and the right to access and use infrastructure of other concessionaires (Art. 35-36 of the LRSF). Prices have to be set based on non-discriminatory basis, with the only obligation to submit them to DGDFM (former DGTFM) (Art. 46 of LRSF). If the SCT or another party considers that the prices do hamper fair competition, they can request an opinion from the Federal Economic Competition Commission (COFECE) about the market conditions; during this period, the SCT will temporally fix tariffs of services (Art. 47 of LRSF). These tariffs have to be registered within the DGDFM (former DGTFM) and can increase according to inflation and operator's costs.

Non regarding this, a number of shippers have claimed that railway rates are too high. SCT has the legal power to set maximum rail rates and the power to collect data on payments by shippers to railways, to audit that actual rail rates do not exceed posted maximum rates. The regulatory powers are in respect to maximum rates, and rates are assessed based on inflation in railway costs, but no analysis is made to determine whether the rate levels before inflation are too high or too low. Neither does SCT track the profits of the railways or make determination as to whether railways are revenue adequate or earning returns above their cost of capital. As railway regulator, SCT has not determined an allowed cost of capital for the railways.

In the US and Canada rates are confidential and shippers can and do pay different rates for similar shipments. Even if service levels and commodities are identical, difference in rate is on its own, no basis for complaint to the regulator. In Canada if a shipper is unhappy with a rate it goes to arbitration. The arbitrator will probably not seek to equalise rates, especially if they were set on different dates. In the United States, some commodities are eligible for maximum rate review, but not in relation to rates applied to other shippers.

No OECD country regulates freight tariffs systematically. Where countries do regulate all freight tariffs, in the Russian Federation and India for example, the railways are seeing their share of freight carriage and their income eroded, as they are unable to respond to price competition from road haulage in the higher yielding markets (ITF, 2004). In both these countries railways have traditionally enjoyed systemic monopolies in freight carriage over parts of their networks. In Russia, rail is the only option in large parts of Siberia, and the nature of the heavy industrial products carried over much of the rest of the network prior to 1991 was much better suited to rail than road haulage. In India, poor road quality with low standards of traffic management and regulatory enforcement resulted in systemic congestion, and this provided the railways with a significant advantage. In both countries freight profits have traditionally been used to support passenger services. In these circumstances freight tariff controls were seen as necessary to protect shippers. Investment in rapidly expanding highway systems is removing the advantage for railways in both countries and both are seeing increasing difficulty in covering costs. Freight tariff regulation persists, despite the changed circumstances and the rigidities it creates prevent the railway companies from being able to respond to competition from road hauliers.

Ending freight tariff regulation was one of the keys to success in the deregulation of the US and Canadian railways. The US and Canada's today competition, between railways and from road haulage and shipping, is primarily relied on to prevent abusive pricing. Regulatory authorities oversee tariffs, but intervene to cap prices only in very limited circumstances.

US regulation accepts Ramsey pricing, and focuses on identifying and rectifying cases in which market power has been abused. US regulations specify in some detailed the circumstances that might constitute abuse. These are:

- total revenues that exceed those required to recover costs including a reasonable return on investment
- prices for a shipment that exceed stand-alone costs

- a revenue to marginal cost ratio greater than 180%
- inefficient operating costs
- or abrupt changes in tariffs that would cause disruption.

Contract rates and a range of services are exempt of any regulation. Combined with the definition of effective competition, exemptions mean that only about 10% of traffic is actually eligible for regulation (see ITF, 2016).

Canadian regulation has a less clearly defined set of parameters for delimiting the circumstances in which tariffs can be regulated but follow similar lines. Under the Canadian National Transportation Policy, competition (including from other modes) and market forces are primarily relied on. Canadian regulatory remedies (inter-switching, final offer arbitration, level of service adjudication and arbitration) are intended to provide shippers with additional leverage in their negotiations with railways, rather than replacing negotiation with rate setting.

Alternative models that include systematic regulation of track access charges (prices for train operators) and separation of track management from train operation have been introduced elsewhere in the world. In the United Kingdom, where the infrastructure manager (Network Rail) is separate from the train operators, the regulator (ORR) sets the access charges that Network Rail can apply on its infrastructure over a 5-year period. Infrastructure use charges are based on the calculated Regulatory Asset Base (RAB), which is determined taking into account expenditures, debt and depreciation. Freight rates (prices for shippers) are not regulated in the United Kingdom, but passenger fares are subject to a price cap. Passenger fares can increase year-on-year only insofar as the weighted basket of all available fares to passengers does not exceed the price cap, typically linked to inflation.

The other countries in the European Union have also separated infrastructure management from train operations and adopted similar charging principles, based on non-discrimination and some of cost-reflection. Many charge freight trains only the marginal costs of using the infrastructure, leaving passenger trains to cover fixed costs (ITF, 2008). All the railways with the exception of the freight-intensive railways of the Baltic States require large public subsidies. Governments generally subsidise passenger services on all but the most intensively used inter-city routes. Governments also cover a large part of capital investment costs in rail infrastructure and in some countries also subsidise track maintenance costs.

In Europe many railways have accumulated very large debts. These have generally been taken off the railway balance sheets, at least in part, but remain in special financial options. In some cases governments have failed to pay even the interest on the debt and debt has continued to grow.

Implementation of trackage rights and rail rates

Although the LRSF mandated the award of trackage rights, confirmed in each concession contract, it did not specify the terms to be applied to trackage rights. Operators are required to negotiate terms (charges, types of service allowed, permissible volumes of traffic, dispatching priority, etc.). If agreement cannot be reached within 90 days of the start of negotiations, SCT has authority to impose the terms of access (Art. 35 LRSF), but the basis on which terms should be established is unclear.

The difficulty in developing the terms of trackage rights reflects the core issues of railway cost structures and pricing policy. Railways are an industry of high fixed costs and low marginal costs, leading to prices that can range from just above marginal cost to well above that level.

Mexican concessions allow freight tariffs differentiation following well-established principles (often called "Ramsey Pricing"). This implies that for maximum efficiency in the long run, prices should be market-based and differentiated to reflect the value of the service to the customer, subject to the limit imposed by competitive alternatives. Customers who are highly sensitive to transport costs (such as sand and gravel producers) will be charged low prices, while customers who are less sensitive to transport costs (such as containers or auto parts shippers) will pay higher prices.[5] This principle is also fundamental to US and Canadian rail regulation.

Whereas Mexican companies are free to apply Ramsey Pricing, they are subject to a requirement to file a table of maximum tariffs in order to prevent individual abuse of dominance. Tariffs below this maximum are unregulated and agreed in commercial contracts (that are voluntary and confidential). The use of confidential contracts was also a key principle employed in the successful deregulation of the US railways in 1980 (the "Staggers Act") and in Canada (1987).

Box 2.1. **Regulatory oversight of abuse of market power in the United States**

Overall income and cost recovery

Revenue adequacy (a normal return on capital invested) is not guaranteed for any US railroad, nor is earning revenue greater than a normal return prohibited. The US Surface Transportation Board (STB) annually measures the rate of return earned by each Class I railroad and also determines an industry wide cost of capital. From this, it can be inferred whether a given railway has become revenue adequate. Revenue adequacy is a factor considered in maximum rate regulation cases. US freight railroads generally receive no subsidy. Passenger services (either Amtrak or metro regional) are provided by freight railways for a fee. The passenger rail authority may be subsidised by federal or regional governments, but there is no direct subsidy for passenger services paid to freight carriers. Generally there is no capital subsidy paid to US freight railroads, although they may qualify in certain cases for partial financing under some specific federal, state or metro infrastructure programmes.

Individual cases

Certain shippers have the right to appeal a rail carrier's tariff to the US Surface Transportation Board.* A rate can be appealed only if the ratio of the rate to unit long-run variable cost exceeds 180%. The shipper must then prove that the railroad has market dominance (a rate exceeding the 180% threshold does not necessarily constitute market dominance). Determining maximum rates generally involves use of the stand alone cost (SAC) test. This test is costly for the shipper, carrier and the STB alike with some proceedings requiring several years, costing millions of dollars. A simplified SAC is available but generally not used where the transport revenues being contested fall within a medium range. Rates involving smaller revenues can be contested using a three benchmark test, but this too is not frequently used. In assessing the contested rate, a major factor is whether or not the railway has achieved revenue adequacy.

*. Congress empowered the STB to develop a list of commodities or shipment types that are considered to have competitive transportation alternative, and these are not eligible for a rate review. These include, for example, anything shipped in containers and box cars (wagons), any forest or automotive products, amongst others.

Source: Elaboration by the OECD Secretariat based on the Surface Transportation Board.

By comparison, in the US and Canada prices are allowed to be differentiated in this way, so long as overall income generated does not exceed that needed to recover total costs and earn an acceptable rate of return on investment (see Box 2.1). Prices are also subject to ensuring there is no abuse of market power in individual cases by setting maximum limits for carriage that cannot be exceeded, commodity by commodity. The principle promotes efficient operations by railways and helps recover the fixed costs of infrastructure in the most economically efficient way. To be clear, discrimination is permitted on the basis of service level provided and type of cargo carried, with types of freight that are less sensitive to price that are charged more.

The Ramsey Pricing principle also has implications for charges for using trackage rights. Although exclusivity of train operations reduces rail-versus-rail competition, it does not reduce intermodal competition, and it gives an operator a somewhat better chance of recovering fixed costs. Trackage rights can erode the ability to cover fixed costs if they are not well designed and efficiently priced. If a tenant train operator does not pay enough, or if the terms of access do not permit the tenant's traffic to be efficiently integrated with the existing operator, the existing operator will be damaged. If this occurs in a major market, the financial and operational viability of the concessionaire will be damaged.

Very shortly after the concessions were initiated in Mexico, the concessionaires commenced negotiations on trackage rights. Until 2010, however, negotiations remained unproductive because the stakes were high for the concessionaires and because the basis on which to formulate them was undefined. In 2010, Ferromex and KCSM finally reached agreement on the most important segments: access by KCSM to Guadalajara and Silao, and access by Ferromex to the main KCSM line from Viborillas to Ramos Arizpe. These agreements can expand competitive access for domestic traffic. However, the companies agreed not to use these trackage rights for export/import traffic. Whether or not this represents a significant loss of potential competition is something that warrants further examination.

A potential issue in network industries, known as foreclosure, can take place when a dominant firm denies proper access to an essential good it produces, with the intent of reinforcing or extending its monopoly power. As discussed in the large literature on this topic (see, for example, Rey and Tirole, 2006) foreclosure can arise when the essential facility is an input, such as infrastructure in rail services.[6] Even when access to interconnections is granted, foreclosure can take place in the form of price discrimination, since the vertical monopolist may have an incentive to raise the rival firm's costs and hence create an artificial competitive advantage for the rail services it offers. Examples of this behaviour are common and an example from Germany is often referred to: in an earlier version of its track access charging system (removed in 2011), the infrastructure manager DB Netz was found by the German Competition Authority to have favoured the integrated railway undertaking DB Regio over rivals by means of volume discounts.

Given the potential incentive for an integrated monopoly to foreclose, Mexico should systematically review the instances in which interconnection is granted in order to verify that:

- Access to the infrastructure is only ever denied based on objective justifications, and not motivated by an intention to foreclose, and;

- Access prices as expressed in the interconnection agreements are not modulated so as to raise the rival company's costs and, if discrimination takes place, this is based on objective criteria and does not disproportionately benefit the integrated company.

Potential reforms

Issues over interlining arrangements led the Chamber of Deputies to propose an extensive revision to the 1995 railway law in December 2013, amended by the Senate in December 2014 and approved by Deputies on 15 December 2014. In its original formulation the revision of the law would have dramatically restructured the railway industry. It was designed to facilitate the use of trackage rights and allow railways to run their trains on the tracks of other railway concessionaires and included open access provisions to allow shippers or other parties to run trains. These open access provisions were removed by the Senate in order to safeguard property rights accorded to existing rail concessions and preserve incentives for investment on the part of concessionaires. On 26 January 2015, it was published in the Official Gazette, a decree by which was reformed the Law of the Rail Service. This reform includes the creation of the Regulatory Agency of Rail Transport and the National Security Fund for rail crossing roads.

The reform as originally proposed would have been unique in the world. Neither the US nor Canada (both of which share the North American rail network with Mexico and use a common technology) allow comprehensive trackage rights. While some trackage rights exist in the US, they are limited and almost uniformly the result of voluntary agreements among the carriers, often as a result of mergers. In Canada, the only major trackage rights are due to operational agreements between carriers.

Both Canada and the US have legislation that empowers the railway regulator to impose trackage rights on the railways. However, even after 125 years of such power, these governments have not imposed such rights on the track owning carrier. In Canada, where there have been a small number of requests from shoreline operators for trackage rights on mainlines, such rights have been viewed as similar to the expropriation of property, and the regulatory agency has not granted any such applications. It clarified in its decisions that such rights, even if granted, would not extend to traffic solicitation in competition with the mainline carrier, but would be limited only to transit rights. In any event, this has been a moot point since the Agency has not granted such rights. While there have been recommendations in Canada to enhance the legislative power to award trackage rights, as a means to enhance rail competition, governments (of both major political parties) have consistently rejected such legislative change, even as they made other changes to the railway sections of the Transportation Act.

It should be noted that if railway trackage rights are used to increases competition between railways, this removes the need for regulation of the rates shippers pay the railways. The literature in this area (Vickers, 1995; Gabel and Weiman, 1998) emphasises that competition is the first-best option to reduce the exercise of market power by a single operator. This provides incentives for productive, allocative and dynamic efficiency, in turn achieving lower prices and higher quality for consumers, as well as greater technical innovation. It is often the responsibility of sector regulators and/or competition authorities to determine whether sufficient competitive pressures are present in the market. If either excessive dominance or abuse of market power is detected (e.g. in the form of excessive profits), then the potential for some form of regulation arises. Either competition is used to limit exercise of carrier market power, or price regulation is used, but not both.

It is important to note that both Canada and the US have rejected running rights as a solution to railway rate concerns. One reason for this is that such a regime mixes two different governance models for railways. One model, the one used in North America (Canada, US and Mexico) to date, involves vertically integrated railways, where a rail company owns (or leases) track and runs trains on its own track. There are important economies from vertical integration of a railway, including elimination of double marginalisation in railway rates, optimisation of train operation and track investment, and coverage of fixed costs. Carriers will do this optimisation differently, depending on the market conditions they face. Vertical integration also eliminates the need for establishing the prices for track access, which if done by a regulator can be a time consuming and expensive undertaking, with major negative consequences if access prices are set incorrectly.

The alternative railway governance model involves complete vertical separation of the railway into a track company (usually government owned) and one or more train operating companies. This model is used, for example, in the United Kingdom where Network Rail operates the track and various other companies operate trains on the track, including freight operating companies. The freight operating companies include the German freight railway and freight forwarder DB Schenker and specialty train operating companies, such as Devon and Cornwall Railways (owned by Iowa Pacific Holdings that also owns short lines in North America) and GB Railfreight (owned by Eurotunnel). The vertically separated railway governance model requires a regulator to establish rates for access to track. This is not a trivial undertaking. In the United Kingdom this is the responsibility of the Office of Rail Regulation, with a staff of around 280 and an annual budget of GBP 30 million (USD 47 million).

The advantage of the vertical separation regime is the absence of ambiguity on the rates to be charged. A mixed regime suffers greatly from ambiguity. It is difficult for a regulator to establish rates for the "host railway", as it earns revenues not only from fees from guest railways operating on its track, but also from its own train operations. The latter includes revenues which must be used for track cost contributions. Separating this out is not an easy task. One of the most important aspects of any railway governance regime is the price signals for investment. If these are not efficient, then investment is reduced, service deteriorates, productivity falls and rates rise. This in turn undermines the logistics chain for a nations export and domestic trade. This is not a hypothetical concern. It is exactly what happened in the United States, Canada and Mexico over many decades, and was only rectified by policy changes in the 1980s and 1990s.

The mixed regime also is likely to have ambiguity, as it is left to the host railway to establish a wide range of operating procedures, investment and maintenance policies, amongst others. While there may be an attraction to implementing a mixed regime in Mexico, there is high risk that the policy will fail and reverse the gains achieved in the past 18 years, gains which were critical in enabling Mexico's export growth. The inward investment in the automobile industry, for example, would not have been possible without the improvement in quality of rail service (especially in reliability), and the reduction in tariffs achieved as a result of the productivity increases unlocked by deregulation in Mexico.

A potential remedy to allow for interline rail traffic can be the application in Mexico of the Rail Tariff Rule 11, see Box 2.2.

Box 2.2. **Rail Tariff Rule 11: a potential remedy for interline rail traffic**

What is Rail Tariff Rule 11

An alternative policy remedy to limit the issues faced by shippers requiring an interline movement is available elsewhere in North America. "Tariff Rule 11" is used by railways and shippers in both the US and Canada and is simple to use in practice. Rule 11 is one of the Railway Accounting Rules published by the Association of American Railroads (AAR).The rule can be used by shippers as a means to argue for a more favourable rate for a movement that requires connecting services between two carriers.

In most cases, a shipper requests a rate from the originating carrier, who then negotiates with the connecting rail carrier for the cost of moving the traffic on the second carrier. The originating carrier then quotes a single through-rate to the shipper, which combines the charge of the originating carrier and the connecting carrier. The shipper generally will not know the rate break down and the split between revenue to the originating and connecting carriers. Sometimes the connecting carrier will not know the breakdown either.

With a Rule 11 rate, the shipper is charged separately by the two carriers for the portion of the transport service provided by each. Rule 11 can be initiated by the originating carrier or by the shipper. If the shipper-carrier contracts are confidential, then Rule 11 protects the confidentiality of the rates for the shipper. The US Association of American Railroads (AAR) notes that: "Rule 11 is intended for use by the rail industry to protect confidential prices and/or meet customer requirements by providing multiple freight bills on shipments covered by a through Bill of Lading." Rule 11 is the default rate rule that enables a shipper to combine negotiated rates from two carriers for an interline move where a joint-line rate is not available. The carriers bill the shipper separately, which enables the confidentiality of the rates charged to be maintained.

The shipper can also use Rule 11 to combine published rates of two carriers to achieve an interline service where no existing interchange arrangements exists, which may be the case between short lines and major carriers. The effectiveness of Rule 11 carriage depends on the availability and effectiveness of interchanges but in the US and Canada interchanges have not proved an obstacle.

Rule 11 can be a powerful remedy for a shipper, in some cases, for a shipper who is unsatisfied with a through rate quoted by an originating carrier. It is always a remedy when the posted public tariffs sum to a charge less than the originating carrier's quoted through rate. For other cases, it eliminates the opportunity for the originating carrier to add a mark-up to the fee it (the originating carrier) will pay to the connecting carrier. If the shipper has a choice of routings, it may be able to use Rule 11 both to get more competitive rates from the candidate connecting carriers and to put some pressure on the originating carrier for its part of the rate, as the shipper might choose an option that results in a shorter movement on the connecting carrier.

A final advantage is that the competitive benefit of Rule 11 can be present even if the rule is not used or seldom used. An originating carrier knowing the shipper has a Rule 11 option may be less likely to quote a high through rate.

Potential application in Mexico

Tariff Rule 11 might provide a useful tool to address the perceived issues faced by shippers requesting interlining services. At the same time, the Regulatory Agency for Rail Transport established in 2015 should develop the competence and capacity for a more comprehensive approach to ensuring that rail tariffs are set in a non-discriminatory and transparent way through full implementation of the existing railway law.

Box 2.2. **Rail Tariff Rule 11: a potential remedy for interline rail traffic** (*cont.*)

The implementation of Rule 11 could in theory also present some disadvantages. It might encourage tacit collusion between the originating and the connecting carrier by artificially inflating costs for customers seeking to interline. It might also result in longer waiting times if the carriers are not able to agree on a tariff in due course, potentially damaging the competitiveness of rail freight vis-à-vis other modes. This does not, however, appear to have been the case in the United States.

Should Mexico adopt a Rule 11 model, the exclusion of import/export services from these regulations as is the case in the United States and Canada would deserve more analysis, given the large share of imports and exports carried by Mexican rail freight companies.

Source: Elaboration by the OECD Secretariat based on Rail Accounting Rules. Association of American Railroads 2015.

Regulatory capacity

A reform to the LRSF published in the Official Gazette of Mexico on 26 January 2015, includes the creation of the Railway Transport Regulatory Agency (*Agencia Reguladora del Transporte Ferroviario*, ARTF). It is a de-concentrated body of the SCT, with technical and operational autonomy, but without legal personality or financial independence—it will remain financially and legally dependent on the SCT.

In fact, the reform split the DGDFM (former DGTFM) in two organisations, one in charge of the promotion of the industry (SCT's General Direction of Rail and Multimodal Transport) and the other in charge of the regulatory affairs (ARTF). The main challenges to the new agency, however, as it is stated in the law, are to overcome the limited designated budget and the independency over the technical decisions, as they are under the umbrella of the SCT.

The government does not presently collect the data necessary or conduct the analysis required to make determinations on access conditions and tariffs, where trackage rights are disputed, or shippers believe they are captive under the current law. *A fortiori* the government would not be equipped to set rates and conditions under extended access provisions.

Effective regulation requires adequate and accurate information, much of it made public to ensure the credibility and transparency of regulatory decisions. To be able to implement the current law fully, Mexico needs to adopt a suitably adapted version of the regulatory information reported to US and Canadian authorities. The key information that the US law requires railways to provide is as follows:

The US Surface Transportation Board (STB) form R-1,[7] has been filed annually by every Class I (large) US freight railway for many years, and provides the information for detailed comparisons among railroads and analysis of changes over time. As both Ferromex and KCSM both have US Class 1 railways as significant shareholders, preparing and filing the required information should be well understood and well within their capability and resources. The R-1 forms are sworn statements that are also prepared in support of filings before the Securities and Exchange Commission (SEC), so they are reliable. They include a wide range of financial information, as well as employment, wage and salary, tariff, commodity and operational indicators.

- US Class I railroads also file an electronic copy of all freight waybills. The freight waybill contains a wide range of information including commodity type, number of carloads, shipment weight, shipment distance, origin and destination stations by railroad, tariff revenue and tariff type (contract versus public tariff), among other data. The waybills permit the STB to analyse commodity flows by route, commodity flows by origin and destination pair, tariffs by commodity and a virtually unlimited range of other questions
- The STB can combine the waybill data with the R-1 data to estimate the cost of a shipment in order to assess the relationship between revenue and cost for a particular shipment, or for a particular commodity, or for particular railways. Waybill data also identify export and import traffic in fully usable detail.

Using this data, the US STB publishes annual Revenue Stratification reports that indicate the share of railway revenues by category of commodity and the percentage of traffic (by revenue) carried at rates above and below long run variable cost. This reveals that in 2011, for example, the average mark-up over all types of freight was 45% and that:

- 12% of US rail traffic by revenue moved below variable cost
- 53% was carried with a mark-up over variable cost of between 0 and 80%
- 36% was carried with a mark-up of over 80%.

Traffic carried below an 80% mark-up is deemed not to be subject to market power, following a ruling by Congress. The data extracted from the stratification reports in Figure 2.8 and Figure 2.9 illustrates the kind of broad picture of the freight market that the data collected and made public provides. STB's waybill data covers all (confidential) contract tariffs providing the information needed to arbitrate when rates are contested.

Collection and analysis of Mexico's waybill data would allow assessment of the degree of interchanging and the use of trackage rights, in order to determine the extent of national network and service integration. Equally importantly, it would allow informed decisions to be made about any proposed changes in industry structure or regulation.

The regulatory agency created by Decree on 18 August 2016 and published in the Official Gazette will need to develop a data collection system along these lines as a matter of priority, in order to carry out its responsibilities towards ensuring interconnection of services and efficient tariffs (DOF, 2016).

The agency will also need to develop a methodological basis for limiting the ability of railroads to "refuse to deal" with competing railroads regarding the traffic of captive shippers, and determining efficient charges for inter-switching services that treat shippers fairly. This requires judgement in relation to overall transport and competition policy goals and is an area of policy that will be contested regularly, just as it is in the United States (Pittman, 2010).

Regulations like the LRSF and the Bylaw of Rail services will need to be updated if the regulatory agency is to implement these last two recommendations: to establish the faculty to the agency to collect data, giving it the power of enforcement and the capacity to audit the rail companies if need it.

Figure 2.8. **Distribution of carriage by rate band for top 21 commodity groups, 2011**

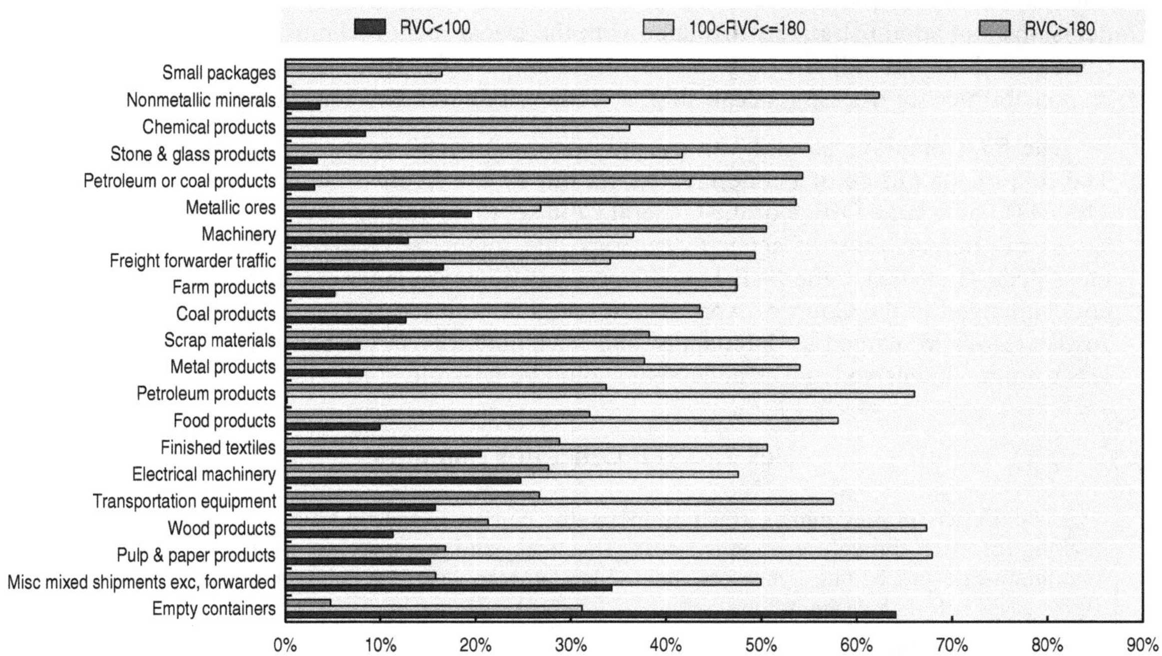

Source: US STB Commodity Revenue Stratification Report for 2011.

Figure 2.9. **Distribution of US rail traffic across rate bands in 2011**

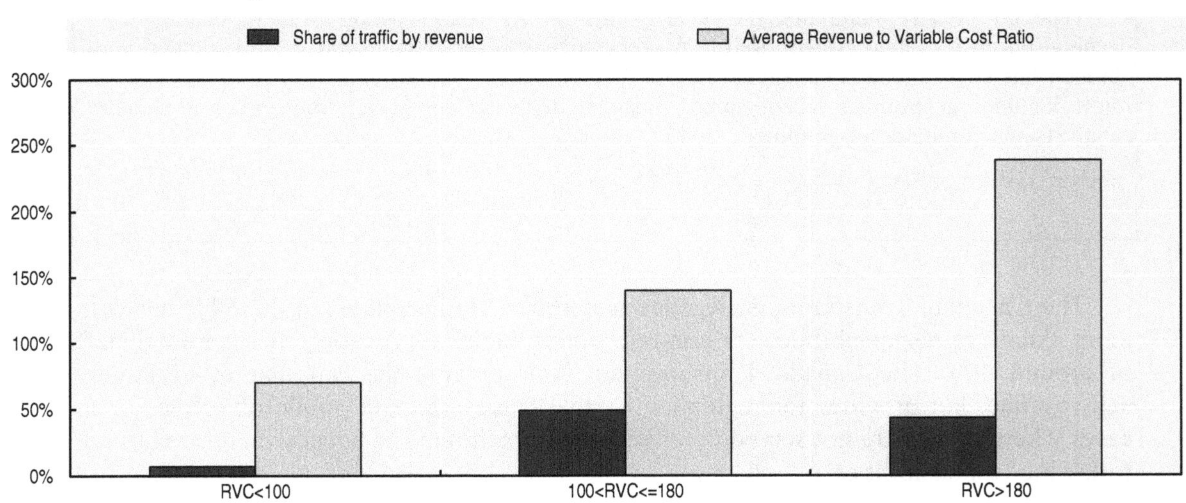

Source: US STB Commodity Revenue Stratification Report for 2011.

Rail regulatory agencies in North America

This section describes the North American regulatory agencies given that they have been contributing to the performance of the vertical integrated systems they regulate, systems that have performed better in comparison with the other models, and that share the structure with the Mexican system.

The US Surface Transportation Board was established by Congress to resolve railway rate and service disputes and review proposed rail mergers. It is independent in making decisions, but administratively affiliated with the Department of Transportation. The STB serves as both an adjudicatory and a regulatory body. The agency also has some responsibilities for trucking, ocean shipping, intercity buses and certain pipelines.

The STB employs around 135 people[8] with around 50 in the Office of Economics. The role of the Office of Economics, as set out by the STB, is summarised in Box 2.3. The STB has a large Office of the General Counsel to defend its decisions in court and to assess the defensibility of agency decisions that might be challenged in court. Unlike most Federal agencies, the STB has independent litigating authority and when decisions are challenged in the Court of Appeals attorneys of both the STB and the Department of Justice (DoJ) are named as defendants, and have authority to appear in court. A simpler, less resource intensive legal arrangement should be possible in Mexico.

Box 2.3. **STB Office of Economics**

The Office of Economics (OE) supports the Surface Transportation Board's decision-making process through economic, cost, financial, and engineering analyses in railroad maximum-rate proceedings, mergers, line abandonments, and line-construction and trackage-rights cases before the agency.

OE oversees accounting and reporting rules and requirements for regulated railroads and maintains an audit programme to ensure compliance; provides up-to-date information on the financial condition of individual railroads and the overall industry; and maintains informational databases, including the railroad waybill file, and railroad annual and quarterly financial and operating data.

The Office also maintains the STB's Uniform Railroad Costing System, the agency's general-purpose costing system used in matters such as rail maximum-rate cases, calculation of branch-line costs in abandonment cases, and cost estimates in other regulatory contexts. The OE staff includes economists, accountants, financial analysts, engineers, transportation industry analysts and computer programmers.

Source: STB, https://www.stb.gov/stb/about/office_oe.html.

The Canadian Transportation Agency undertakes similar duties to the STB but with more extensive responsibilities for non-rail modes, including aviation. It has a total staff of around 400. The Canada Transportation Act, permits the rail market to largely self-regulate, but provides for regulation by the agency to meet public objectives or in cases where parties are not served by effective competition. The agency therefore has the following responsibilities:

- licensing rail carriers
- approving railway line construction
- setting railway revenue caps for moving western grain
- establishing financial and costing frameworks for certain railways
- setting inter-switching rates to increase competitive options available to shippers

- establishing the net salvage value of railway lines to facilitate their orderly transfer.

Border crossing and inspections

Boarding crossing inefficiencies or any regulation which is not supported by any risk control justification (or other), lower or delay traffic flows of merchandise unnecessarily between countries. Thus, this situation has an impact on business creation and trade. Of course a situation like this is not desirable and regulation to cross borders should be based on risk management of perfectly identified issues.

Border crossing issues are dealt with in the chapter on border regulation of this report, but rail is particularly affected by a number of aspects of the way border controls are implemented. There are 15 rail border crossing points with the United States. One of these, Nuevo Laredo, is equipped with single window IT systems. The electronic exchange of data does work. However, the Mexican authorities require duplicate paper manifests for the time being. More generally, practices vary somewhat from one border station to another, and border agency personnel are often unfamiliar with rail working practices and constraints. Inspections outside standard office hours are often not available, despite the size and value of loads carried by block trains operating 24 hours a day.

The use of bonded inland warehouses and bonded transit transport is increasing rapidly in Mexico; for auto parts, for example, or for Chilean fruit in transit to the United States by rail through the Port of Lazaro Cardenas. Customs authorities sometimes fail to waive in-country inspection as is provided for by bonded containers (see Border Management chapter).

Large block trains require significant investments in infrastructure for stopping for inspection. A grain train might count 100 cars and be 3km long. Sidings to park such a train do not exist at borders and inspections need to take place at terminal depots, where there are suitable facilities. Inspection services in Mexico, US and Canada are discussing possibilities for reciprocal inspections to avoid stopping trains at borders.

Recommendations

Regulatory capacity

Establishment of a regulatory agency with responsibilities for conditions of access to the freight rail services under revisions to the Railway law adopted in December 2014 is welcome. Development of capacity to collect and analyse the data needed to form judgements on issues of competition should be pursued without delay and sufficient resources provided for this important task. Establishment of a Mexican equivalent of the US STB form R-1 and collection of data from electronic waybills are the priority. These would allow: more in-depth analysis of traffic flows; better assessment of the degree of interchanging and the use of trackage rights in order to determine the extent of national network and service integration, and; more informed decision-making for changes in industry structure or regulation.

Trackage rights and interline services

The new regulatory agency should establish timelines as soon as possible for the development of analytical capacity for determining conditions for the use of trackage rights in cases where agreement is not reached voluntarily.

The reform of January 2015 of the Railway law should be monitored for effectiveness in addressing complaints from shippers over charges for interline services. Should further reform be contemplated "US style tariff rule 11" opportunities might be considered as a first option.

Border crossings and inspections

Given the value of goods carried on a single train, border agencies should develop a specific set of inspection practices suited to railway operations with the aim of standardising procedures and making services available to suit railway timetables, including outside regular office hours.

Practices need to be standardised in relation to bonded goods in transit to minimise or eliminate en-route inspections inside Mexico.

Rail system should increase the statistic information gathered and reported to the public

Statistic information permits to assess rail performance and evaluate possible public policy changes. Thus, the SCT has to enhance efforts to gather and report available information of friendly formats.

A good alternative is to get closer to the US framework to collect information. For instance, the US has the same vertical integrated model in the rail system and information can be aligned according to such model. In order to comply with such recommendations, the LRSF and the Bylaw of Rail Services should be amendment, together with other implementation rules and procedures.

Notes

1. Railway Statistical Yearbook, SCT 2012 (*Anuario Estadístico Ferroviario, Dirección de Transporte Ferroviario y Multimodal*).

2. For instance, the General Law of Health (*Ley General de Salud*), Law of Acquisitions, Leasing and Public Service (*Ley de Adquisiciones, Arrendamientos y Servicios del Sector Público*), Federal Law of Administrative Procedures (*Ley Federal de Procedimiento Administrativo*), Law of Public Works and Related Services (*Ley de Obras Públicas y Servicios Relacionados con las mismas*), Law of Timing System in the United States of Mexico (*Ley del Sistema de Horario en los Estados Unidos Mexicanos*), Law of Insurance Contract (*Ley del Contrato de Seguro*), Law of International Treaties (*Ley de Tratados Internacionales*), Federal Law of Labour (*Ley Federal del Trabajo*), Federal Law of Measures and Standards (*Ley Federal de Metrología y Normalización*), Civil and Penal Codes, amongst others.

3. Interconnection services include: 1) interchange of rail equipment; 2) interlineal traffic between concessionaires; 3) movements and any other activity to provide continuity to rail traffic; 4) delivery or return of rail equipment to origin or destiny; and 5) terminal services (Art. 104 of RSF). An access-right is a permit which allows a concessionaire after paying compensation, the transit on the network of another concessionaire with its own crew and equipment (Art. 105 of RSF). A dragging-right is a permit which allows a concessionaire after paying compensation, transit on other's concessionaire network with its own equipment but tractive equipment and crew of other's concessionaire. Concessions prevent compulsory access-rights but allow concessionaires to agree on access-rights freely (Art. 106 of RSF).

4. The merger in question between Ferrosur and Ferromex was not initially approved by the Competition Commission of Mexico on competition grounds, and the authorities opened a case against the merging parties alleging collusion. Eventually, the case was closed following a judgment of "silent is consent rule" and the merger was approved.

5. Expressed in economists' terms, the railway should add a mark-up to the marginal costs of individual customers to cover fixed costs and overheads in inverse proportion to price elasticity of demand.

6. The "foreclosure of essential facilities" doctrine was first elaborated in the US in Terminal Railroad Association v. U.S. (1912), in which a coalition of railroad operators formed a joint venture owning a key bridge across the Mississippi River and the approaches and terminal in Saint Louis and excluded non-member competitors. The Supreme Court ruled that this practice was a violation of the Sherman Act.

7. See annual reports and financial statement at the following webpage: www.stb.dot.gov/econdata.nsf/f039526076cc0f8e8525660b006870c9?OpenView.

8. See annual reports www.stb.dot.gov/stb/docs/AnnualReports/STB%20FY2012%20AR%20Final%201-7-14.pdf.

References

DOF (2016), "Decreto por el que se crea la Agencia Reguladora del Transporte Ferroviario, como un órgano desconcentrado de la Secretaría de Comunicaciones y Transportes", *Diario Oficial de la Federación*, 18 August.

ECMT (2004), *Regulatory Reform of Railways in Russia*, OECD Publishing, Paris, http://dx.doi.org/10.1787/9789282123119-en.

IDB (2013), "Información Estadística sobre los Sistemas Ferroviarios Latinoamericanos" (Statistical Information on Latinamerican Railway Systems), Observatorio Regional de Carga y Logística (Freight Transport and Logistics Regional Observatory), http://logisticsportal.iadb.org/.

IMT (2014), "Diagnostico del Sistema Ferroviario de Carga Mexicana al año 2013", (Diagnosis of the Mexican Freigh Railway System), prepared for the Texas A&M Transportation Institute (*Instituto Mexicano del Transporte* – IMT).

IMT (2013), "Manual estadístico del sector transportes 2013", (Statistical Manual of the transport sector), IMT.

ITF (2016), "Establishing Mexico's Regulatory Agency for Rail Transport: Peer Review of Regulatory Capacity", *International Transport Forum Policy Papers*, No. 17, OECD Publishing, Paris, http://dx.doi.org/10.1787/5jlwvz8ws3bq-en.

ITF (2014), "Freight Railway Development in Mexico", *International Transport Forum Policy Papers*, No. 1, OECD Publishing, Paris, http://dx.doi.org/10.1787/5jlwvzjd60kb-en.

ITF (2008), "Charges for the Use of Rail Infrastructure", OECD, www.itf-oecd.org/content/charges-use-rail-infrastructure.

Pittman, R.W. (2010), "The Economics of Railroad Captive Shipper Legislation", *Economic Analysis Group Working Paper* EAG 10-1.

Ray, P. and J. Tyrole (2007), "A primer on foreclosure", Handbook of Industrial Organization III, Vol. III, North Holland, pp. 2145-2220.

US Department of Transportation (2016), Bureau of Transportations Statistics website, https://transborder.bts.gov/programs/international/transborder/TBDR_QA.html (accessed 3 August 2016).

Vickers, J. (1995), "Concepts of Competition", *Oxford Economic Papers*, No. 47, pp. 1-23.

Chapter 3

Regulation of air freight transport in Mexico

Demand for air freight is largely driven by the economic climate, and as a result, air freight transport in Mexico has grown broadly in line with both GDP and the number of passengers carried by airlines. Regulatory challenges facing by the air freight sector concern, amongst others: i) landing and take-off slot allocation at congested airports: Mexico should facilitate the implementation of auctions for primary slot allocation or replace the auction mechanism with international standards on airport slot allocation; ii) transposition of international regulations into national one: Mexico should publish aviation standards immediately in their original language in the Official Gazette, with acknowledgement that they are legally binding until replaced by official translations; iii) limits to market development imposed by restrictive air service agreements: Mexico should pursue a policy that seeks open skies agreements with other nations, in order to accrue benefits in trade and tourism of expanded air service.

Overview of ports in Mexico

Market organisation

Dynamics of the air industry is intense; actors and its organisation react quickly to perceived or actual changes. Airline organisation is complex as they need essential facilities like airports and terminals, and they transport passengers, freight or both in trunk, low cost and specialised services, through direct or indirect origin-destiny segments. Beyond that, the key elements that shape the market organisation of the industry are the multiproduct and multimarket condition, the network effects, the economies of scope and density and the possible sunk costs involved (Bailey and Friedlaender (1982).

Passengers choose an airline based on quality of service, time departures and time arrivals, price, interconnection with complementary flights, and frequent flying awards. For cargo, the determining factors are different, since cargo owners do not mind intermediate points in which cargo is being distributed, but is mainly interested in the total time to final destiny.

Airlines

The airline industry (freight and passengers) can be categorised into *hub-and-spoke* airlines (network carriers) or *point to point* airlines (e.g. low-cost airlines). *Hub-and-spoke* airlines operate to and from their principal or secondary hub airports, which are normally the biggest of the country, in order to maximize scale economies—for example; Aeromexico can be considered the network carrier based in Mexico City. Part of the flights of network carriers is done via their partner airlines in international alliances. Low cost airlines on the other hand, base their strategy on direct point to point flights. Normally the low cost aircrafts use narrower decks aircrafts, which limits the possibility to carry cargo at the same time. Passenger aircrafts (apart from low-cost or regional airlines) usually also carry freight, mainly on long-haul flights (taking advantage of the airplane's size), but these airlines can also operate aircrafts only for cargo, sometimes with integrated door-to-door transport services. Similarly, there are airlines focusing only on cargo. In Mexico, the three modalities are present.

Passengers and freight airlines compete with other national firms in local (nation-wide) and origin-destination (segment) but also compete internationally, connecting with overseas destinations.[1] In the air industry an origin-destination can be reached by direct flights or indirectly through many segments. Thus, a price segment would be influenced by direct or indirect flights, between trunk and low cost carriers, but also between other modes of transportation in certain segments.

State-intervention on air transportation in Mexico has been present almost since its foundations. Government involvement has gone from price controls to acquisition of firm's shares—sometimes because of danger of firm bankruptcy. National entry in this market has been through concessions and permissions, and the difficulty to acquire them strengthened the position of incumbents. The first two airlines in Mexico, Aero México (1934) and Mexicana de Aviación (1921) started as private firms operating as the only option for some routes, but they move from private to government participation in their life operation. On the other hand, facilities for air transportation also have been regulated since the entry of private funds on airports and complementary service.

Inside the country, Mexican airlines operate under permissions and international airlines through bilateral country-agreements—an open sky policy in Mexico is not implemented although a bilateral agreement with the United States was signed on December 2015 to open the skies to all operators of such countries without limits of routes and frequencies.[2] Until 2015, Mexico has signed 48 agreements to operate international flights.[3]

Figure 3.1. **Air freight transported in Mexico by national and foreign carriers on scheduled and non-scheduled flights**

Tonnes and % of the total

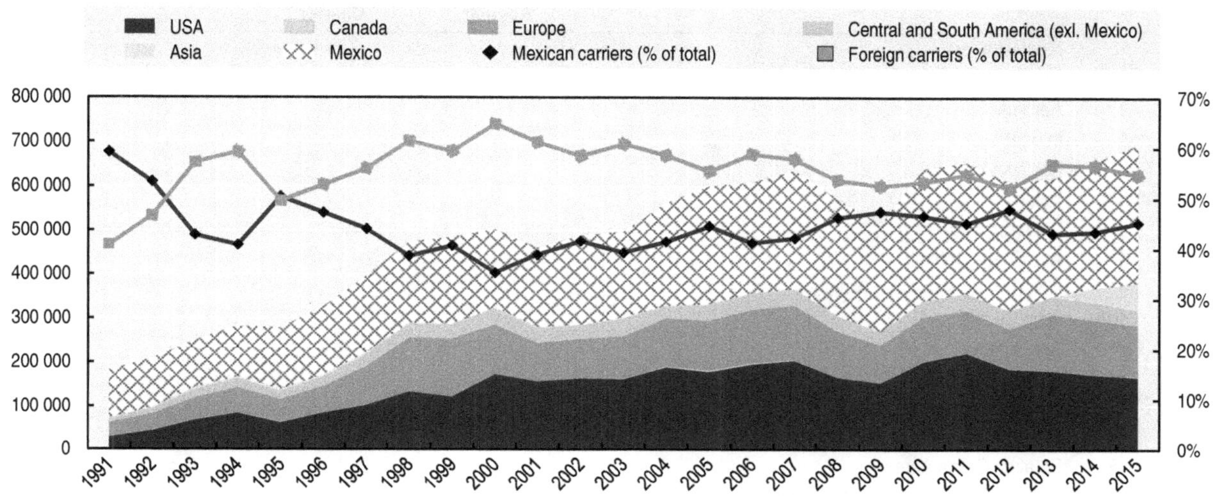

Source: Air statistics of the Ministry of Communications and Transport (SCT), www.sct.gob.mx/transporte-y-medicina-preventiva/aeronautica-civil/5-estadisticas/51-aviacion-mexicana-en-cifras-89-15-only-in-spanish/.

The Mexican air freight market is open to entry from national and foreign companies and for the past two decades over half of the cargo volume has been carried by foreign companies — Figure 3.1. The market is supplied by a diversified range of players, as 11 out of Mexico's 15 national carriers provide air freight services with Aeroméxico (Figure 3.2), the Mexico's flag carrier, currently capturing the highest market share among the national carriers —9% of all air freight volume carried. The biggest foreign players are FedEx, UPS and Air France (with 10%, 6% and 5% air freight market share respectively).

The openness of the air freight market in Mexico is illustrated by a constantly changing composition of market shares among the national carriers. Over the past two decades a number of national carriers have exited the industry, creating opportunities for other market players, including relatively young low cost airlines. For example, in the aftermath of Mexicana's[4] shutdown of its operations in August 2010, its slots at Mexico City Airport were promptly taken over by its biggest competitors – the flag carrier Aeroméxico, as well as two low cost carriers, Interjet and Volaris, see Figure 3.2.

Mexicana's demise has presented Aeroméxico and its SkyTeam partner Delta[5] with opportunities to grow their US-Mexican connections. Mexicana's exit left SkyTeam partners as the only carriers serving such an important connection as New York-Mexico City. Low cost carriers have also used the growth opportunity and have been expanding their international connectivity from Mexico City. The exit of Mexicana's domestic subsidiary, MexicanaClick, helped Aeroméxico and other carriers grow their domestic connections. The biggest Mexican low cost carrier, Interjet (established at the end of

2005) has also tapped into the domestic market and captured a 25% share in the first year after Mexicana's collapse, hence becoming the second largest domestic carrier in Mexico by the number of passengers carried. Other low cost carriers, such as Volaris and VivaAerobus have also used the opportunity to expand domestically.[6] It is now expected that that the biggest players will be allocating most of their capacity growth to international markets, potentially growing their network of connections.[7]

Table 3.1. **Types of services provided by national carriers in Mexico in 2015**

No.	Airline	Passenger Regular	Passenger Charter	Freight
1	Magnicharters	√	√	
2	Aerolitoral	√	√	√
3	Aeromar	√	√	√
4	Interjet	√	√	√
5	Aeroméxico	√	√	√
6	Volaris	√	√	√
7	Viva Aerobús	√		
8	Aerolíneas Damojh	√	√	
9	Link Conexión Aérea S.A de C.V	√		
10	Aéro Calafia	√		
11	Aero Unión			√
12	Aeronaves TSM			√
13	Aeroservicios de la Costa			√
14	Aerotransportes Mas de Carga (MasAir)			√
15	Estafeta Carga Aérea			√
16	MCS Aerocarga de México, S.A de C.V.			√

Source: Ministry of Communications and Transport (SCT) (2016), General Direction of Civil Aviation, www.sct.gob.mx/transporte-y-medicina-preventiva/aeronautica-civil/5-estadisticas/51-aviacion-mexicana-en-cifras-89-15-only-in-spanish/

Figure 3.2. **Air freight transported by a selection of national carriers on national and international services (tonnes)**

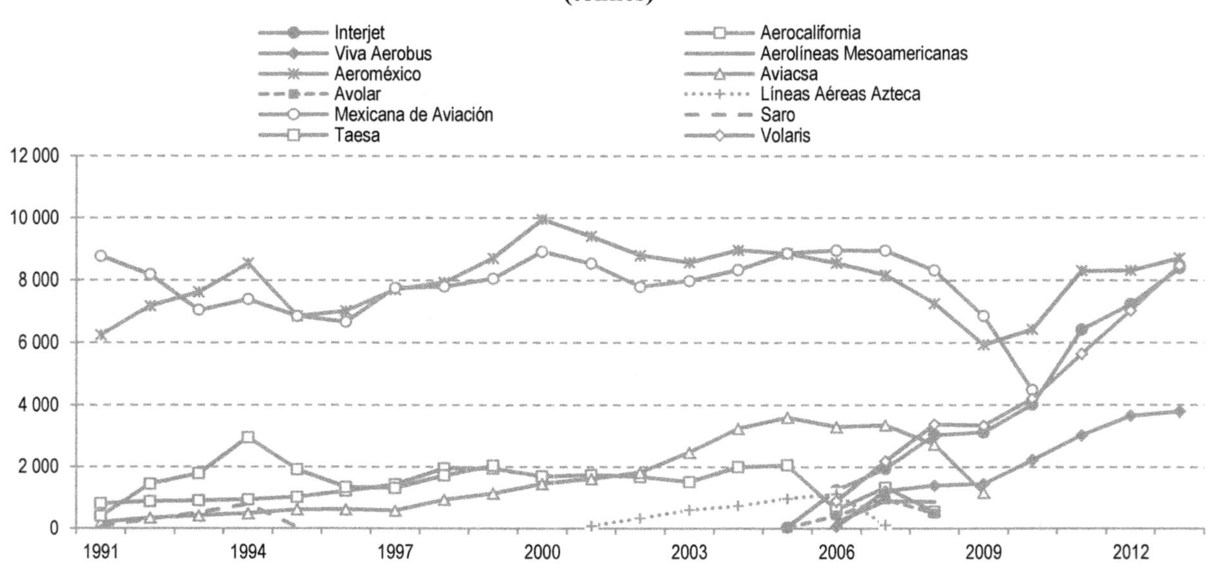

Source: Air statistics of the Ministry of Communications and Transport (SCT).

Airports

In aviation, a relevant issue arises with the existence of a natural monopoly position on airports—which would be an essential facility as airlines need landing infrastructure. Due to the low competition between close airports, regulatory solutions are being set across the world to solve such concerns, including price caps (limits on prices), rate of return regulation (limits on profits), approximations to Ramsey prices (prices considering social welfare), amongst others. According to Forsyth (1997) regulation is needed because airports have no close substitutes and it is difficult to build an airport that could compete with hubs established in Paris or Frankfurt for example, which have a monopolistic position. On the other hand, Church and Ware (2000) argue that the theory of market failure applied to airports gives the justification to regulate.

Inside airports there could also be monopoly positions for certain services and regulation is also an alternative. In New Zealand for example, there is no regulation for services on airports and instead the government applies a monitoring on prices with penalties when there is not good performance. However, there is not a clear regulatory criterion for evaluation.

Airports have capacity constraints with few opportunities to increase it. Then, price regulation has to take it into account that a low price scheme can trigger the demand for services. But also, prices have to be higher enough to recoup investments. In the same way, prices are also a mechanism to redistribute flow of people and merchandise to reduce congestion.

In some circumstances, competition can be viewed as a substitute of regulation. Competition on airports arises when these facilities fight for:

- Particular traffic
- Hub establishment
- Operational bases
- Concessions revenue
- Across the board competition.

Auxiliary services in airports are essential in the logistic chain, because sometimes a long-haul flight needs to distribute cargo through the hub with a medium or small-haul aircrafts, or even with trucks. Because of airports can be congested, plus the fact that passengers have priority over cargo in slot distribution, cargo airlines can move to the less congested airports with few passenger operations. Consequently, co-ordination between different agencies and concessionaire holders on airports (freight forwarders, custom services, pick up and integration services, for example) is also crucial to achieve efficiency in transport.

The airport system in Mexico comprises 76 airports. The 43 main civil airports are operated by private (and one public) firms through concessions.[8] Eighteen airports are operated by an independent national organisation of the federal government: Airports and Auxiliary Services (*Aeropuertos y Servicios Auxiliares*, ASA). The remaining airports are operated by the SCT, the Ministry of Defence (SD), the Ministry of Marine and Mexican Army (SMAM) and state or municipal governments.

Mexico City airport accounts for the largest share of both passenger and freight transport: in 2014. The Mexico City Airport handled almost 400 metric tonnes of freight (about 64% of total freight volume handled by airports in the country). The 43 civil airports under concession are operated by twelve companies:

- Airport Group of Mexico City (*Grupo Aeroportuario de la Ciudad de México*, GACM), 1 airport
- Southest Airports (Aeropuertos del Sureste, ASUR), 9 airports
- Centre North Airport Group (*Grupo Aeroportuario Centro Norte*, OMA), 13 airports
- Pacific Airport Group (*Grupo Aeroportuario del Pacífico, GAP*) 12 airports
- Airport of Cuernavaca (*Aeropuerto de Cuernavaca*), 1 airport
- Consumer Cooperative Society Air Services (*Sociedad Cooperativa de Consumo de Servicios Aéreos*), 1 airport
- State Airport Operator (*Operadora Estatal de Aeropuertos*), 1 airport
- Cortes Sea Airport (*Aeropuerto del Mar de Cortes*), 1 airport
- Intercontinental Airport of Queretaro (*Aeropuerto Intercontinental de Querétaro*), 1 airport
- Mexiquense Administrator of the International Airport of Toluca *(Administradora Mexiquense del Aeropuerto Internacional de Toluca*), 1 airport
- International Airport Angel Albino Corzo Operator Company (*Sociedad Operadora del Aeropuerto Internacional Ángel Albino Corzo*), 1 airport
- Chichen Itza Airport of the Yucatán State *(Aeropuerto de Chichen Itzá del Estado de Yucatán*), 1 airport.

Mexico City airport is operating at close to capacity. In 2014 the Federal Government took the decision to construct a new airport on a larger site 5 km from the existing airport. All passenger and freight operations will be transferred to the new airport on completion in 2020 or shortly thereafter. Conflicting runway alignments rule out the operation of both airports simultaneously. The new site will be developed in stages, and is sufficiently large to accommodate three independent parallel runways, with the potential to carry the traffic of the largest airports in the world.

These facilities have to serve 9 751 registered aircrafts in Mexico for their operation in 2015 (563 officials, 6 893 private and 2 295 commercial). The commercial aircrafts are operated by 15 airlines: 4 of those focusing exclusively on passengers, 6 exclusively on freight and 5 transporting both passengers and freight. Airlines of passengers are divided in four trunk lines, three regional and eight of fleet. International firms that brought freight and passengers totalled 101 lines—on fleet or regular services. The commercial airlines use 1 469 registered airfields, 12 national airports and 64 international airports.

Economic performance

Air freight transport in Mexico has grown broadly in line with both GDP and the number of passengers carried by airlines— Figure 3.3. This is because demand for air freight is largely driven by the economic climate (both at home and abroad), and the sector's capabilities are very much dependent on the passenger demand for aviation, as freight mostly travels in the belly hold of passenger aircraft. Although most of freight is currently carried in the latter, air freight transport channels are strongly reliant on where passengers want to travel. At the same time, whether a service is attractive to freight forwarders may make the difference between a route being profitable or unviable (see, for example, Doganis, 2009, p. 315).

The growth in the number of passengers (3.2%) in Mexico has been consistent with the evolution of the economic added value of the subsector of air transportation (4.8%) and the freight in tonnes (4.1%) for the period 1994-2015.[9] Thus, as the number of people increases it would have a positive impact on cargo.

Figure 3.3. **The volume of air freight transported on scheduled and non-scheduled flights tracks, passenger demand and GDP in Mexico**

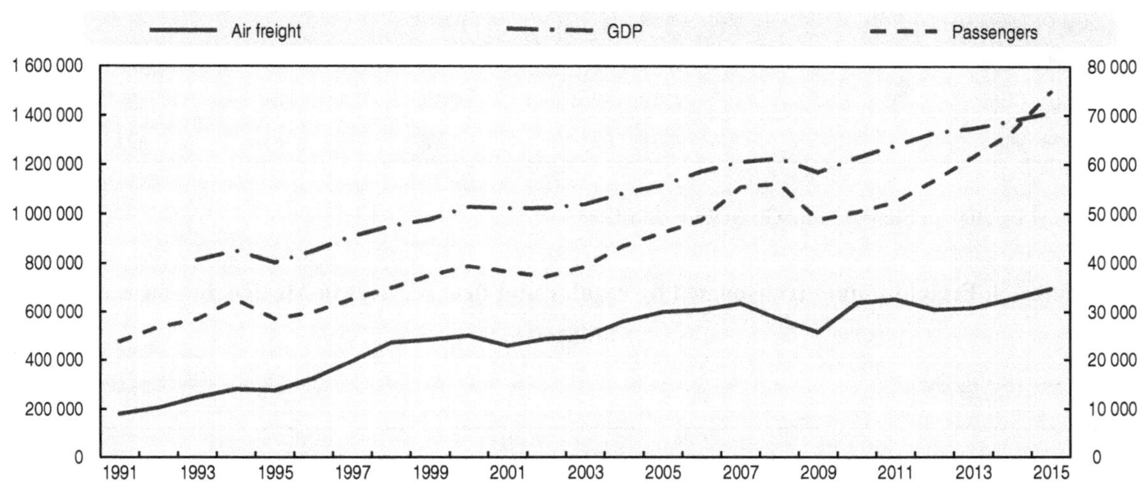

Source: Air freight and passenger numbers – air statistics of the Ministry of Communications and Transport (SCT), available in Spanish at: www.sct.gob.mx/transporte-y-medicina-preventiva/aeronautica-civil/estadisticas/aviacion-mexicana-en-cifras-89-14-only-in-spanish/; GDP statistics – IMF World Economic Outlook Database (April 2015).

Table 3.2 shows that the economic value of air transportation is the second on relevance in the sector, just after maritime transportation. However, it is the second with the highest average growth from 1995-2015 (5.2%) after road transportation, and it has the highest net growth for the period with 189.4%. The salience of this performance is underlined by considering that air transportation is an expensive but efficient option.

A zoom-in on air freight performance indicates that it has increased the amount of tonnes transported for national airlines by about 4.60% on yearly average for the period 1993-2015, and 7.1% for international firms (Figure 3.4). As mentioned before, these results also have been influenced by the increase in passengers; in fact, the trend of passengers and freight seems to follow the same path in relative terms.

Mexico's most important trading partners are the United States and the European Union. Mexico, the second largest Latin American economy after Brazil, is the United States' second biggest export market and third largest source of imports.[10] The Boeing World Air Cargo Forecast 2014-15 predicts that Mexico's air trade with the United States will be growing at an average 5.4% year for the next 20 years.[11] Mexico is also the most important Latin American trade partner of the European Union after Brazil[12] – according to Boeing in 2013 almost 20% of all air freight volume between the EU and all Latin American economies was between the EU and Mexico.[13]

Table 3.2. **GDP by mode of transport in 2015**

Concept	GDP (MXN)	Share of total GDP	Average growth 1995-2015	Total growth 1995-2015
Total GDP	14 664 491.85		2.8%	78.6%
Tertiary sector	8 962 800.11	61.1%	3.1%	90.7%
Transport, mail and storage	852 321.87	5.8%	3.1%	84.0%
Air transport	30 391.34	0.21%	5.2%	189.4%
Rail transport	17 134.60	0.12%	3.9%	99.4%
Maritime transport	8 480.08	0.06%	2.1%	11.7%
Road transport	689 057.05	4.7%	6.1%	83.6%
Freight	420 099.12	2.9%	4.4%	128.1%
Passengers	268 957.93	1.8%	1.6%	40.8%

Source: National Institute of Statistics and Geography (INEGI).

Figure 3.4. **Freight tonnes transported by regular and fleet services in Mexico and passengers**

Millions

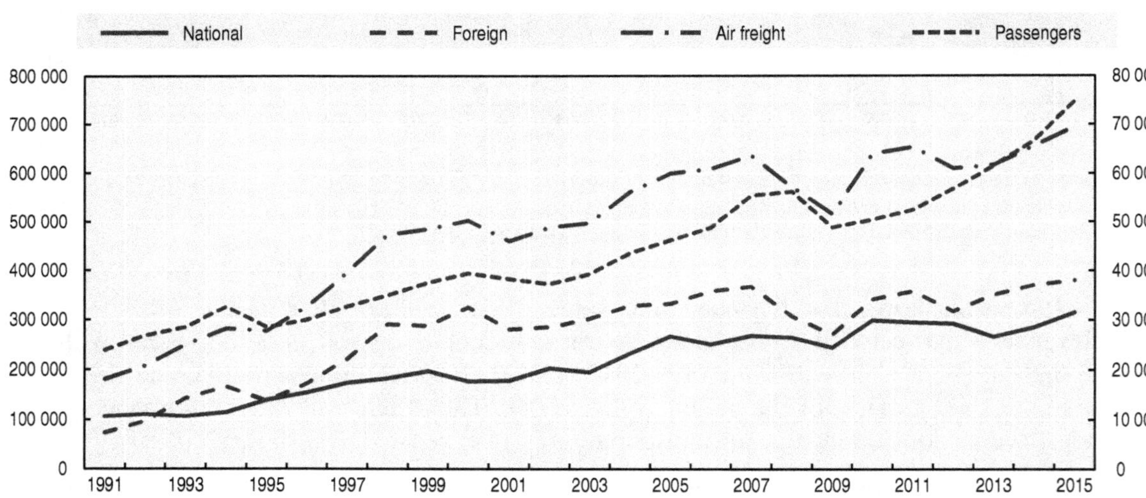

Source: Air statistics of the Ministry of Communications and Transport (SCT)

General regulatory framework

National airlines operate under licences issued by the SCT and international airlines serve Mexican airports under bilateral agreements—Mexico has signed 50 agreements.[14] The SCT is the responsible to promote, administrate and follow-up the activities derived from such agreements and permits.[15]

The airline market in Mexico opened to new entrants in 1993 and it brought about new challenges to the SCT, which is the regulatory agency for air and auxiliary services through the DGAC.[16]

One of the most important challenges was the set-up of a regulatory framework which would allow for an efficient market organisation with benefits for firms and users. The regulatory framework has been constructed on such direction, but there are still many challenges to address. Currently, the challenges facing by the air freight sector concern:

- Landing and take-off slot allocation at congested airports
- Transposition of international regulations into national law
- Relaxing limits to market development imposed by restrictive air service agreements.

These issues are addressed in this chapter in turn, but a general context of the relevant regulatory framework will be presented first. The general regulatory framework of air transportation and logistics over facilities in which airplanes operate, mainly inside airports comprise:

- Law of Airports (*Ley de Aeropuertos*, LA)
- By-law of the Law of Airport (*Reglamento de la Ley de Aeropuertos*, RLA)
- Law of Civil Aviation (*Ley de Aviación Civil*, LAC)
- Law of National Security (*Ley de Seguridad Nacional*, LSN)
- General Law of Communication Routes (*Ley General de Vías de Comunicación*, LGVC)
- Other complementary laws.[17]

Some of these laws have specific regulation and are also supplemented by Mexican Official Standards (*Normal Oficial Mexicana*, NOM), ministerial agreements and other legal documents. Particularly important in this respect are Policy Letters (*Cartas Políticas*), which are documents to establish specific and technical guidelines that should assure that operation in Mexico is conducted according to international standards.

Slots

Slots are time periods attributed to airlines to use airports, and their allocation is one of the most salient regulatory features in civil aviation. There is not a single administration model around OECD countries and they all face relevant challenges (see next section). In Mexico, the LA indicates how the administration of slots has to be conducted. Article 61 of the LA requires an Operation and Schedule Committee (*Comité de Operación y Horarios*, COH), led by the airport administrator[18] that will issue recommendations regarding:

- Airport operation and schedules
- Tariffs and prices
- Rules for efficient operation
- Master planning
- Conditions to providing airport services, amongst others.

Article 63 of the LA also indicates that the COH has to determine landing and departure schedules, including aircrafts priority, according to the regulation, and under equitable and non-discriminatory criteria. The COH also has the legal power to issue recommendations for conflicts between the airport administrator and service providers, and solve user complains about airport administration. The airport administrator however, is the president of the COH which raises possible conflict of interest-issues.

According to the RLA, the SCT establishes the capacity of the airports based on safety and efficiency (Article 94), whereas the airport administrator (Article 95) assigns landing and arrival schedules according to safety, capacity and availability. Concession holders which have previously used those slots will have priority—passengers have priority over freight services. A main issue about slots and their regulation, however, is related with the priority in auctions in favour to incumbents, which seems contrary to the non-discriminatory criteria stated by the LA.

The LA (Article 98) also permits exchange of slots or giving them up in favour of other concession holders after one year of operation. If the regulator determines that the airport is saturated, he can take away the slots from concessionaires during the first four years of the schedule assignation under certain conditions—when the concessionaire has been using the slots at less than 85% of capacity during the previous year, or if they accumulate 15% of delays on its attribution. Thus, the slots can then be auctioned again.

Prices and tariffs

Article 67 of the LA states that the SCT can establish the regulatory basis for airport-service tariffs and prices for leasing and compensations; for contracts between concessionaires or permission holders; and for complementary services if the COFECE considers that competition conditions are not present. When the SCT considers there is a lack of adequate competition, it will request the opinion of COFECE so as to establish the regulatory basis (Article 68), and the tariff or price regulation will only be valid until the originated conditions are still present. Thus, the service providers can request the COFECE for an opinion of these conditions. Tariffs for airport and complementary services in public airfields have to be registered in the SCT before their application (Article 69).

Maximum tariffs or prices can be set for single or joint services with their validity and adjustment mechanisms (Article 70 of the LA). Similarly, Article 102 states that revenues of the concessionaires and permit holders from landing and departures schedules are considered in the joint maximum tariff.[19] Article 141 indicates that the regulatory basis for a maximum joint tariff covers: 1) the services, leasing and compensations (with exemption of non-permanent and parking services); 2) traffic units; 3) a tariff which reflects the forecasts of income, costs and investments; 4) the efficiency factor per airfield; 5) validity; and 6) specific tariffs per service or bundle of services. The joint maximum tariff can be checked at any moment by SCT and if it finds discriminatory conditions it can establish the joint maximum tariff and specific tariffs for all services.

Concerning transport tariffs, Article 42 of the LAC indicates that concession and permit holders can set air-services tariffs freely (freight and passengers) and that international tariffs will be approved by the SCT according to the treaties. The same law allows SCT to reject those tariffs if they rise due to lack of competition and when it considers there is not a competitive environment. Thus it can request the opinion of the COFECE so as to establish the regulation of tariffs—Article 43. In all cases, permit and concession holders have the duty to submit tariffs to the SCT. An important difference in comparison with rail services is that Article 42 of the LAC states that tariffs include clearly and explicitly the restrictions they are liable to and their validity.

Slot allocation on airports

Introduction

A slot is generally defined as an authorisation to land or depart an aircraft at a specific time at a specific airport. One slot is required for a landing and another (at a different time) is required for a take-off. Sometimes the term *slot* is used to represent a pair of slots, both for landing and departing. There are a number of subtleties in defining slots. For example, the actual flight operation might be at a different (usually later) time than authorised due to adverse weather conditions, need for maintenance or flight loading delays.

At the heart of slot allocation lays the issue of distributing access to scarce airport capacity at peak hours of demand. The constraints may arise due to insufficient runway or terminal capacity, or due to the limited processing capacity of the customs hall. Terminal facilities, such as the number of gates, may also create constraints. At a few airports, air navigation constraints may also exist. For example, both in the US and Canada, airport capacity constraints tend to arise to due airspace-related, rather than ground infrastructure, issues. Airport capacity may also be constrained due to regulation. In particular, limits on capacity utilisation may be imposed due to noise considerations. For example, at Düsseldorf Airport the total number of slots in use is restricted as means to limit the impact of noise on the neighbouring communities. At Washington Ronald Reagan National Airport, there is a cap on the number of operations allowed per hour. At Frankfurt, Amsterdam and some other European airports there is a noise quota that cannot be exceeded, effectively also limiting the number of movements. Flights are assigned a number of noise points based on how noisy an aircraft is and what time of day/night it operates. Slot allocation to each carrier is a function of the number of points collected.

In almost all jurisdictions, there is ambiguity as to whether the right to operate a slot constitutes its ownership. As slot sales at several airports have revealed, there is a monetary value to the entitlement at slot restricted airports. Indeed, US airlines have pledged slot entitlements as collateral to financial institutions and trustees of bankrupt airlines have sold slots under "Chapter 7: bankruptcies" leading to liquidation of the company.

The costs and benefits of slot concentration

An airport operating at or near its slot capacity requires finding some means to ration that capacity. Providing new slots at congested airports by increasing capacity does not remove the need to allocate slots – when new capacity comes on stream a way of allocating new slots needs to be agreed.

National policies stipulate who determines whether an airport is congested, how the determination is made and, thus, whether or not the slots at the airport should be managed. Depending on the country, there are different ways of establishing capacity. In Mexico and Germany, for example, establishing airport capacity is a legislative requirement for certain airports. There are also some "slot controlled" airports in the United States. In Canada, the capacity of Toronto International Airport is established by the minister. For most airports it is the airport itself that declares capacity.

Almost all major airports have the biggest part of their capacity utilised by a single carrier or alliance—this is for example the case for hub airports in Europe and the Middle East (Airports Commission, 2013). The policy debate on how slots should be allocated to carriers has therefore focussed on the welfare analysis of the potential costs (higher fares) and benefits (positive network externalities) of increased concentration of airport capacity in the hands of one hub carrier or alliance (see, for example, Borenstein, 1989).

On one hand, such slot concentration leads to higher fares and congestion (see, for example, Borenstein, 1989; Kahn, 1993; and Starkie, 2006). On the other, it induces positive network externalities—improved connectivity outcomes due to an increased number of destinations offered and increased frequencies (see, for example, Caves, Christensen and Tretheway, 1984) as well as better quality of service due to more convenient booking options when interconnecting and minimised connecting times at the airport.[20]

As Starkie (2006: 1) remarks the "effects of slot concentration are complex". For example, while numerous studies confirm that slot concentration leads to higher fares and congestion, the average price mark-up may arise not only due to the market power of the dominant carrier but also as a result of, for example, the services provided being more desirable by a certain group of users (who, for instance, value higher frequency of service provided by a hub carrier) or of the scarcity of airport capacity, and the resulting scarcity rents accruing to the carriers (see, for example, Burghouwt, 2013). It is thus debatable whether reducing slot concentration would lead to better price outcomes for passengers.

Due to these findings, the current policy making in the area of slot allocation mostly focuses on ensuring that the mechanisms to allocate slots at capacity constrained sites maximise economic efficiency i.e. slots are allocated to those airlines that can use them to the greatest benefit to the consumer, both passengers and air freight. This in practice means balancing a system in which the benefits of slot concentration and the benefits of competition are maximised.

Advantages and disadvantages of different mechanisms to allocate slots

In general, there are three ways in which slots can be allocated to airlines: the usage of a pricing mechanism, an administrative mechanism (a combination of administrative and pricing mechanisms can be used as well) or by neither. Each with advantages and disadvantages:

No allocation mechanism

At all US airports except for four designated as 'high density' (JFK and LaGuardia in New York, O'Hare in Chicago, and Ronald Reagan in Washington, D.C.),[21] carriers schedule flights as they wish. The most obvious advantage of having no particular allocation mechanism at a congested airport is its administrative simplicity, while the disadvantage is the potential for delays created by over-subscription of airlines to airport slots during the busiest periods during the day.

As Starkie (2006) points out, however, the marginal costs of delays due to congestion are often overstated as the costs of delay that an airline imposes on its own operations when it decides to include an additional flight in the peak. These costs are internalised into the airline's business equation so they do not constitute a negative externality to that airline (although they do to other carriers).[22] Hence, the more slots are concentrated in the hands of one carrier or alliance, the smaller the externality.

Slot auctioning

Slot auctioning, as a market-based allocation mechanism, enables the scarce airport capacity to be allocated to the carrier who values it most (or has the highest "willingness to pay"). If the auctioning is appropriately designed and administered, it may provide incentives for airlines to exchange the already-allocated slots in a way that may enhance efficiency and encourage competition between carriers—from peak slots to off-peak slots,[23] or from a more desirable airport in an airport system to a less desirable one for those carriers that can do it most easily.

In an auction, the price of a slot will rise until only the carrier with the highest value use for that slot purchases it.[24] Auctions come in many different formats, e.g. the "English auction" in which bidders successively offer higher prices until one bidder who offered the highest price remains, or the "Dutch auction" in which the auctioneer starts the auction with a high price and gradually lowers it until one bidder is willing to pay.

The literature suggests a number of ways in which slots could be auctioned to airlines. For example, Grether et al. (1989) suggests a 'sealed-bid, one price auction' in which sealed bids indicating the highest price that the bidder is willing to pay are submitted and then arranged from the highest to the lowest. The highest bids are then accepted (if five slots are auctioned, then five number of highest bids are accepted), but the winning bidders pay the price of the lowest accepted bid. If the bids reflect carriers' maximum willingness to pay, which is derived from the expected revenue for prospective flights, then significant efficiency gains can be achieved.

Pricing slots is strongly opposed by airlines who perceive them as another way for the airport or the ministry in charge (or whoever sell the slots) to erode the already wafer-thin airline profit margins. In the literature, an argument that airports could finance new infrastructure through slot sales is pitched against the argument that the airport may be incentivised to ensure that the infrastructural development lags behind demand in order to maximise the rents collected from selling scarce airport capacity (see, for example, Sentence, 2003). An alternative would be for the government to sell slots and use these funds to develop new infrastructure or compensate local communities for the adverse environmental impacts of aviation (such as noise or pollution).

Earmarking revenues collected from selling slots at Mexico City Airport to finance the new airport implies that airlines and their customers would be contributing to financing of the assets, ahead of their coming into use. Such a mechanism would likely be opposed by the incumbent airlines who would not like to pre-fund new capacity that would most likely disproportionately benefit new entrants, once new capacity comes on-stream. Financing new airport infrastructure from current airport charges may also affect the competitiveness of the hub in Mexico City, as carriers may decide to move part of their operations to other airports in the region (e.g. Toluca), hence creating additional costs to the network.

Administrative slot allocation

Administrative slot allocation is the most commonly used method of distributing scarce airport capacity to airlines, in which slots are allocated by a co-ordinator using a prescribed set of allocation criteria. Administrative slot allocation reduces congestion and, if appropriately designed, can achieve significant welfare benefits for aviation users (such as maximising hub connectivity or ensuring that new entrants can enter the market). However, it is widely viewed to be economically inefficient, as it does not reflect the scarce nature of airport slots and does not include a specific mechanism to ensure that slots are allocated to those who attach the highest value to them, or can deliver the highest benefits to the consumers (see, for example, DotEcon, 2006).

The IATA's World Scheduling Guidelines for administrative slot allocation

Most of the administrative slot allocation mechanisms follow the World Scheduling Guidelines (WSGs) set up by the International Air freight Transport Association (IATA)—an airline industry association[25] with focus on how slots should be allocated at constrained airports.

The need for WSGs originates in airlines' financial and operational interest to reduce airport congestion, and in the need to create one single set of standards for the management of airport slots, in order to facilitate slot matching at the origin and destination airports in different countries. The latter is facilitated by a process of a central clearinghouse and twice annual meetings between airlines and slot co-ordinators to discuss the global interconnectedness of slot times. The WSGs thus has an important role in providing an arena for discussion between different stakeholders.

A slot co-ordinator is designated for each airport that requires slot allocation. A slot co-ordinator may be an employee of the largest airline operator at the airport, a government slot allocation representative,[26] an airport representative,[27] or a private/independent slot allocation company.[28] There is a schedule and procedure for how carriers make requests to each airport's slot co-ordinator. There are roles and responsibilities defined for airport slot co-ordinators whose main goal is to develop draft slot allocations prior to the scheduling conference for each six month period.

The WSGs have a number of key principles. One important feature of the system is the prescription of 'grandfather rights' stipulating that carriers that historically were assigned slots are free to keep those slots as long as they utilise them at least 80% of the time (the 'use it or lose it' rule). In practice that means that almost all slots at co-ordinated airports are reallocated to the carriers who have already been using them.[29] A system of grandfather rights plays an important role in providing the degree of stability and continuity needed for planning and long-term investment by airlines and airports, this stability can in turn be enjoyed by aviation users: passengers and freight forwarders.

Related to grandfather rights is the principle that an airline wishing to retime an existing slot will have a priority in allocating a slot over an entrant to the market.[30] The WSGs recommend that slots should be first allocated to the carriers with grandfather rights and only then allocated to airlines wishing to swap an existing slot for a slot at a different time. The WSGs establish preference for assigning slots to carriers operating frequent (e.g. daily) services, with charter flights and infrequent services having lower priorities.[31]

A criticism of the original version of grandfather rights under the WSG is that it creates barriers to entry. For that reason, a number of governments, and in particular the European Commission, imposed regulations to provide for access of slots to new entrants.[32] The EU regulation accepted the principle of grandfather rights, but ruled that after grandfather rights (and slot re-timing), priority in the award of half of all other slots is given to new entrants, in order to foster both the benefits of competition and the benefits of having a stable schedule and investment prospects for airlines, as well as the benefits of the relatively high allocative efficiency that incumbent carriers can achieve.[33]

The IATA WSG designates three levels of airports:

- Level 1: airports are those without significant capacity constraints. Slot allocation at these airports is not subject to any specific slot allocation guidelines
- Level 2: or 'schedule facilitated' airports, which are approaching full capacity, especially at peak times, and where there are benefits to carriers from participation in the IATA system[34]
- Level 3: or "co-ordinated" airports, which are capacity limited and congested. Slots at these airports are allocated according to the IATA WSGs and their slot co-ordinators are required to participate in bilateral slot co-ordination conferences.

IATA recommends that, before an airport becomes "co-ordinated", it should first become a 'schedule facilitated' airport. In order to become a Level 3 airport, the site has to undergo a capacity study which examines options for increasing airport capacity and documents any capacity constraints which cannot be relaxed. This is to discourage airports from seeking Level 3 status when not all options for increasing capacity have been pursued.

The IATA WSGs are not legally binding, unless a nation makes them a requirement in law or under operating regulations. A number of jurisdictions employ alternative slot allocation systems, or modifications to the IATA WSGs.

Alternatives to the IATA WSGs

A number of Governments have imposed their own slot allocation rules on airports and airlines. In Australia, the Sydney Airport Demand Management Act of 1997 (updated in 2008) recognised the power of the Transport Minister of the New South Wales State government to establish regulations for slot allocation. The minister has the authority to appoint a slot management company, which the Act specifies it must not be neither an agent of the Government nor a public authority.[35]

In the United States, the Federal Government through the Federal Aviation Administration has the power to manage the slots at certain designated airports. Out of concern for the potential anti-competitive consequences of the activities of the airline industry when acting collectively, the US removed antitrust immunity for some of the IATA slot allocation rules. Slot allocation at six congested airports (later reduced to four) was established under the powers of the Federal Aviation Act.[36]

Slot co-ordinators in those countries that have established their own guidelines for slot allocation usually attend IATA scheduling conferences, and the processes that they follow normally parallel many aspects of the IATA process. For example, the slot controlled US airports have US government representatives at the IATA slot allocation conferences to facilitate slot co-ordination for international routes, but they apply their own national guidelines rather than the IATA WSGs.

Although a slot co-ordinator may be following the IATA WSGs, there may be reasons for departure from the IATA guidelines – for instance, when flights to remote areas need to be secured or when carriers seek approval for antitrust immunity for a merger, an acquisition or an alliance.

In Canada, following the acquisition of Canadian Airlines International Ltd by Air Canada in 1999, slots at Toronto Pearson Airport were allocated to other domestic carriers under a consent order between Air Canada and the Competition Commissioner.[37] A private-sector slot co-ordinator for Toronto Airport facilitated this transfer, which technically did not meet the IATA WSGs (it gave preference to slots relinquished by Air Canada to domestic carriers and excluded international carriers from access). In a number of jurisdictions a proportion of slots are allocated on a priority basis to services to small communities.

In the US, a number of slots at all small airports are earmarked for essential air service operations. In Australia, a number of slots at Sydney Airport are assigned to regional air services. EU member states may impose public service obligations (PSOs) on air routes which are vital for the economic and social development of the region, in order to maintain appropriate air services. Their policy on establishing these services is governed by European legislation. This legislation broadly sets out, but does not fully define, the criteria under which EU governments can protect air services.[38] In the UK, for example, the Government imposes PSOs to protect certain regional air services to London.[39]

In Europe and the US, competition authorities often require carriers seeking antitrust immunity for alliances to surrender slots, either generally (e.g. British Airways and American Airlines were required to shed a number of slots at London Heathrow as a condition for government approval of their application for antitrust immunity for their alliance), or for specific services (e.g. Swissair and Sabena were required to make slots available at Zurich and Brussels to accommodate any new entrant on that specific city pair route).

US slot allocation policies depart from the IATA WSGs in some other respects. To begin with, the US has tended not to establish limits to slot allocation at most airports. Thus it has favoured competition with congestion over reduction of delays. All US airports except for four designated as 'high density' (JFK and LaGuardia in New York, O'Hare in Chicago, and Ronald Reagan in Washington, D.C.) have no slot limits imposed on their available capacity and the FAA does not allocate slots to carriers, with some exceptions – the FAA, for example, has before compelled a dominant carrier to surrender a number of slots in order to accommodate new competition.

Slot allocation in Mexico

Mexico City's, Benito Juárez International Airport is a severely slot constrained airport. In 2014, its two runways operating in a segregated mode (i.e. the runways are too close to each other to be operated independently), handled about 34 million passengers and over 400 000 aircraft movements.[40] In September 2014 the government announced plans to build a new airport with two and ultimately three independent runways. Although this project is expected to significantly expand airport capacity in Mexico City when it is completed in six years, slot allocation will continue to be required in the interim, and it is also likely that it will be required in the Mexico's airport system after the new capacity comes on-stream, as the aviation sector is currently experiencing high levels of growth.

In Mexico, the 2010 Law on Airport contains provisions (articles 95-100) governing the allocation of airport slots. Key aspects of the law are:

- Slots are assigned by the airport administrator, Article 95
- The objective is achieving safety and efficiency, Article 95
- Slots should be allocated to (scheduled) passenger flights, non-scheduled passenger flights, scheduled all-cargo flights, and charter cargo flights (in order of priority), Article 95

- The airport operations committee must have a subcommittee to investigate airport delays and must identify reasons for delay and perpetrators of delay, Article 97
- Carriers may trade slots among themselves, provided a slot has been used for one year, Article 98
- If slots are not adequately utilised by a carrier, the airport administrator will reallocate the slot, Article 99-I
- Any reallocated slots will be auctioned to the highest bidder who demonstrates a financial ability to pay the fees, Article 99-I.

Auctioning, rather than rationing, is used to distribute slots a) whenever slots become available due to non-use or under-use and b) every three years, when there is to be an auction of 10% of slots. The law specifies that, if an airport has continued to be congested for three consecutive years, the airport manager should remove 10% of slots from each carrier, with the carrier able to choose which slots in congested time periods it will yield, and auction these slots (Article 99-II). The determination as to whether the airport is congested (both terminal and airfield congestion are taken into account) or not, will be made by the SCT (Article 100). The SCT however, has never removed slot rights due to congestion of usage.

This approach is a major departure from the IATA guidelines. The use of auctioning for slot allocation has potential to achieve higher economic efficiency if slots go to those who create the highest value from their use. Auctioning, if appropriately designed and undertaken, also creates revenues for the airport operator which potentially could be used to invest in facilities or procedures that increase airport capacity

Auctioning is not a commonly used policy tool for slot allocation.[41] Although auctions are used for secondary trading of slots between airlines (e.g. at Heathrow or Gatwick), so far no nation other than Mexico has adopted an auction based approach for primary allocation of airport slots. For instance, Article 95 of the LA indicates that slot assignation has to be conducted by the airport administrator, according to some criteria which includes efficiency, security and availability. Article 99-I-b indicates that new slots have to be auctioned by the airport administrator. Although the law in Mexico makes provision for slot allocation, a different process has been used historically, following the laws' prioritisation of air services, but following IATA guidelines in respect of grandfather rights and new entrance. For example, slots have been granted when airlines were passed from state control to private initiative. As Article 95 indicates, an airline has preferences if it held the slot previously.

As a consequence of the high level of congestion at the Benito Juárez Mexico City International Airport and the airport administrator's prioritisation of passenger over cargo flights (as required by the law), new air cargo flights to Mexico City airport have not been facilitated. This has led to rapid growth at Toluca Airport, in the neighboring city 50 km away. This airport serves both low cost passenger carriers (i.e. Volaris, Interjet, Spirit) and FedEx.

The stakeholders (the airport and its airlines) so far have not been enthusiastic about the policy to auction slots. Airlines would prefer a slot allocation policy based on the IATA WSGs or on a set of similar principles. If auctioning is to be implemented, a strengthening of regulatory capacity will be required, and clarification of the policy on allocating airport capacity in the run-up to opening of the new airport would reduce risk in commercial planning by air carriers operating or seeking to operate from Mexico City.

Recommendations on the way forward for slot allocation are developed at the end of the chapter.

Adoption of international standards and their incorporation to national regulation

In Mexico, as in most nations, regulations and other orders of government do not carry the force of law until they are officially published by the Government. In Mexico this entails publication in the Official Gazette (*Diario Oficial de la Federación*).[42] All publication in the Official Gazette must be in Spanish.

The formal process for establishing standards in Mexico involves oversight by the Directorate General of Standards of the Ministry of Economy. [43]This process involves advanced publication of the proposed standard, a formal consultation process with stakeholders, and an analysis that shows that the benefits of a new regulation or standard exceed the costs or other negative impacts. This process is not unlike what is required in other countries, including the United States at least for some government agencies.[44]

Mexico allows adoption of international standards (e.g. standards from multi-nation organisations such as the International Civil Aviation Organization – ICAO), or adoption of foreign standards (e.g. aircraft standards established by the US Federal Aviation Administration – FAA), as long as it is done through the process to issue technical standards according to the regulatory framework, and they are in Spanish. Other countries have also formal procedures for this. For example, in Canada, all official documents must be in French and English. However, external documents that are not bilingual can be referred to officially as the basis for regulation, known as incorporation by reference.

In fields such as aviation the resources required to establish standards (e.g., maintenance standards for a new type of aircraft) are so large that often these standards can only be developed by international co-operation through international organisations such as ICAO, or by a large nation such the United States or by the European Union's Joint Aviation Authority. Thus most nations in the world adopt international or foreign standards for much of its aviation sector rules and regulations. The adoption of such standards is so relevant that if Mexico does not adopt them, it can loss in efficiency, security and safety. In fact, the obligation to accomplish a delayed standard would promote the maintenance of old technology and disincentive the adoption of innovation. Of course, a delay in the adoption of standards affects the economic performance of the industry.

Since 2012 Mexico has allowed reference to international standards that are published in a language other than Spanish. Nevertheless, we are advised that until a standard is published in the Official Gazette in Spanish it will not carry the full force of law.

This requirement is particularly challenging for regulation of the aviation sector which is characterised by a relatively high number of standards pertaining to different types of aircraft, airports, air traffic control, pilot qualifications, maintenance procedures, etc. Many of these standards are frequently updated and time-sensitive: for example to allow a new aircraft model to be flown within or into the country or to urgently change a maintenance procedure.

Furthermore, some of the international standards for aviation stipulate an official language to be used. An important example is the IATA Safety Audit for Ground Operations (IASGO) standard, which aims to improve safety and cut airline costs by drastically reducing ground accidents and injuries. The standard's official language is

English. IATA points out that a reason for adopting an official language for the standard is due potential misinterpretations of the standard in other languages. The IASGO standard states (Section 7):

> "The GOPM requires Auditors to ensure the English language version of this GOSM and/or ISAGO Checklists is always used as the basis for a final determination of conformity or nonconformity with the GSSAPRs during the conduct of an Audit. Versions of the GOSM or ISAGO Checklists that have been translated into another langue are subject to misinterpretation; therefore any translated ISAGO document is considered an unofficial reference." (Emphasis added.)

As the formal process required by the Directorate General of Standards for publication of official standards is very time consuming and requires significant resources, the Civil Aviation Authority has issued Mandatory Circulars (*Circulares Obligatorias*) for immediate adoption of new or changed international or foreign standards. Civil Aviation (and some other authorities) has also sometimes used Policy Letters for immediate adoption of standards. These have not undergone the process to issue a standard according to the LFMN, including pre-publication, stakeholder consultation and cost-benefit analysis. Thus they are not published in the Official Gazette. Policy letters and Mandatory Circulars are not the same as published standards, and do not carry the full force of the law.

The desire of the Directorate of Standards of the Directorate General of Economy is that all standards be formally published and this means adhering to the formal process. The Directorate of Standards also has an obligation to monitor standards, with review every five years, although in practice this may depend on the level of resources available. Establishing and evaluating standards can require a large number of experts in the specific field or technology, and each individual requires extensive professional training and experience. It can be challenging to develop and retain such capabilities within government departments, and when human resources for establishing standards are limited, publication of standards can be severely delayed, often with delays that are unacceptable for aviation safety and operational efficiency.

Limits to market development imposed by restrictive air service agreements (ASAs)

International air services are governed by bilateral and in some cases multilateral air service agreements that determine which airports are open to which airlines. Open skies agreements relax the controls on routes, frequencies of service and size of aircraft operating services imposed by traditional air service agreements. Liberalisation of ASAs can produce strong economic benefits for tourism and trade, as well as reduced air fares (see Box 3.1). However, the adoption of open skies is not immediate, as the regulatory framework involved has to be updated to such policy, in order to bring the potential benefits.

The transition from more restrictive agreements, however, may need managing to reduce the risk of placing national air carriers at a competitive disadvantage with respect to other foreign carriers. The degree of liberalisation of ASAs is often perceived as a trade-off between deriving the benefits of competition and, on the other hand, providing national carriers with conditions enabling them to compete with foreign carriers.

Box 3.1. **Economic benefits of liberalising air service agreement**

Gonenc et al. (2000) were among the first to examine the effects of bilateral air services agreements on air fares. They concluded that both at the national and route level there 'is clear evidence that fares tend to decline as the regulatory and market environment becomes friendlier to competition'. In addition, they found that fares react to changes in the level of regulation independent from the market structure, which suggests that potential entry instead of actual competition might have a disciplining role in setting prices. Furthermore, they conclude that economy fares tend to be higher for non-stop routes that are dominated by an airline alliance and they find that airport congestion and dominance tend to raise fares, in particular for business passengers.

Doove et al. (2001) extended the work of Gönenç et al. (2000) and found a positive and significant effect of restrictiveness on airfares, with larger effects for developing countries than for developed countries. A differentiated effect of air service liberalisation for developed and developing countries is also found by Micco et al. (2006). Focusing on the US Open Skies Agreements (OSAs), they investigate the impact of these agreements on airfares and on the share of US imports arriving by air. They found that for developed and upper-middle income countries, signing Open Skies Agreements on average reduces airfares by 9% and increases the share of imports arriving by air by 7% three years after the OSA is signed. They do not find, however, significant effects of OSAs for low income countries.

In work undertaken for the World Trade Organisation, Piermartini and Rousova (2008) use a gravity model to explain international passenger traffic and estimate the impact of liberalising air services agreements on air passenger flows for a sample of 184 countries. In order to assess the effective degree of liberalisation of the bilateral air services agreements, the Air Liberalisation Index, constructed by the WTO, was used. The authors found robust evidence of a direct and significant relationship between the volumes of traffic and the degree of liberalisation of the aviation market. An increase in the degree of liberalisation from the 25th percentile to the 75th percentile increases traffic volumes between countries linked by a direct air service by approximately 30%. The study finds that the most traffic-enhancing provisions of air services agreements are the removal of restrictions on the determination of prices and capacity, cabotage rights and the possibility for airlines other than the country's flag carrier to operate a service (WTO, 2008).

Bosch and Montalvo (2006) analyse the free and non-discriminatory access to airports with the objective to make a proposal to Latin America. In this context, the authors analyse the European Union case, as an example of good practices but lessons to learn from the three package liberalisation, which finished with community licences, free access to markets for carriers with community licences and price freedom. The EU community system includes the single European space and a single regulator.

Source: Elaboration by the OECD Secretariat based on Gonenc, R. and G. Nicoletti, (2000), "Regulation, market structure and performance in air passenger transportation", *OECD Economic Studies*, 32 (2001), pp. 183–227; Doove, S. et al. (2001), "Price Effects of Regulation: Telecommunications, Air Passenger Transport and Electricity Supply", Productivity Commission Staff Research Paper; Micco, A. and T. Serebrisky (2006), "Competition regimes and air freight transport costs: the effects of open skies agreements", *Journal of International Economics*, 70 (2006), pp. 25–51; Piermartini, R. and L. Rousova (2008), "Liberalization of Air freight transport Services and Passenger Traffic", Staff Working Paper ERSD-2008-06, World Trade Organization; Boch, A.D. and G.J. Montalvo (2006), "Free and Non Discriminatory Access to Airports: A Proposal to Latin America", *International Journal of Transport Economics*, Vol. 33/2, pp. 211-255.

The evidence of adoption of open skies agreements to date, and more generally incremental liberalisation of ASAs, is that the airlines of many relatively small or less developed nations have fared very well in competition with global mega-carriers, for example:

- US-Canada open skies (Canada's market is only 10% of the size of the US market) resulted in Air Canada becoming the largest carrier in the trans-border market, using the open skies agreement to develop 6th freedom traffic (see Box 3.2 for definition of air freedoms)
- Open skies with Gulf states have seen the smaller Gulf carriers growing fastest
- Australia-New Zealand open skies agreement has seen Air New Zealand not only maintains its market share, but also become the largest carrier in New Zealand.

Box 3.2. **Freedom in the air**

When countries negotiate air services agreements, they grant traffic rights to airlines that are referred to as "freedoms of the air." With these rights, a Mexican air carrier could:

- Overfly the territory of the other nation (first freedom)
- Land in the other nation to refuel or perform maintenance on the aircraft while en route to a third nation (second freedom)
- Carry traffic from Mexico to the other nation (third freedom)
- Carry traffic from the other nation to Mexico (fourth freedom)
- Carry traffic from the other nation to a third nation as an extension of a service to or from Mexico (fifth freedom)
- Carry traffic from a third nation to the other nation (or from the other nation to a third nation) through Mexico (sixth freedom)
- Carry traffic between the other nation and a third nation on a flight that does not serve Mexico (seventh freedom)
- Carry domestic traffic between points in the other nation as an extension of a service to or from Mexico (eighth freedom) or as purely domestic service with no connection to Mexico (ninth freedom). This is also known as Cabotage.

Source: Elaboration by the OECD Secretariat based in the *Manual of the Regulation of International Air Transport* published by the International Civil Aviation Organization.

In open skies agreements between two nations of different size, the carrier of the smaller nation has the advantage of improved access to a large market, whereas a carrier from the larger nation usually sees marginal benefits in having unrestricted access to the smaller market. The three examples above illustrate that phenomenon. One rationalisation for restrictive ASAs is that the home carrier lacks access to adequate financial capital to expand. However, access to equity capital can be solved, in part, by easing foreign ownership restrictions. While Mexico only allows 25% foreign ownership (the same as the US and Canada), most other nations allow 49%, almost double the foreign equity capital. In the EU, ownership of an EU airline by a non-EU national must be limited to 49.9%, leaving majority ownership in the hands of EU nationals. Some countries have gone further and allowed 100% foreign ownership of their national carriers. For several decades, New Zealand has enjoyed competition in its domestic market from a foreign owned, domestic carrier. Australia also allows 100% foreign ownership of domestic carriers and this enabled the establishment (with UK financing) of a low cost carrier (Virgin Australia). Restrictive agreements are not an appropriate instrument to address issues of access to foreign capital.

Another rationalisation for restrictive ASAs is if the market for aviation itself is restricted. Mexico City Airport, for example, has been suffering from capacity constraints, and an open ASA might fail to achieve gains since no additional air services are possible. In such a situation, a nation might decide to use a restrictive ASA as a means to ration airport capacity. However, this is another clear example of using restricting ASAs as an inappropriate policy tool to address a legitimate issue. Airport capacity constraints can be solved through either new infrastructure and/or better use of the existing infrastructure. Until capacity is increased, it will be considered a scarce resource and should be managed as such. The slot allocation system described previously is designed to manage this scarce resource. While an open ASA will not acerbate the existing capacity shortage, but if appropriately designed, it may foster the benefits of competition. In principle, Mexico City airport has such a renewal system, although it has not been implemented. There is also capacity at the neighbouring Toluca airport that could accommodate traffic growth as capacity constraints are lifted under ASAs.

When the dominance of one of the parties to the open skies agreement is a concern, the governments may decide to phase it in. For example, the Canada-US open skies agreement was gradually phased in due to the concern of Canada that US carriers would be able to expand into its market with its relatively much larger fleets, hence capturing the vast portion of the market, while the Canadian carriers would require a few years to ramp up their operations. Thus the 1995 Canada-US open skies agreement restricted US carrier access to the three largest Canadian markets (Toronto, Vancouver and Montreal) for three years. In the end, a Canadian carrier (Air Canada) became the largest passenger carrier in the trans-border market. On the air cargo side, fear of domination by US cargo carriers also resulted in a phase in of cargo rights. US cargo carriers were denied certain access in the 1995 treaty, specifically 5th and 7th freedom rights, as well as co-terminalisation of cargo services. These rights required another round of negotiations and were not implemented until 2005. In the end, the fear of domination of the US cargo carriers was misplaced and the US carriers did not use the co-terminalisation or beyond rights.[45]

There is another important aspect of restrictive ASAs: they can deny carriers the ability to enter into alliances, with price and capacity agreements, with foreign carriers. Such alliances require the granting of anti-trust immunity (ATI) from competition authorities in the home nations of both parties. But such immunity is normally contingent upon open skies ASAs to remove entry barriers for competing carriers (the only cases in which alliances have received ATI without an open skies agreement in place was when an open skies ASA was in the process of being phased in). Thus, there is a nexus between ATI for alliances and open skies agreements (ITF, 2014).

Alliances can be a desirable element of market structure for Mexico's airline industry. Aeromexico is already a member of SkyTeam, the only member located between the United States and Argentina, and the more open Mexico's air service agreements are, the more it can play a strategic role in channelling traffic from Europe and Asia to Latin America. There is a growing literature that demonstrates that airline alliances can produce significant benefits for both carriers and consumers.[46] However, to achieve these benefits, there must be an open market so that the aligned carriers do not operate in the absence of competition.

In our discussions we heard stakeholders distinguish between unrestricted air service agreements for 3rd/4th freedom traffic rights versus agreements that include 5th freedom services and also 7th freedom traffic rights for air cargo. With regard to 3rd/4th freedom traffic rights, there is a willingness to embrace unrestricted rights for these services and the OECD advice is not to limit 3rd/4th freedoms based on capacity, but rather use a slot allocation system to efficiently allocate scarce capacity where it will be economically most profitable.

The issue with 5th freedom services is that of foreign 5th freedom carriers potentially "dumping" seats into the market at very low fares, thus undermining the businesses of Mexican 3rd/4th freedom carriers on the same route. If 'seat dumping' were to materialise, however, the Government could cap the proportion of seats available for 5th freedom traffic, for example, at 25%, which could change the economic dynamics of such a route and prevent any significant dumping of capacity.

While 5th freedom services are relatively rare today,[47] such services could develop through Mexico in the future due to its geographical location – for example, Asian carriers operating a 5th freedom sector between a US or Canadian point and an airport in Mexico, or Latin American carriers operating through Mexico on the way to the United States (or Canada). However, the strong consumer preference for non-stop flights make the latter unlikely and while there was some use of 5th freedom rights by Asian carriers in the past (e.g. Japan Airline's Tokyo-Vancouver-Mexico City service), such rights are all currently unused.

The issue of 7th freedom rights is confined to air cargo. Air cargo routing is very complex as goods normally travel only one way, contrary to passengers. Thus, freight carriers will often be forced to vary the routing in each direction to maximize their loads (and profits). An example of this in Mexico City is Lufthansa's freighter flights that arrive in Mexico City from Frankfurt via Chicago or Caracas but fly back to Frankfurt via Dallas. With greater 7th freedom rights for cargo, airlines could more easily integrate a leg between Mexico City and a 3rd country on a flight where the carrier does not serve its home country. This would enable Mexican exports to enjoy greater global connectivity in reaching far-flung markets while at the same time facilitating the import of goods for the Mexican market. In addition, through ASA reciprocity, this could enable Mexican MasAir (part of the LATAM group) to leverage its secondary hubs in Miami and Los Angeles and possibly operate a freighter between one of those airports and a 3rd country.

Mexico has negotiated restricted ASAs with most countries. In 2014 a modified agreement with the United States was initialled by the aeronautical authorities, to provide for unrestricted use of 3rd/4th freedom rights for all services (regular and charter passenger and cargo services), and unrestricted 5th and 7th freedom rights for cargo services (regular and charter). The agreement comes into force in 2016, upon confirmation of the agreement on both sides, which in Mexico requires approval by the Senate.

Recommendations

Airport capacity allocation at congested airports

It is recommended that the key elements of the existing slot allocation law be retained and effectively implemented. These would include 1) the slot allocation by the air operator; 2) slot trade between airlines in the secondary market to increase the efficiency of their use—for example to enable better times for flights; 3) the *use it or lose it* principle in which airlines making inadequate use of assigned slot should lose it; and 4) allowing airline families to reassign slots to other family members—through ownership families and global and bilateral alliances.

Slot allocation rules need to strike a balance between the benefits of competition fostered by ensuring that new entrants will be able to enter the market; and the network benefits, where a hub carrier may create high value from an additional slot due to its large network of connections and economies of scale.

The 2000 Law on Airport Regulation should be amended to, or regulations should be issued, to facilitate the implementation of auctions for primary slot allocation (as prescribed by the law); or to replace the auction mechanism with either, the adoption of the international standard on airport slot allocation, the IATA World Scheduling Guidelines or any method that embraces its key elements.

The primary slot allocation should consider introducing a cap on overall aeronautical revenues at Mexico City airport (and any other airport operating primary slot auctions) in order to prevent economic rents accumulating to the airport operator. Capacity in a regulatory agency should be created to establish the level for the cap on aeronautical revenues and adjudicate in case of disputes between airlines and the airport, regarding the tariffs of airport services. The first candidate to be in charge of such duties would be the Federal Agency of Civil Aviation (AFAC) which is in plan to be created since the 2015. Thus, the AFAC would have in its duties the establishment of price caps between other technical and economic regulations—with the exemption of the security matters which will be assigned to a specialised agency in process to be formalised. Of course, the auctions conducted for primary slot allocation should provide information about the price cap regulations, so as to internalise the cost of regulation in the bid. The precise auction design and mechanism should be developed by such agency. An example of such price caps can be found in the telecommunications industry, in which weighted average caps have been used.

A regulatory cap on aeronautical revenues would work by requiring the airport to reduce its landing, terminal and other charges so that its overall income is not increased by the implementation of auctions for primary slots and the new income stream that would generate. Without a regulatory cap on aeronautical charges the airport would have incentives to accrue disproportionately high rents from auctioning of slots – airlines would very strongly oppose such as system. The cap would serve consumer as well as airline interests, as uncapped charges would be largely passed on to passengers and freight users in higher fares. The Government will have an interest in ensuring the way aeronautical charges are reduced as well as in the overall reduction so that changes in charges are structured to be in line with the government's overall objectives for development of the market for air services in Mexico City.

If the new airport is to be financed by the operator of the existing airport, the price cap could be designed to allow for generating funds for investment in expansion of capacity. Pre-funding of new capacity through charges on use of existing capacity is resisted by airlines and establishing a suitable asset base for regulation is a far from trivial task. The government would need the regulatory capacity to be able to determine what level of overall aeronautical charge increase is efficient and in line with overall policy. Adequate staffing and access to expertise would need to be provided for and sufficiently resourced.

Adoption of international standards and their incorporation to national regulation

Publish aviation standards immediately after they are adopted in their original language in the Official Gazette (*Diario Oficial de la Federación*) with acknowledgement that they are legally binding until replaced by official translations.

In short order, translate those standards to Spanish and republish them in the Official Gazette.

Conduct a study of Spanish and Latin American civil aviation authorities to review their publishing practices identify best practices and adapt those to Mexican requirements.

Air Service Agreements

Mexico should consider the adoption of a policy that seeks open skies agreements with other nations. In addition to the trade and tourism benefits of expanded air service, open skies agreements can enable Mexican air carriers to enter into alliances with antitrust immunity, producing both carrier and consumer/trade benefits for Mexico.

Including 5th freedom rights in open skies agreements should be seen as an opportunity. Experience suggests they are unlikely to be used extensively by entrants competing on existing routes but they are likely to enable new services to emerging markets such as China to open earlier than they would otherwise. This will be important to fostering development of Mexico City's new airport as a global hub.

Seventh freedom rights for cargo should be included in open skies agreements and other revised air service agreements as they are essential to competitive dedicated cargo operations. It is important for growth of the airfreight market and growth opportunities for Mexican air freight carriers operating from US hubs that the Senate ratifies the ASA agreed between Mexico and the United States in 2014.

Notes

1. According to the SCT, until January of 2016, there were 298 routes-destinies for regular national flights, http://busca.datos.gob.mx/#!/conjuntos/infraestructura-aeroportuaria/.

2. Convenio sobre transportes aéreos entre el Gobierno de los Estados Unidos Mexicanos y los Estados Unidos de America, consulted on www.sct.gob.mx/JURE/doc/31-eua-transp-aereo.pdf.

3. SCT, Aviación Mexicana en cifras 1993-2015. Subsecretaría de Transporte, Dirección General de Aeronáutica Civil.

4. Mexicana was Mexico's oldest network carrier, operating a diversified domestic and international route network.

5. Mexicana is a founding member of the SkyTeam alliance.

6. See http://centreforaviation.com/analysis/mexicos-interjet-plans-further-expansion-with-new-superjet-fleet-targeting-thinner-routes-78548.

7. See http://centreforaviation.com/analysis/aeromexico-and-volaris-remain-cautiously-optimistic-that-a-domestic-yield-rebound-will-hold-213789.

8. SCT, *Aviación Mexicana en cifras 1993-2015. Subsecretaría de Transporte, Dirección General de Aeronáutica Civil.*

9. In 2013, the number of air passengers in Mexico was 61.4 million; 38% of these were served by foreign airlines and 61% by domestic airlines.

10. See www.trade.gov/mas/ian/build/groups/public/@tg_ian/documents/webcontent/tg_ian_003364.pdf.

11. See Boeing World Air Cargo Forecasts 2014-15, www.boeing.com/resources/boeingdotcom/commercial/about-our-market/cargo-market-detail-wacf/download-report/assets/pdfs/wacf.pdf.

12. See http://trade.ec.europa.eu/doclib/docs/2006/september/tradoc_122530.pdf.

13. Estimate is based on Boeing World Air Cargo Forecasts 2014-15.

14. Under the Civil Aviation Law (*Ley de Aviación Civil*).

15. Airport Law (*Ley de Aeropuertos*).

16. At least until the project of the new regulatory agency is formalised. The SCT submitted to the COFEMER a decree project, by which the Federal Civil Aviation Agency is created, in August, 2014, in order for the regulatory impact assessment of the draft to be evaluated, and receive comments from the public. However, the final decree has not been published.

17. Law of Professional Service in the Federal Public Administration (*Ley del Servicio Profesional de Carrera de la Administración Pública Federal*); Federal Law of Public Fees (*Ley Federal de Derechos*); Federal Law of Administrative Procedure (*Ley Federal*

de Procedimiento Administrativo); Federal Law of Administrative Argumentative Procedure (*Ley Federal de Procedimiento Contencioso Administrativo*); Federal Law of Administrative Responsibilities of Public Servant (*Ley Federal de Responsabilidades Administrativas de los Servidores Públicos*); Federal Law of Transparency and Governmental Public Information (*Ley Federal de Acceso a la Información Pública Gubernamental*); and Federal Law of Measures and Standards (*Ley Federal sobre Metrología y Normalización*).

18. The Operation and Schedule Committee is formed by the airport concession holder, which is the airport administrator; the airfield captain; civil and military authorities; and representatives of the concession and permission holders of air transport and other services.

19. Article 133 of the Regulation of LA includes a definition of specific and joint maximum tariff. Specific tariff is the compensation paid by the user of airport and complementary services providers, which includes applicability basis and conditions and restrictions according to the services or leasing contract. Joint maximum tariff is the maximum total income that a concessionaire can receive for a group of services, leasing and contracts for a specific period of time.

20. There are also some negative impacts on the network, such as longer journey times and the inconvenience of having to change flights to some passengers. See Starkie (2006).

21. See https://www.law.cornell.edu/cfr/text/14/93.123.

22. See Brueckner (2002, 2005), Mayer and Sinai (2003).

23. A peak slot is the available during the busiest time in the day in which the demand for slots normally exceeds supply.

24. Another way in which scarce slots may be allocated at peak times to the carriers who place the highest value on it would be through pricing as a rationing device (see, for example, Matthews and Menaz, 2003) to distribute capacity to airlines.

25. See IATA's website, https://www.iata.org/policy/slots/pages/slot-guidelines.aspx. This section draws on material in IATA World Scheduling Guidelines, Effective January 2010, 19th edition. This document is attached to the Affidavit of Alain Boudreau 8 February 2010.

26. E.g., at the slot controlled US airports such as Chicago or the German federal slot co-ordinator.

27. E.g., at airport in Calgary and Montreal.

28. E.g., Slots at congested London airports are allocated by the Airport Coordination Ltd.. In Canada there is Airport Coordination Canada, and independent private company which manages the slots at Toronto Pearson International Airport.

29. According to the DotEcon report, in the 2006 summer schedule, 2.2% of slots at Heathrow and 6.4% of slots at Gatwick were allocated using a slot allocation mechanisms, the rest of them were reallocated to the carriers who were already using them previously. See DotEcon (2006, p. 35).

30. A new market entrant is defined by the IATA WSG as an airline that holds less than 3% of all slots at a given airport.

31. By this principle, for example, a carrier seeking to increase its weekly frequency of service toward daily will be given priority over scheduling new flights (whether by incumbents or entrants).

32. Slot allocation in the European Union is governed by European Council Regulation 95/93, later updated (in 2004) by regulation 793/2004.

33. IATA decided to adopt this externally imposed policy into its own WSGs.

34. For example, a capacity constrained airport serving both short-haul and long-haul traffic, in which long haul slot requests have s matching pair at Level 3 airport.

35. Sydney Airport Slot Management Administration Manual', https://infrastructure.gov.au/aviation/airport/planning/files/sydney_airport_slot_administration_manual.pdf.

36. 14 CFR Part 93, subpart K, established the "high density rule," https://www.law.cornell.edu/cfr/text/14/part-93/subpart-K.

37. See 'Airline Restructuring in Canada', Parliament of Canada, www.parl.gc.ca/Content/LOP/ResearchPublications/tips/tip45-e.htm.

38. EU member states that impose PSOs must respect the conditions and the requirements set out in Article 16 of the Air Services Regulation 1008/2008, http://ec.europa.eu/transport/modes/air/internal_market/pso_en.htm.

39. See "Guidance on the Protection of Regional Air Access to London", https://www.gov.uk/government/uploads/system/uploads/attachment_data/file/266383/pso-policy-guidance.pdf.

40. See Mexico City Airport (AICM), www.aicm.com.mx/en/.

41. Although there have been cases where airport slots assigned to a carrier were sold and transferred to the highest bidder when the carrier ceased operations due to a bankruptcy, but this is a rare event and most governments would reclaim the slots rather than allow them to be auctioned.

42. See www.dof.gob.mx.

43. Article 40 of the LFMN indicates the requirements for a standard and what a standard must entail. In general, anything that involves the safety of users must have a standard established.

44. While in Mexico, however, oversight of standards is by a single agency, in the US there are more than 100 agencies that are able to independently set and publish standards. The agencies, whose approach may differ, generally use cost benefit analysis (CBA) as a decision-making framework for assessing the merits of a proposed policy change. The US Congress requires that any regulation introduced by the government is supported by a CBA which indicates clearly what social benefit will result from adopting the regulation. Any new regulation must be supported by a CBA which shows a clear net benefit from the regulation. See: www.whitehouse.gov/the-press-office/2011/01/18/improving-regulation-and-regulatory-review-executive-order.

45. See http://internationaltransportforum.org/Pub/pdf/14AirServiceAgreements.pdf.

46. See IATA's Economic Briefing on The Economic Benefits Generated by Alliances and Joint Ventures: https://www.iata.org/whatwedo/Documents/economics/Economics%20of%20JVs_Jan2012L.pdf.

47. Such services were more common in the past when aircraft ranges were much more severely restricted and intermediate stop were required for many long-haul connections.

References

Airports Commission (2013), "Discussion Paper 04: Airport Operational Models", London, https://www.gov.uk/government/publications/discussion-paper-on-airport-operational-models.

Bailey, E.E. and A.F. Friedlaender (1982), "Market Structure and Multiproduct Industries", *Journal of Economic Literature*, Vol. 20/3, September, pp. 1024-1048.

Boch, A.D. and G.J. Montalvo (2006), "*Free and Non Discriminatory Access to Airports: A Proposal to Latin America*", *International Journal of Transport Economics*, Vol. XXXIII/2, pp. 211-255.

Borenstein, S. (1989), "Hubs and high fares: dominance and market power in the US airline industry", *RAND Journal of Economics*, Vol. 20/1, Autumn.

Brueckner, J.K. (2002), "Airport Congestion When Carriers Have Market Power", *American Economic Review*, Vol. 92/5, pp. 1357-1375.

Brueckner, J.K. (2005), "Internalization of airport congestion: A network analysis", *International Journal of Industrial Organization*, Vol. 23, pp. 599-614.

Canadian Airport Council (2005), "The Next Stage for Canada-U.S. Air Transportation: Open Skies or Beyond?", http://westac.com/pdfs/thenextstage.pdf.

Doganis, R. (2009), *Flying off course: airline economics and marketing*, 4th edition, Taylor & Francis e-Library.

Doove, S. et al. (2001), "Price Effects of Regulation: Telecommunications, Air Passenger Transport and Electricity Supply", *Productivity Commission Staff Research Paper*.

DotEcon (2006), "Alternative allocation mechanisms for slots created by new airport capacity", Final Report by DotEcon, www.dotecon.com.

Gönenç, R. and G. Nicoletti (2000), "Regulation, Market Structure and Performance in Air Passenger Transportation", *OECD Economics Department Working Papers*, No. 254, OECD Publishing, Paris, http://dx.doi.org/10.1787/163610427241, pp. 183-227.

International Civil Aviation Organization (2004), "Manual on the Regulation of International Air Transport", 2nd edition.

ITF (2014), "Air Service Agreement Liberalisation and Airline Alliances", ITF.

Kahn, A.E. (1993), "The Competitive Consequences of Hub Dominance: A Case Study", *Review of Industrial Organisation*s, Vol. 8, pp. 381-405.

Matthews, B. and B. Menaz (2003), "Airport Capacity: The Problem of Slot Allocation", *Institute of Transport Studies*, University of Leeds.

Mayer, C. and T. Sinai (2003), "Networks Effects, Congestion Externalities, and Air Traffic Delays: Or Why All Delays Are Not Evil", *American Economic Review*, Vol. 93, pp. 1194-1215.

Micco, A. and T. Serebrisky (2006), "Competition regimes and air freight transport costs: the effects of open skies agreements", *Journal of International Economics*, Vol. 70, pp. 25–51.

Piermartini, R. and L. Rousova (2008), "Liberalization of Air freight transport Services and Passenger Traffic", *Staff Working Paper*, ERSD-2008-06, World Trade Organisation.

SCT (2015), "La Aviación Mexicana en Cifras 1992-2015", General Direction of Civil Aviation, Ministry of Communications and Transport, www.sct.gob.mx/transporte-y-medicina-preventiva/aeronautica-civil/5-estadisticas/51-aviacion-mexicana-en-cifras-89-15-only-in-spanish/ (accessed 22 November 2016).

Sentence, A. (2003), "Airport slot auctions: desirable or feasible?", *Utilities Policy*, Vol. 11, pp. 53–57.

Starkie, D. (2006), "The Dilemma of Slot Concentration at Network Hubs", in *How to make slot markets work*, eds A. Czerny et al.

Chapter 4

Regulation of ports in Mexico

Mexico has 117 ports and terminals that handled 288 million tonnes of goods in 2013. Four ports are considered to be national hubs: Manzanillo, Lazaro Cardenas, Altamira and Veracruz. The SCT has the legal attributions to granting concessions, permits and authorisations for building, establishing, administrating, operating and exploiting works and goods in ports, maritime terminals and port installations. Challenges include: to develop an integrated logistics strategy for the main four Mexican ports to increase the volume of containers that could be carried on railroads; to increase port efficiency by: establish a dedicated areas free of border controls for coastal shipping; to introduce a specific regime to facilitate transhipment; to open customs and other inspection agencies more often 24 hours per day; to develop policies to simplify port gate operations; and to consider opening up the maritime cabotage market.

Overview of ports in Mexico

Market organisation

Mexico has 117 ports and terminals that handled 289 million tonnes of goods in 2013—102 ports and 15 terminals outside ports. And 74 of these facilities are either under the administration of subnational governments or by the private sector, while 32 are administrated by the federal government. From those 74 facilities administrated by an API, in 32 of them, the concessionaire is a legal firm owned by the federal government as the largest stakeholder; in 36 APIs the control is exerted by a regional government, 3 by the National Fund of Tourism and one by private capital, see Table 4.1.

According to Article VII of the Law of Ports (*Ley de Puertos,* LP) in 1993, the federal government may create state-owned limited companies to which the concessions could be assigned. There is no legal mandate stating whether or when these concessions would be transferred to private entities.

Table 4.1. **Ports of Mexico and their administrative structure**

No.	Federal APIs	State APIs	FONATUR	Private
1	Altamira	Baja California Sur	Huatulco	Acapulco
2	Coatzacoalcos	Campeche	Zihuatanejo	
3	Chiapas	Quintana Roo	Los Cabos	
4	Dos Bocas	Tabasco		
5	Ensenada	Tamaulipas		
6	Guaymas			
7	Manzanillo			
8	Mazatlán			
9	Lázaro Cárdenas			
10	Progreso			
11	Vallarta			
12	Salina Cruz			
13	Tampico			
14	Tuxpan			
15	Topolobampo			
16	Veracruz			

Source: OECD elaboration.

The most important ports are administered by 16 APIs, 9 of which are on the Pacific Coast and 7 on the Gulf Coast (see Table 4.1). Of these 16 ports, 4 are considered to be national hubs: Manzanillo and Lazaro Cardenas on the Pacific Coast and Altamira and Veracruz on the Gulf Coast. These four national ports are the largest in terms of tonnage if petroleum is excluded (see Table 4.2). A large share of the cargo in Mexico is handled by a few ports inside the country, which indicates a more concentrated activity compared to similar sized countries, despite the large number of ports and terminals in Mexico. A precise measure of concentration would require a market definition approach but in such case, the probable result would be on the same direction. This concentration is particularly visible in containerised cargo and oil products. Approximately, 95% of the total container volume of 4.9 million TEUs is handled in four hub ports (Table 4.3). Comparable concentration tendencies are apparent in the oil terminals where the four top oil ports and terminals account for 74% of the volume. Considering that their maritime forelands and terrestrial hinterlands are hardly overlapping, these ports can be considered to have a quasi-controlling position with respect to oil. For container traffic a concentration tendency is more limited as Manzanillo, Lázaro Cárdenas, and Veracruz all compete to serve the very large market of Mexico City. Monterrey, the second major market, is however, dependent on Altamira. Competition between terminals inside the port is particularly important, considering the fairly concentrated nature of the ports in Mexico. As seen in Table 4.2, in case oil is included, the largest port in Mexico is Cayo Arcas, an off-shore oil terminal owned by Petróleos Mexicanos (PEMEX), a Mexican state-owned company.

Table 4.2. **Overview of main federal ports in Mexico**

Name of port	State location	Coast location	Type	Nearest ports
Altamira	Tamaulipas (North of Mexico)	Gulf of Mexico	Hub Port	Tampico
Coatzacoalcos	Veracruz	Gulf of Mexico	Regional Port	Veracruz, Dos Bocas
Dos Bocas	Tabasco (Southeast of Mexico)	Gulf of Mexico	Regional Port	Coatzacoalcos
Ensenada	Baja California (Northeast of Mexico)	Pacific Coast	Regional Port	Guaymas
Guaymas	Sonora (Northeast of Mexico)	California Gulf	Regional Port	Topolobampo, Ensenada
Lázaro Cárdenas	Michoacán	Pacific Coast	Hub Port	Manzanillo
Manzanillo	Colima	Pacific Coast	Hub Port	Lázaro Cárdenas, Puerto Vallarta
Mazatlán	Sinaloa	Pacific Coast	Regional Port	Puerto Vallarta, Topolobampo
Progreso	Yucatán (Southeast of Mexico)	Gulf of Mexico	Regional Port	Dos Bocas
Puerto Chiapas	Chiapas (South of Mexico)	Pacific Coast	Regional Port	Salinas Cruz
Puerto Vallarta	Jalisco	Pacific Coast	Regional Port	Manzanillo, Mazatlán
Salina Cruz	Oaxaca (South of Mexico)	Pacific Coast	Regional Port	Puerto Chiapas
Tampico	Tamaulipas (Northeast of Mexico)	Gulf of Mexico	Regional Port	Altamira, Tuxpan
Topolobamo	Sinaloa (Northeast of Mexico)	California Gulf	Regional Port	Guaymas, Mazatlán
Tuxpan	Veracruz	Gulf of Mexico	Regional Port	Tampico, Veracruz
Veracruz	Veracruz	Gulf of Mexico	Hub Port	Tuxpan, Dos Bocas

Source: Ministry of Communications and Transport (SCT).

A large share of the cargo in Mexico is handled by a few ports inside the country, which indicates a more concentrated activity compared to similar sized countries, despite the large number of ports and terminals in Mexico.

Table 4.3. **The top 10 ports in Mexico in 2015**

Port	Tonnes (incl. oil)	% of total	Port	Tonnes (excl. oil)	% of total
Coatzacoalcos	30 250 853	10.44%	Manzanillo	25 243 881	15.16%
Cayo Arcas	29 838 800	10.30%	Lázaro Cárdenas	23 681 785	14.22%
Manzanillo	27 998 504	9.67%	Veracruz	21 423 898	12.87%
Lázaro Cárdenas	26 430 356	9.12%	Altamira	18 038 940	10.83%
Veracruz	23 157 615	7.99%	Isla de Cedros	15 283 901	9.18%
Dos Bocas	22 290 449	7.69%	Punta Venado	12 996 494	7.80%
Altamira	18 038 940	6.23%	Guerrero Negro	7 720 025	4.64%
Isla de Cedros	15 283 901	5.28%	Coatzacoalcos	6 007 921	3.61%
Salina Cruz	13 814 960	4.77%	Guaymas	5 274 962	3.17%
Tuxpan	13 288 420	4.59%	Topolobampo	3 799 567	2.28%

Source: OECD elaboration based on data from the Ministry of Communications and Transport (SCT). The data included in the table came from the *Informe Estadístico Mensual: Movimiento de Carga, Buques y Pasajeros*. At the moment of this draft, statistics have been published until August 2016. This table has been updated up to December 2015 for two reasons: comparability with other figures in the chapter and to grasp the dynamics of a whole year in the Ports System. The following link shows the latest set of available statistics: www.sct.gob.mx/fileadmin/CGPMM/U_DGP/estadisticas/2015/Mensuales/12_diciembre_2015.pdf.

Table 4.4. **The top 10 container and oil ports in Mexico**

Port	Container (TEUs)	% of total	Port	Oil volume (tonnes)	% of total
Manzanillo	2 136 157	43.3%	Cayo Arcas	47 944 077	39.1%
Lazaro Cardenas	1 051 183	21.5%	Coatzacoalcos	18 625 413	15.2%
Veracruz	866 966	17.7%	Salina Cruz	12 929 555	10.5%
Altamira	597 760	12.2%	Tuxpan	10 959 279	8.9%
Ensenada	131 054	2.7%	Dos Bocas	7 660 759	6.2%
Progreso	64 928	1.3%	Tampico	5 520 165	4.5%
Mazatlan	28 094	0.6%	Rosarito	2 547 415	2.1%
Guaymas	8 370	0.2%	Topolobambo	2 205 767	1.8%
Puerto Morelos	7 271	0.1%	Guaymas	2 191 372	1.8%
Puerto Ciapas	762	0.0%	Lazaro Cardenas	1 987 705	1.6%

Source: OECD elaborations based on data from the Ministry of Communications and Transport.

The cargo mix of Mexican ports is dominated by petroleum (43% of the total tonnage), followed by bulk minerals (27%) and containerised cargo which represented 14% of the total tonnage of Mexican ports in 2013 (Figure 4.1). The last decade has seen, however, significant changes in the cargo categories: the share of petroleum in the total port cargo has declined from 61.5% in 2002 to 42.5% in 2013, whereas the shares of both, bulk minerals and containerised cargo have increased in the same period. Cargo in minerals increased 7 points from 20.3% to 27.2% and containers from 4.7% to 13.9%. The other cargo types remained relatively stable (Figure 4.2).

Figure 4.1. **Cargo mix of Mexican ports 2015**

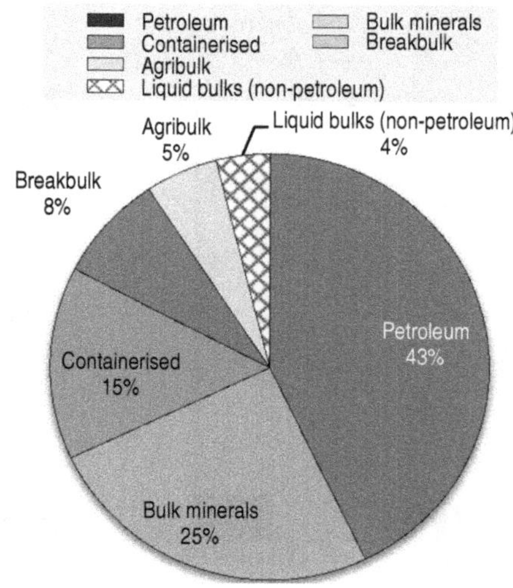

Source: Elaboration of the OECD Secretariat based on data from the Ministry of Communications and Transport.

Figure 4.2. **Cargo mix of Mexican ports 2002-2015**

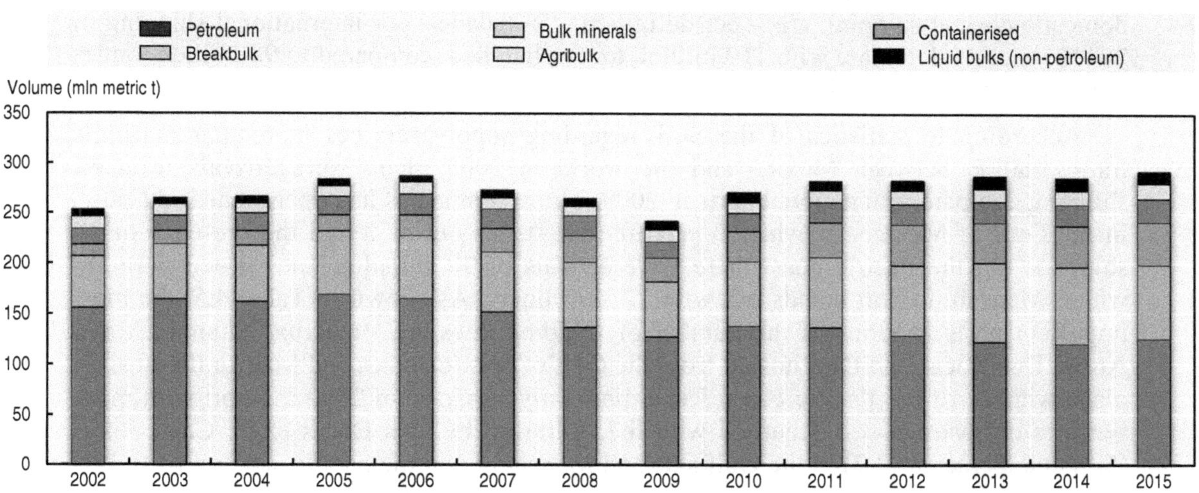

Source: Elaboration of the OECD Secretariat based on data from the Ministry of Communications and Transport.

There are few ports in Mexico that resemble this average cargo mix (Figure 4.3), due to port specialisation. Some of the largest ports in Mexico are specialised in oil (Cayo Arcas, Coatzacoalcos, Dos Bocas)). The main four non-oil specialised hub ports have different profiles with respect to their cargo mix, with pre-dominance of container traffic, representing between 26% of tonnage in Lázaro Cárdenas to 65% in Manzanillo. The exception is Lázaro Cardenas, where minerals form the largest cargo type, taking up 52.5% of total tonnage. The cargo type for which most of the competition takes place is in the container sector. As the section on Port Competition (below) indicates, the four main container ports have hinterlands that overlap to some extent, in particular Mexico City.

Figure 4.3. **Cargo mix of seven largest ports in Mexico (2015)**

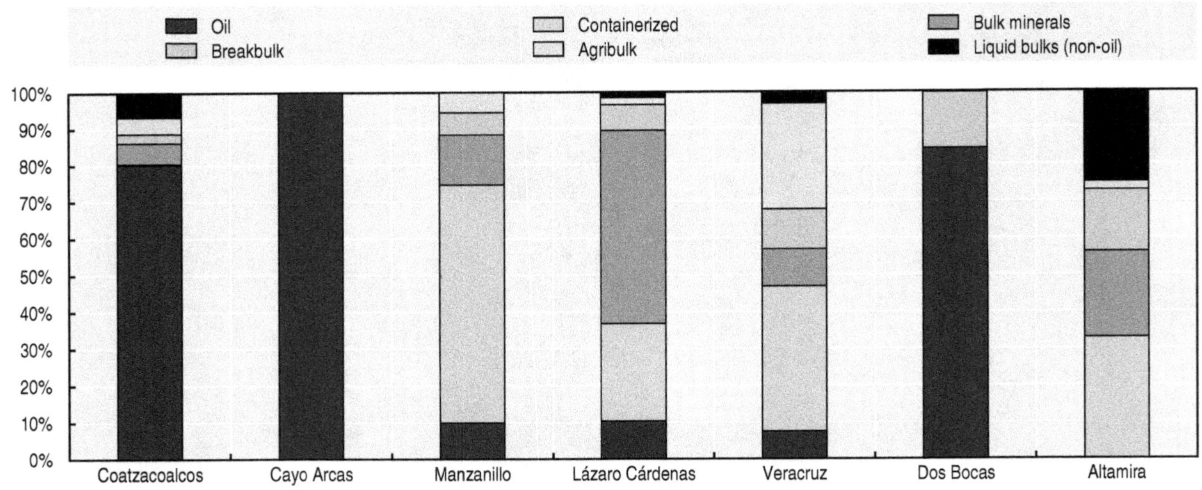

Source: Elaboration of the OECD Secretariat based on data from the Ministry of Communications and Transport.

Coastal shipping represented around 25% in 2015 of the total volume transported by maritime transport in Mexico; this is down from 30% in 1996. Imports and exports from domestic coastal shipping are – per definition – in balance; for international shipping in 20115, exports dominate with 119 million tonnes handled, compared to 98 million tonnes for imports from international shipping.

According to statistics of the SCT regarding supply services in regular maritime transportation between Mexico and the world in 2009, there were arrivals from 82 shipping companies in national ports in 2009. These companies had operations in 11 ports in the Gulf of Mexico, in which Veracruz port stands out as it had the presence of 37 shippers. On the Pacific coast there were arrivals of 30 shipping lines in ten ports, in which Manzanillo port stands out with 22 ship liners. As shown in Table 4.5, the most important ports in terms of the number of shipping lines are Veracruz, Altamira, Cayo Arcas, Dos Bocas and Pajaritos all from the Gulf of Mexico coast and Manzanillo in sixth place with 22 of the Pacific coast. Regarding daily services, in 2009 the port with more services on average was Pajaritos with 6.7, followed by Dos Bocas (5.7), Cayo Arcas (5.6) and Veracruz (4.2) in the Gulf side and Manzanillo on the pacific side with 4.0. It is worth mentioning that Dos Bocas and Cayo Arcas are two of the most important petroleum ports in the country.

As shown in Table 4.6, in 2009 the highest number of shipping lines was concentrated in the routes between Mexico and North America with 64 lines, which also had the highest daily average of services with 11.2, but the second lowest number of destinies with 43, just above Oceania with 18 destinies. It stands out that the largest number of destinies goes to Asia with 194 through 25 shipping lines that make 3.2 services every day on average. Central and South America and Europe also had an important number of destinies with 113 and 106 respectively, with 44 and 25 shipping lines. In summary, lines that transport to North American destinies would face more competitive pressure because of the largest number of lines. On the contrary, Oceania and Africa would face lower competitive pressures from the point of view of the number of participants in the market.

Table 4.5. **Shipping lines by port in Mexico in 2009**

Gulf of Mexico			Pacific		
Port	Shipping line	Average daily service	Port	Shipping line	Average daily service
Tampico	19	2	Ensenada	12	1.8
Altamira	31	3.8	La Paz	2	0.5
Tuxpan	11	1.7	Guaymas	2	1.3
Veracruz	37	4.2	Topolobambo	2	1.3
Coatzacoalcos	5	0.8	Mazatlán	5	0.8
Dos Bocas	25	5.7	Manzanillo	22	4.0
Cayo Arcas	27	5.6	Lázaro Cárdenas	10	1.6
Pajaritos	25	6.7	Acapulco	1	0.3
Cd. del Carmen	2	0.5	Salina Cruz	8	3
Progreso	6	1.9	Puerto Madero	2	0.4
Puerto Morelos	3	0.6			
Total	**191**		**Total**	**66**	

Source: Ministry of Communications and Transport (SCT).

Table 4.6. **Ship arrivals in national ports on regular services in 2009**

Ship liner services	Total of shipping lines	Daily average services	Total monthly average	Destinies
Mexico-North America	64	11.2	335	43
Mexico-Central, South America and the Caribbean	44	5.4	163	113
Mexico-Africa	13	1.5	45	58
Mexico-Asia	25	3.2	97	194
Mexico-Europe	25	2.6	79	106
Mexico-Oceania	10	1.4	41	18

Source: Ministry of Communications and Transport (SCT).

Port organisation

Ports in Mexico are relatively specialised, which means that a limited number of ports dominate the traffic of different cargo categories, as illustrated in Table 4.4 for containerised cargo and oil. Ports compete with each other if they have overlapping hinterlands and forelands. For three of the four main container ports in Mexico the main port hinterland is the metropolitan area of Mexico City (Table 4.7). Considering that Veracruz is on the Gulf Coast, unlike Manzanillo and Lazaro Cardenas, it has a completely different maritime foreland that is difficult to replicate for the two other ports. Rail concessions were structured and designed to ensure competition between the ports in the rail container and intermodal markets; this objective however, should be assessed in order to know to what degree the objective has been achieved.

Table 4.7. **Mexico City as container port hinterland in 2007**

Port	Flows to/from Mexico City (in mln TEUs)	% of TEUs destined to Mexico City
Manzanillo	0.72	51%
Veracruz	0.54	74%
Lazaro Cardenas	0.19	71%
Altamira	0.10	25%

Source: Elaborations based on Peyrelongue and Martinez (2011) and data from Ministry of Communications and Transport.

The geographic limitation on inter-port competition would be compensated to some extent by intra-port competition. The main ports in Mexico all have concession agreements and contracts with private terminal operators that handle services for the different cargo categories. This would provide competitive pressures, especially for terminals with similar cargo types such as containers. For instance, several of the largest global terminal operators are active in the main Mexican ports and compete with each other for cargo, especially in the container sector (see Table 4.8).

Table 4.8. **Global terminal operators in Mexican ports**

Global terminal operator	Port	Terminal	Cargo type
Hutchison Port Holdings (HPH)	Manzanillo Lazaro Cardenas Veracruz Ensenada	Terminal Internacional de Manzanillo (TIMSA) Lazaro Cardenas Terminal Portuaria de Contenedores (LCT) Internacional de Contenedores Asociados de Veracruz (ICAVE) Ensenada International Terminal (EIT)	Containers Containers Containers Cont. & bulk
APM Terminals	Lazaro Cardenas		Containers
SSA	Lazaro Cardenas Manzanillo Veracruz Acapulco		RoRo Containers Multipurpose Cars
ICTSI	Manzanillo	Contecon Manzanillo	Containers

Source: Elaborations of the OECD Secretariat based on data from terminal operators.

One of the areas where port competition is played out is in port hinterland connections. As Table 4.8 shows, many of the global terminal operators are present in the ports that compete with each other, in particular Lazaro Cardenas and Manzanillo, indicating the competition between the terminals of HPH, APMT, SSA and ICTSI. It is reasonable to assume that the knowledge transfer from global terminal operators such as HPH and SSA, benefits terminals in both ports (Lazaro Cardenas and Manzanillo), so one would expect that the main differences between the ports will not be so much with respect to terminal operations. However, these ports differ in their connections to freight rail. Although all major ports in Mexico are connected to rail lines, the way that freight rail is organised in Mexico implies that major ports have a different rail company taking care of the cargo service. For instance, Ferromex is the rail company that serves the port of Manzanillo to Mexico City, KCSM for is the firm connecting the port of Lazaro Cardenas and Mexico City (ITF, 2014), see Table 4.9.

Table 4.9. **Port-railway connections in Mexico**

Firm	Kilometres of lines	Ports covered	Border cities covered[2]	Inland cities covered
Kansas City Southern de México (KCSM)	4 283	Lázaro Cárdenas (Pacific) Veracruz (Gulf of Mexico) Matamoros (Gulf of Mexico) Guaymas (Pacific) Manzanillo (Pacific)	Matamoros (United States) Nuevo Laredo (United States) Mexicali (United States)	Mexico City Hermosillo Guadalajara Irapuato Silao Puebla Monterrey Torreón Chihuahua
Ferrocarril Mexicano (Ferromex)[1]	8 643	Altamira (Gulf of Mexico) Guaymas Topolobampo Mazatlán Tampico (Gulf of Mexico) Manzanillo Coatzacoalcos (Gulf of Mexico) Veracruz (Gulf of Mexico)	Piedras Negras (United States) Mexicali (United States) Nogales (United States) Ojinaga (United States) El Paso (United States) Ciudad Juárez (United States)	Puebla Mexico City Querétaro Irapuato Tepic Guadalajara Chihuahua Los Mochis Culiacán Hermosillo Saltillo Monterrey Torreón Aguascalientes Colima
Línea Coahuila Durango	974	-	-	Sabinas Barroterán Ciudad Frontera Escalón Torreón Felipe Pescador Durango
Ferrocarril y Terminal del Valle de México	297	-	-	-
Compañía de Ferrocarriles Chiapas-Mayab	1 550	Villahermosa (Gulf of Mexico) Coatzacoalcos (Gulf of Mexico) Progreso (Gulf of Mexico) Puerto Madero (Pacific) Salina Cruz (Pacific)	-	-Campeche Mérida Izamal Escárcega Ixtepec Arriaga Tonalá
Ferrocarril del Istmo de Tehuantepec	219	Salina Cruz (Pacific)		
Administradora de la vía corta Tijuana- Tecate	71	-	Tijuana (United States)	Tecate

1. Including the lines of Ferrosur, due to its merge.
2. Parenthesis on the "Border cities covered" column states the country that the city has a border with.

Source: Ministry of Communications and Transport of Mexico.

Hinterland connections

The lack of capacity of hinterland connections is a widely-recognised issue and infrastructure expansion is well underway in several ports and critical links. Ports are clearly identified as critical nodes in the logistic infrastructure of the country and, as it is often the case, road connections appear more developed than rail. Several sections of the road, however, need to be upgraded and as cargo volume increases, it is likely that road congestion will become an issue. While there seems to be substantial efforts carried out by the government to improve the quality of the infrastructure, some issues appear which require further attention: in particular, the favouring of the growth of intermodal nodes, the prioritisation of infrastructure needs, and the involvement of the private sector in the financing of road and rail infrastructure.

An important consequence of the current structure of Mexican hinterland transport is that major ports act as gateway to specific areas or corridors in the country, with limited competition being allowed by the current network structure, Mexico City being the exception as it is served by various ports. While in the United States or in Europe, ports on major ranges compete for cargo as the hinterland is competitive, the more limited development of transport infrastructure in Mexico implies that the captive hinterland of some of the ports is substantial. While the road network connects major nodes, distances and the quality of infrastructure in the end leaves transport service providers with only a few alternatives.

The national development plan has the objective of providing an infrastructure investment strategy so as to resolve some of the bottlenecks in the country. Table 4.10 displays the assessment of the government on the current access to major ports of the country, as described in the national transport programme (*Programa Sectorial de Transportes y Comunicaciones 2013-2018*). With the exception of Veracruz, Lazaro Cardenas and Guaymas, all other ports have infrastructural issues that need to be resolved. Even in those cases where infrastructure is indicated as in good state, the rapid growth of transport volumes will create new bottlenecks. One of the main policy challenges remains prioritisation.

On the Gulf of Mexico, the ports of Altamira and Tampico appear to have sufficient connections, although the access by rail could be improved. Veracruz seems to have effective connectivity in terms of rail and road and adequate intermodal capabilities, although the railway access to the port by the two competing railway companies could be improved. Other ports, however, such as Progreso are poorly connected. The port of Dos Bocas, although mostly focusing on liquid bulk cargo, does not have adequate hinterland connections. Coatzacoalcos is one of the few cases where rail connectivity appears better than road accessibility. The port, however, is not one of the main gateways to the major production areas in the country.

On the Pacific side only Lazaro Cardenas and Guaymas appear to have good connectivity on multiple modes. Mazatlan and Ensenada lack both road and rail connections, while the ports of Topolobampo and Puerto Chiapas have good connections by road and are niche ports in terms of hinterland and cargo. The port of Salina Cruz, on the other side of the Tehuantepec isthmus as Coatzacoalcos, has a similar good connection by rail and poor road connectivity.

Infrastructural needs are being addressed with a large number of projects, both related to the port infrastructure (Altamira and Veracruz), road (new road Mazatlan-Durango, Salina Cruz and Coatzacoalcos, Tuxpan), rail (new tunnel in Manzanillo, Lazaro Cardenas) or logistics (new logistics zone in Progreso).

Table 4.10. **Connectivity of the port system to rail and road networks in Mexico (2012)**

Name of port	Coast location	Direct access to highway	Connectivity to rail	Intermodal terminal
Altamira	Gulf of Mexico	In good shape	Difficult or deficient connexion	In good shape
Coatzacoalcos	Gulf of Mexico	Non existent	In good shape	In good shape
Dos Bocas	Gulf of Mexico	Non existent	Non existent	Non existent
Ensenada	Pacific Coast	Difficult or deficient connexion	Non existent	Non existent
Guaymas	California Gulf	In good shape	In good shape	In good shape
Lázaro Cárdenas	Pacific Coast	In good shape	In good shape	In good shape
Manzanillo	Pacific Coast	Difficult or deficient connexion	Difficult or deficient connexion	In good shape
Mazatlán	Pacific Coast	Non existent	Difficult or deficient connexion	Non existent
Progreso	Gulf of Mexico	Non existent	Non existent	Non existent
Puerto Chiapas	Pacific Coast	In good shape	Difficult or deficient connexion	Non existent
Salina Cruz	Pacific Coast	Non existent	In good shape	In good shape
Tampico	Gulf of Mexico	Difficult or deficient connexion	Difficult or deficient connexion	In good shape
Topolobamo	California Gulf	In good shape	Difficult or deficient connexion	Non existent
Tuxpan	Gulf of Mexico	Difficult or deficient connexion	Non existent	Non existent
Veracruz	Gulf of Mexico	In good shape	In good shape	In good shape

Source: OECD elaboration based on the Sector Program Communications and Transport, SCT (*Programa Sectorial de Comunicaciones y Transportes*, SCT) 2013-18, p. 41, 2012.

Economic performance

Maritime transport accounted for around 30% of the total freight volume in Mexico over 1995-2013. In 1996 maritime freight represented approximately 208 million tonnes; in 2015 it was 290 million tonnes, which represented an increase of 39% in the whole period and an annual average increase rate of 1.65%. In relative terms, the proportion of the maritime transportation increased from 30.7% of the total transport of freight to 31.9%, which meant an increase of 3.9% points over the 20-year period.

As shown in Figure 4.4, high seas transportation increased from 145.1 million tonnes in 1996 to 217.4 million in 2015: a total increase of 49.8% at an annual rate of 2.04%. Coastal trade performance was more modest, going from 63.5 million tonnes to 72.3 million in the same period with a global increase of 13.9% and an annual rate of 0.65%. In fact, coastal trade has presented a decreasing pattern since 1996 in relative terms: it accounted in 1996 for 30.4% of the total freight and in 2015 the share was 25%.

Figure 4.4. **Maritime transportation in tonnes in Mexico (thousands)**

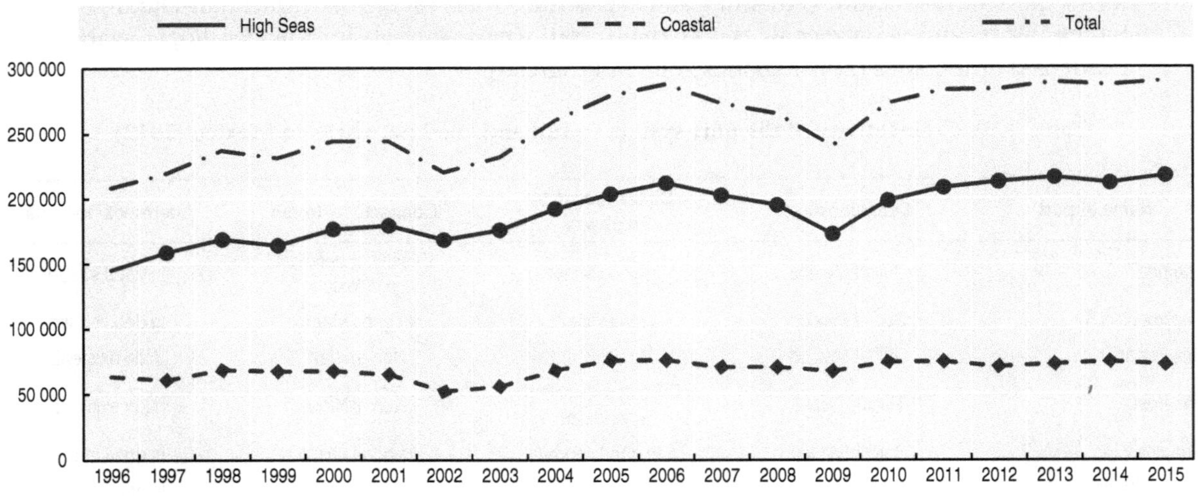

Source: Banco de Información Económica, INEGI.

A comparison of the increase of the economic value added of maritime transportation in real terms versus freight transported from 1996 to 2013, shows that value added in maritime transport had an annual average increase of 3.2%, 1.3 percentage points higher than the pace of total freight, and 0.9 points more than maritime transport volumes. Maritime transport accounted for 6.39 million passengers in 1996 and 13.68 million in 2015, an increase of 114% in the whole period and an average yearly increase of 3.88%.

Maritime transport flows showed a predominance of exports at the end of 2015, representing approximately 120 million tonnes, whereas imports represent around 98 million tonnes. Imports via shipping have increased at an average annual rate of 6.8% over 1996-2013 and the exports at an average rate of 0.7%. During this period export flows were fairly volatile, with growth dips in 1999, 2002 and 2009—imports have also shown similar trends but with less overall impact. In the case of coastal trade, imports and exports have shown almost the same pattern.

Figure 4.5. **Growth paths main ports 1995-2013**

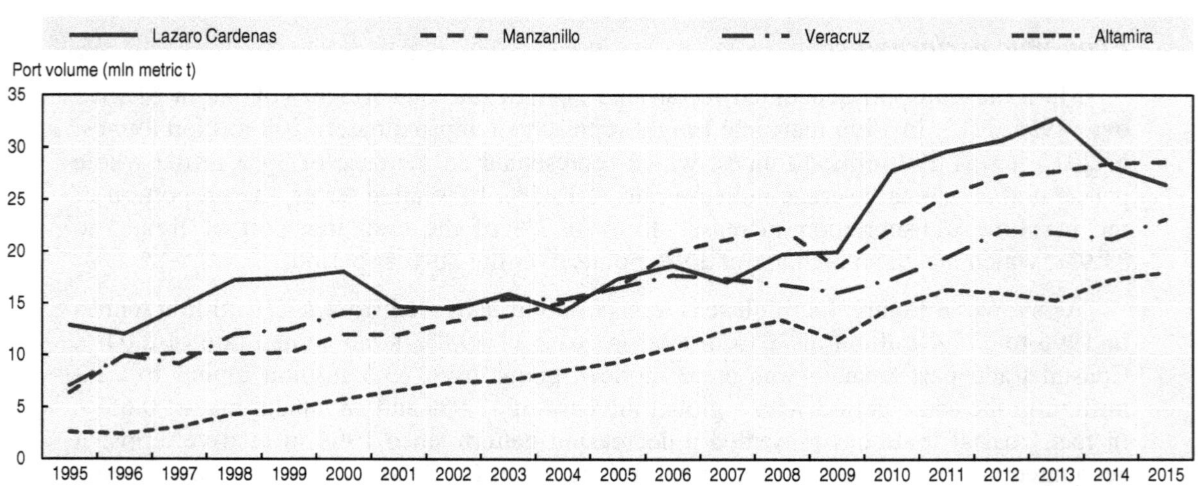

Source: Elaborations of the OECD Secretariat based on data from the Ministry of Communications and Transport.

The largest Mexican ports showed average growth annual rates during 2002-2013 ranged from 3.53% in Veracruz, 4.75% in Lázaro Cárdenas, 6.07% in Manzanillo and the highest rate in Altamira, with 7.10%. Excluding Lázaro Cárdenas (3.67%), long-term growth rates were higher, considering the period 1995-2015: Veracruz (6.11%), Manzanillo (7.80%) and Altamira (10.19%) (Figure 4.5).

The main driver of port growth in Mexico is containerisation. The top-five container ports in 1990 handled 0.21 million Twenty-foot Equivalent Unit (TEUs) and 4.88 million TEUs in 2013. Although container growth increased in the 1990s, higher growth rates in container handling happened from 2000, with average annual growth rates of 13.1% in Manzanillo, 13% in Ensenada and 9.6% in Altamira (Figure 4.6). Container traffic in Lazaro Cardenas was almost inexistent in 2000, but it had grown until 1 million TEUs in 2013. In comparison, growth rates over the same period in Veracruz were relatively slow (3.7%), but this port had seen huge container growth in the 1990s. In Figure 4.6, it can be observed that the growth rates of Lázaro Cárdenas and Manzanillo rose rapidly since the 2000s, outpacing the rates of Veracruz and Altamira. This may be related to increasing trade relations of Mexico with emerging Asian markets, which caused a higher demand of Pacific Coast shipping points. Another reason is the emergence of Manzanillo and Lázaro Cárdenas as transhipment hubs: in 2013, 44% of the containers handled in Manzanillo and 41% in Lázaro Cárdenas were transhipment. Considering the rapid increases of container ship size, and the constraints of the current Panama Canal, increases in trade flows with Asia have benefitted the Pacific ports. The share of Pacific ports in total Mexican container handling rose from 28% in 1990 to 69% in 2013 (Figure 4.7). There have been container port concentration tendencies at the Gulf coast, where ports like Tuxpan and Coatzacoalcos have dropped out the container business, flows which have been absorbed by Veracruz (Martner, 2002).

Figure 4.6. **Growth paths main container ports in Mexico 1990-2013**

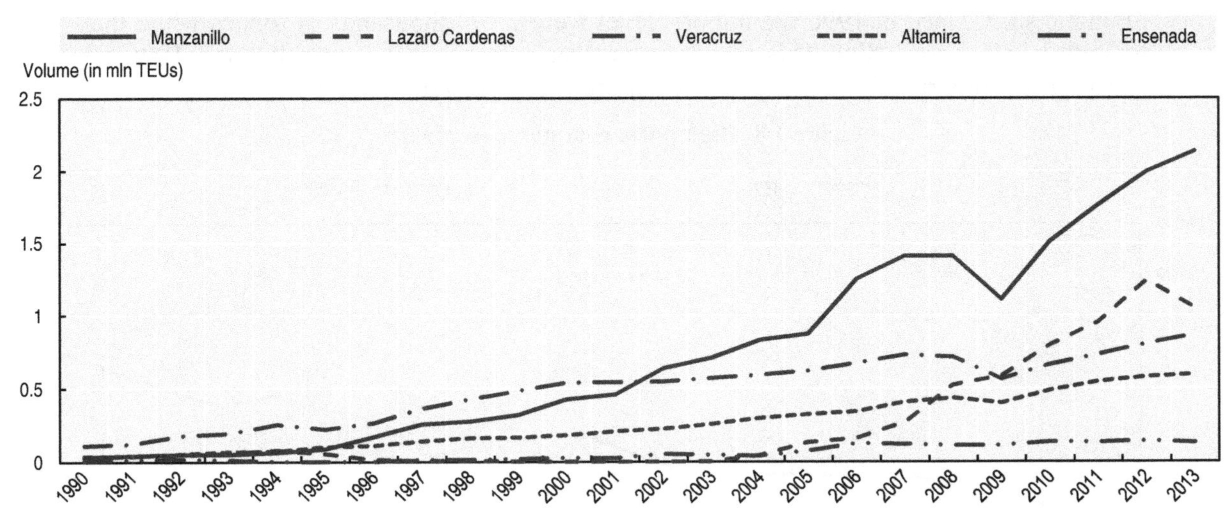

Source: Elaboration of the OECD Secretariat based on data from the Ministry of Communications and Transport.

Figure 4.7. **Distribution of container handling by type of ports in Mexico 1990-2013**

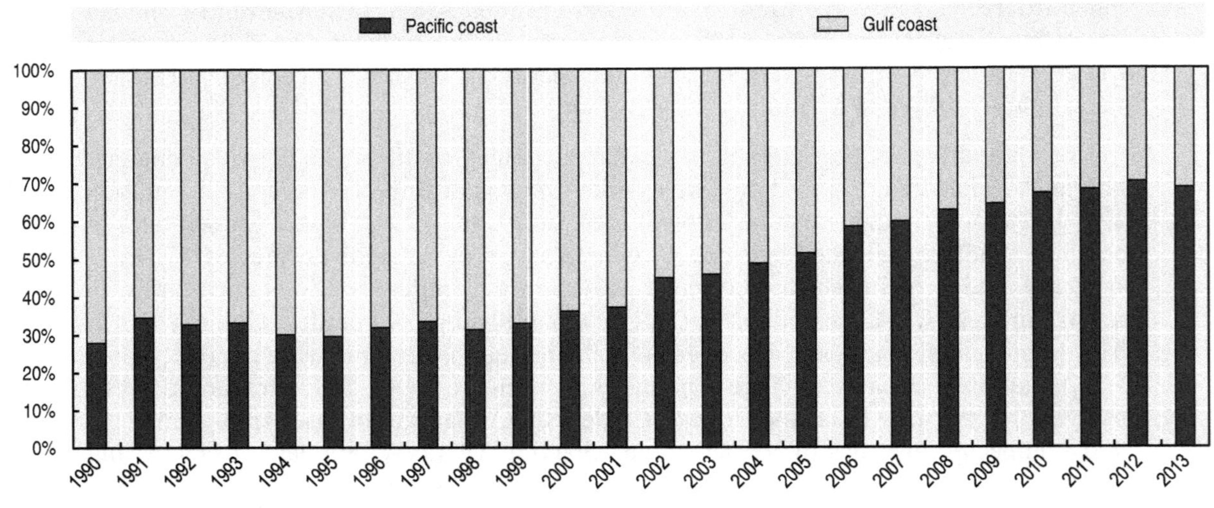

Source: Elaboration of the OECD Secretariat based on data from the Ministry of Communications and Transport.

Determinants of the port growth rates—and port competitiveness in a wider sense—are mainly the performance in maritime forelands and operations within the port, and hinterland connectivity. The performance on these aspects will be assessed in the next section using the following key performance metrics: maritime connectivity, ship turnaround time, port efficiency, cargo release time, and facilities and access.

As it can be observed in Figure 4.8, the volume of exports of high seas has seen a growth far superior that the imports. During 2016 (up to July, the last available figure), the imports average volume has accounted for 8 910 thousands of tonnes, while the exports figure has been 9 976 thousands of tonnes. The growth dynamic has seen a dramatic shift, since in 1996 the imports level were 2 294 thousands of tonnes while the exports levels were 9 800. This translates into an average annual growth from 1996 to 2015 for the imports of 6.93%, while the exports rate has a rate of only 0.07%.

Figure 4.8. **High ports commerce in Mexico**

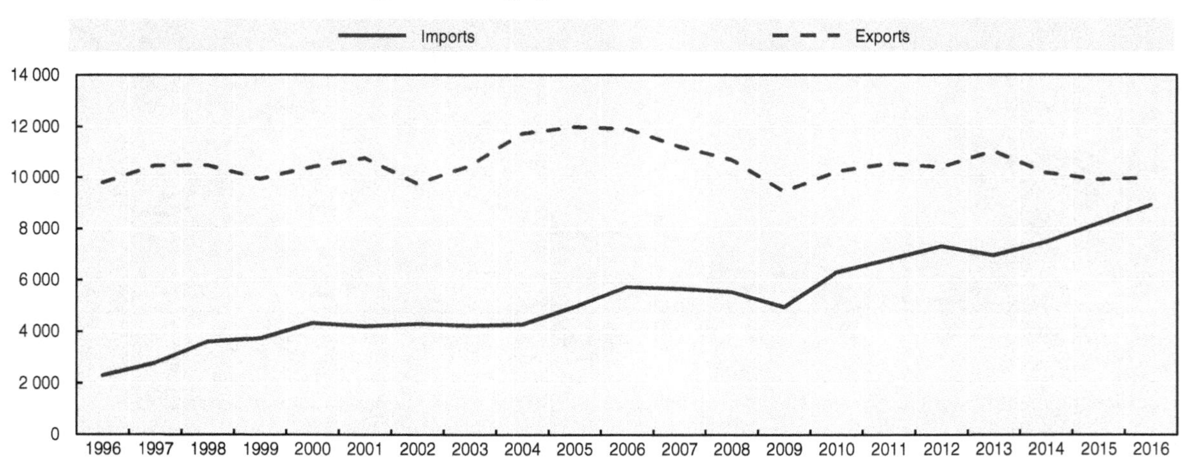

Notes: The figure shows yearly averages of the monthly data presented by INEGI. For the year 2016, the average was constructed with information from January to July. Units: thousands of tonnes.

Source: Bank of Economic Information, INEGI.

The cabotage market is smaller in terms of tonnes moved in ports, as in October of 2015 the volume of entries was 2 693 thousands of tonnes and 2 801 for exits. This market has been rather static in comparison with the High Ports market (see Figure 4.9). The annual average growth rate from 1996 to 2015 of both the entries (0.34%), and the exits (1.03%).

Figure 4.9. **Cabotage commerce**

Thousands of tonnes

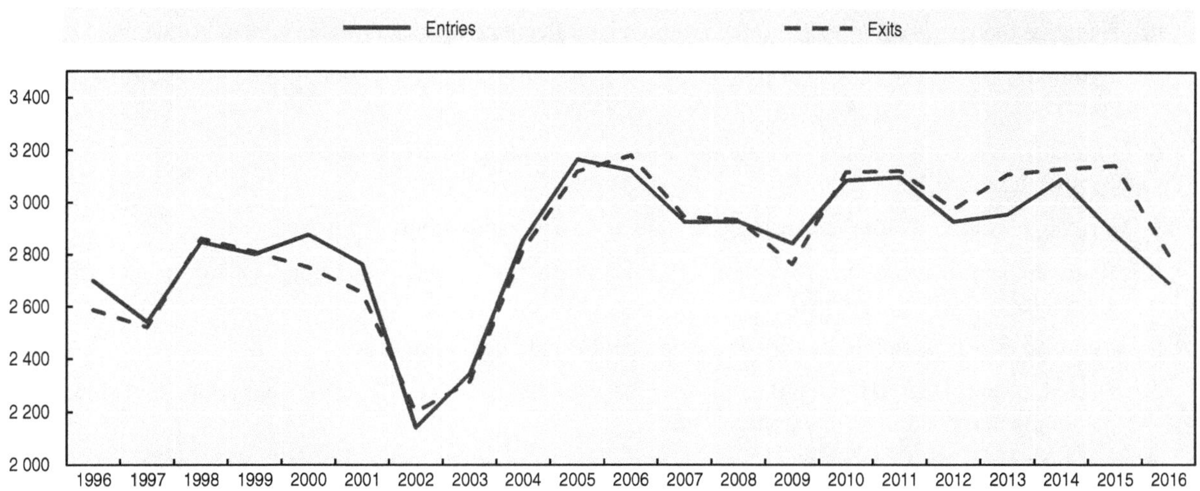

Note: The graphs are yearly averages of the monthly data presented by INEGI. For the year 2016, the average was constructed with information from January to July.

Source: Bank of Economic Information, INEGI.

Regulatory framework

The General Coordination of Ports and Merchant Navy (CGPMN), dependent of the SCT, has by law, the authority on regulation and administration of Ports and Merchant Navy. Created in 1993, the LP and its by-law (*Reglamento*) are the main source of port regulation. For merchant navy the general principles are in the Law of Navigation and Maritime Commerce (*Ley de Navegación y Comercio Marítimo*, LNCM) and its by-law.

As established in the LP, every activity related to the port administration, operation and services is under supervision of the federal government, who also has the obligation to establish and make ports operational.[1] Other relevant legal faculties of the SCT regarding port policies include the promotion and conduction of policies and programmes for the development of the national port system; the promotion of the private industry and subnational governments to exploit the ports, its terminals and installations; the authorisation of deep sea navigation terminals of private use. In matters of construction and operation, the SCT has the legal attributions to: granting concessions, permits and authorisations; build, establishing, administrating, operating and exploiting works and goods in ports, maritime terminals and port installations.[2]

The LP defines ports and terminals given its navigation, installations and services nature. Depending on its navigation, ports may be *deep sea navigation,* which refers to ports handling vessels that cater for people or goods within national and international ports; whereas *cabotage* refers to vessels only moving within national ports. The installation and services classification divides ports into commercial, industrial, fishing, and touristic categories.

Box 4.1. **Legal attributions of the Ministry of Communications and Transport of Mexico on merchant navy**

1. The planning and conducting the policies and programmes for the development of transport by water and Merchant Navy.
2. Intervene in the International Treaty negotiations in maritime issues.
3. Organise, promote and regulate the formation and capacitation of the Navy Merchant personnel.
4. Integrate the statistical information of the merchant fleet, transport and water related accidents.
5. Champion and registering vessels and Mexican naval craft and developing National Maritime Public Registry.
6. Grating navigation permits and authorisations for lending services in general waterways, as well as competency certificates.
7. Grating concessions for the construction, operation and exploitation of waterways.
8. Regulate and oversee that waterways comply with the general conditions of safety and maritime signalling
9. Regulate and oversee the security of the navigation and human life at sea.
10. Organize, regulate and if applicable give service of assistance for the navigation, maritime radio communication and maritime transit control.
11. Establish and organize a vigilance, security and distress body for the navigation of interior waters.
12. Regulate and oversee that the pilotage service is being given in a secure and efficient way.
13. Conducting inspections and certifying Mexican vessels, the compliance of International Treaties, national legislation, by-laws, official Mexican normative in matters of navigation safety, and prevention of marine contamination due to vessels.
14. Conducting inspections on foreign vessels with regard to International Treaties.
15. Granting and supervising authorisations of inspections to physical persons to verify and certificate the compliance of international treaties and national legislation.
16. Establishing basis for regulating tariffs in the provision of maritime services in national territory
17. Request for the intervention of the Ministry of Economy when there may be existence of international trade practices that break the national legislation in foreign trade.
18. Conducting investigation and relevant actions as well as designating experts in matters of maritime regulation and issue opinions on maritime, river and lake accidents.
19. Helping within its faculties the labour authority for the compliance of the maritime conflicts resolution on labour nature.
20. Requesting the intervention of the Competition Commission when there may be practices breaking the Federal Economic Competition Law.
21. Imposing sanctions for breaking the Merchant Navy and Maritime Commerce Law and International Treaties.

Source: OECD elaboration with information from the Law of Navigation and Maritime Commerce.

The SCT may establish basis for tariff regulation when competition issues may arise.[3] This tariff regulation can be applied for services such as port infrastructure, general freight and container handle services, storage services, pilotage, amongst others. The LP also establishes the definition and faculties of the API. According to Article 38, when the entire administration, planning, programming and development activities of the port administration are entitled to a private business they can become an API, having autonomy on its operational and financial management. This legal figure may manage – with the proper concession specifications – more than one terminal, installation and, or port within the same state.

On Merchant Navy issues, the federal government, through the SCT has the faculties indicated in Box 4.1.

As stated in Box 4.1 the maritime regulator is in charge of inspections and certifying that Mexican vessels and navy artefacts comply with the national legislation and international treaties. On doing so, the Law also states that the inspection procedures have to be made by personnel authorised by the SCT. The SCT has a non-transferable obligation of supervising the inspection services for vessels.

On terms of Foreign Investment related to the maritime industry, the Law of Foreign Investment (*Ley de Inversión Extranjera*, LIE) states that foreign investment can participate up to 49% of shares in the following port services: Pilotage, towing, mooring, bunkering, electric power supply, refuse collection, services for handling goods. Those limits according to the article cannot be circumvented through trusts, agreements or any other mechanism. However, a share larger than 49% of foreign investment is possible in other port services than the ones mentioned above, provided that this is authorised by the Foreign Investment Commission.

Maritime issues

As it was mentioned before, the main regulation of ports comes from the LP and its by-law. According to Article 21 of this Law, only Mexican companies can hold concessions for the API administration. The law also considers concessions outside the API administration over assets of public domain, including the construction, operation and exploit of terminals, shores and port facilities and permits to provide port services – as in the case of APIs these concessions will be granted only to Mexican citizens and firms. Meanwhile, Article 20 of the LP states that inside the ports the APIs can also transfer rights or grant specific services contracts to other firms or agents in order to supply port services. Cruises terminal concessionaires can sign contracts with third parties if the concessionaires have the authorisation of the SCT.

Maritime connectivity

Maritime connectivity of ports and their place in global port networks can be quantified with three different measures: *degree centrality*, *betweenness centrality* and *clustering coefficients*. The first two indicators indicate gateway characteristics whereas the cluster coefficient reveals hub characteristics. Degree centrality expresses the number of adjacent neighbours of a node; it is the simplest and most commonly accepted measure of centrality. It often correlates with total traffic (more connections imply more traffic). Betweenness centrality expresses the number of shortest paths going through each node. The clustering coefficient estimates whether the adjacent neighbours of a node are connected to each other (i.e. "my friends are also friends"), thus forming triangles (triplets); the coefficient is the ratio between the number of observed triplets and the maximum possible number of triplets connecting a given node. The ratio goes from 0 (no triplets observed) to 1 (all neighbours connected).

When it comes to hub-functions in a transport system, in theory the "pure hub" will have a clustering coefficient near zero because it serves as a pivotal platform redistributing flows to/from satellite platforms (spokes) which are only connected to the hub (star-shaped network). Conversely, values close to 1 depict a denser pattern with more many transversal (and thus less hierarchical) links.

In a maritime network, transhipment hubs should have low clustering coefficients as opposed to other configurations where links are more evenly distributed among ports (e.g. absence of hubs such as in the Baltic Sea or in the United States). The different port hub-measures are related, but also complementary to each other. Very central nodes (high betweenness centrality) often act as hubs (low clustering coefficient) and it is common to observe a high correlation between degree centrality and betweenness centrality due to the physical constraint of coastlines for circulation. In some cases such as relay and remote hubs, some nodes can have higher betweenness centrality than degree centrality, i.e. they are very central globally but have only a few links locally. This is because they act as "bridge" between sub-components of the network, such as Anchorage in the global network of air freight being a bridge between Asia and North America.

We have calculated these three different measures for a set of 2 177 world ports and their connections in 2011, assessing both absolute values and ranking amongst world ports. Results for Mexican ports are summarised in Table 4.11.

Table 4.11. **Connectivity of ports in Mexico and their place in global port networks**

Port	CC score	CC rang	BC score	BC rang	DC score	DC rang
Altamira	0.284	186	7 731	217	127	123
Coatzacoalcos	0.299	234	2 686	471	71	339
Veracruz	0.315	281	3 337	417	95	221
Manzanillo	0.315	282	9 896	172	101	188
Lazaro Cardenas	0.324	312	9 862	174	77	307
Cayo Arcas	0.351	409	1 876	536	44	572
Tuxpan	0.445	741	787	726	41	630
Salina Cruz	0.458	781	145	1 088	16	1146
Tampico	0.507	969	267	973	27	844
Guaymas	0.600	1 227	2	1 592	6	1 626
Topolobampo	0.603	1 254	143	1 092	13	1 265
Mazatlan	0.639	1 320	22	1 390	9	1 438
Progreso	0.665	1 354	301	944	26	863
LAC Benchmarks						
Santos	0.187	27	54 779	22	216	29
Buenos Aires	0.322	304	19 245	90	96	212
San Antonio	0.323	310	5 145	297	75	318
Buenaventura	0.308	264	8 926	197	72	331
Puerto Limon	0.471	834	2 175	504	63	403

Note: CC: Cluster coefficient; BC: betweenness centrality; DC: degree centrality.

Source: Calculations and elaborations of the OECD Secretariat based on data from Lloyd's Marine Intelligence Unit (LMIU).

The overall picture that emerges from this assessment is the confirmation that the four ports in Mexico that are considered as national hub ports by the SCT, namely Manzanillo, Veracruz, Lazaro Cardenas and Altamira, do indeed score highest on gateway and hub characteristics. It is remarkable the strong hub characteristics of Altamira, the smallest of the four ports. Coatzacoalcos also obtains high scores with respect to hub characteristics. The scores of the main four ports are more and less in line with their peer ports in the LAC region with the exception of the port of Santos in Brazil that has substantially more hub and gateway characteristics than any of the Mexican ports. Not included in this assessment are main transhipment hubs in Central America and the Caribbean, such as Kingston (Jamaica), Colon and Balboa (Panama) that score higher on hub characteristics. Mexican ports hardly have any transhipment traffic due to cabotage legislations, which allows foreign ocean-going vessels only to carry empty containers between Mexican ports, not full containers, which evidently limits the possibilities for transhipment and coastal shipping

Ship turnaround time

The ship turnaround times in ports in Mexico are generally in line with those in United States and Canada; however, some Central American countries have ports with lower ship turnaround times. This can be concluded from ITF/OECD work on ship turnaround times, based on detailed calculations of vessel movements (Ducruet et al., 2014; ITF/OECD, 2015).[4] The main Mexican ports score generally well on ship turnaround times in their container terminals, that ranged from 0.6 days in Altamira to 1.2 days in Manzanillo in 2011. Those represents better scores than those of the main LAC benchmarks, such as Santos, Buenos Aires, San Antonia and Buenaventura (Table 4.12). The score of Altamira has to be nuanced considering that the average container ship called there has much lower capacity, so it is reasonable that its ship turnaround time is lower. With respect to the bulk terminals, the assessment is more mixed and varied. The best score in this respect was 2 days turnaround times in Topolobampo in 2011, up to 4.9 days in Veracruz, which represent both lower and higher scores than those of the main LAC benchmarks. The turnaround time for oil terminals ranges from 1.5 days in Coatzacoalcos to 4.5 days in Cayo Arcas, but this difference could possibly be explained by large differences in the ship sizes calling the two ports. Newly released data on 2014 shows that container ship turnaround times in Altamira and Manzanillo remained stable, that the score of Lazaro Cardenas improved to 0.5 days and that the score of Veracruz went up to 0.8 days.

A related performance metric is berth productivity as measured by the Journal of Commerce (JOC) JOC Group. It is the average container movements per ship, per hour on container ships. In the 2013 ranking, there was one Mexican port in the top 10 for the Americas, namely Lazaro Cardenas, ranked 4th with 82 container movements per ship per hour. The first place in that ranking is the port of Balboa (Panama). However, it has to be mentioned that the average scores in the Americas are lagging those of Europe and particularly those of Asia; Tianjin, the top port in Asia reaches a score of 130. In terms of terminals, there is one Mexican terminal in the top 10 for the Americas, the *Lazaro Cardenas Terminal Portuaria de Contenedores*, ranked 9th (JOC Group, 2014). Other container terminals in Mexico have ship productivity rates that are comparable with this last terminal, e.g. HPH reported a rate of 100 moves per ship per hour for its terminal in Veracruz. Data from SCT (in particular the General Coordination of Ports and Merchant Marine) roughly confirm the data indicated above, indicating a score of 94 container moves per ship per hour in the port of Lazaro Cardenas in 2013, increasing to a score of

111 over January-September 2014 for Lazaro Cardenas, with a score of 82 for the port of Veracruz.

Table 4.12. **Average ship turnaround times in days in Mexican ports (2011)**

Port	Containers	Bulk carriers	Crude oil tankers
Altamira	0.6	2.3	-
Lazaro Cardenas	0.7	3.5	-
Veracruz	0.7	4.9	-
Manzanillo	1.2	3.0	-
Coatzacoalcos	-	4.1	1.5
Cayo Arcas	-	-	4.5
Tampico	-	4.0	-
Topolobampo	-	2.0	-
LAC Benchmarks			
Santos (Brazil)	1.0	3.2	
Buenos Aires (Argentina)	1.4	-	
San Antonio (Chile)	1.0	3.5	
Buenaventura (Colombia)	1.0	3.7	
Sao Sebastiao (Brazil)			1.9
San Lorenzo (Argentina)		2.4	

Source: Calculations and elaborations of the OECD Secretariat based on data from Lloyd's Marine Intelligence Unit (LMIU).

Coastal shipping

Coastal shipping in Mexican waters as a general rule is reserved to Mexican ship-owners with Mexican vessels. If there are no Mexican-flagged vessels available, foreign flagged vessels may engage in cabotage trade under temporary permits[5] granted by the SCT.[6] According to Article 40 of the LNCM, cabotage permits are granted for three-month periods and can be renewed seven times with a maximum of two years. After this period, the vessel would have to be flagged Mexican in order to continue operating in Mexican waters. Flagging and registration for Mexican vessels are allowed only to Mexican citizens or companies. Foreign companies and individuals may incorporate a Mexican shipping company, which would be subject to foreign investment restrictions.

The procedure to award cabotage permits gives priority to Mexican ship-owners and crews. This is a bidding procedure which comprises two stages. In the first stage, only Mexican ship-owners may participate with the priority given to foreign vessels under a bareboat charter, which implies that the whole crew must be Mexican. The second priority is for Mexican ship-owners with foreign vessels under any other charter agreement; under this category priority is given to the vessel having a higher number of Mexican crew members. In the case that no vessels are available under these categories, the second stage of the bidding procedure takes place and foreigners with foreign vessels may participate (Moran, 2013).

The obligation to flag a vessel as Mexican after two years does not apply to what is called "highly specialised" vessels. For these kinds of vessels, the 2006 LNCM does not give a limit to the number of times that the cabotage permit might be renewed. Although the law provides some general provisions on what a highly specialised vessel is considered, more concrete guidelines are given in the revised by-law of LNCM in 2007, but it has not been issued yet. In this draft, the criteria to determine if a vessel is highly specialised is as follows: the state of technology in the international market; the availability of the technology in the international market and construction and equipment reports with respect of vessels and naval artefacts. In practice, the question whether a vessel is highly specialised is determined on a case-by-case basis (Moran, 2013). However, it is clear that tankers and cargo vessels (as well as supply vessels, tugs and crew boats) are not considered to be unique in any case (Enriquez and Moran, 2009). Another exception to the Mexican cabotage regulations relates to tourism, sports and leisure vessels, which may be carried out by foreign ship-owners or operators with foreign vessels, provided there is reciprocity with the relevant country.

The cabotage permits are widely used. In 2009, it was estimated that nearly 500 permits are granted or renewed every year. The great majority of these permits are granted to vessels operating in the offshore oil fields in the Gulf of Mexico (Enriquez and Moran, 2009). The coastal shipping provided by cabotage permits represents around one third of the total domestic shipping in Mexico, the other two thirds is concentrated by Mexican ships transporting gas for PEMEX—the Mexican state-owned oil company. The need for exemptions of the cabotage rules is clear considering the relatively small Mexican-owned and flagged fleet with approximately 115 ships representing 0.06% of the total world fleet capacity, according to UNCTAD (2014). Mexico ranks 54th of the world in ship ownership—which includes foreign-flagged vessels. Mexico holds a similar position with respect to the number of Mexican seafarers.

On the other hand, Mexican companies with more than 49% foreign participation in their capital stock cannot have vessels engage in cabotage in Mexican waters, whereas foreign companies (irrespective of whether they have Mexican owners or not) may obtain cabotage permits. The Foreign Investment Law stipulates that foreign investment cannot exceed 49% in any cabotage business in Mexico. Additionally, in Mexico, it is not possible to register a vessel that remains registered in another country, unlike practices in some other countries.

The cabotage regulation in Mexico can make coastal shipping an expensive mode of transport. Priority is given to Mexican-flagged ships with Mexican crews. In the case of Mexican crews, it is common that certain fringe benefits are paid, which makes wage costs more expensive than if foreign seafarers could be used. Mexican crews are generally expensive and prohibitive unless there are long-term contracts such as in the case of Pemex (Moran, 2013). However, Pemex is not satisfied with the current state, since it initiated a constitutional review (*amparo*) by the Supreme Court on the cabotage regulation so as to examine whether it contravened the Mexican Constitution. Pemex claimed that giving preference to Mexican ship-owners with chartered foreign vessels may violate constitutional principles, such as equality, legal certainty, freedom of employment and commerce, and best value for money in procurement procedures. The Supreme Court found that preferring Mexican shipping companies over foreign ones does not create a monopoly, even though the bidding procedure intends to promote national maritime activities, protect the national shipbuilding industry and benefit the Mexican economy. The procedure, continues the Mexican court, does not force Pemex to hire Mexican vessels, considering that foreign vessels with cabotage permits can be hired when the Mexican vessels available do not fulfil the technical specifications required by Pemex (Enriquez and Moran, 2009). Even if the cabotage regulation provides some flexibility that make it aligned to the Constitution, one could wonder if it serves the greatest interest of the Mexican consumer.

An additional disadvantage for coastal shipping is that there are no dedicated facilities or "fast lanes" for it in most ports. As a result, the cargo is handled in the same way as international cargo, subject to many inspections and controls, leading to unnecessary costs and time loss (considering that the goods are not leaving or entering the country), which make coastal shipping uncompetitive in comparison with truck transport. The creation of "fast lanes" for short sea shipping is underlying the EU Blue Belt initiative to ease custom formalities in EU ports for coastal shipping between EU ports. The lack of dedicated facilities for coastal shipping in Mexico is a circular issue; dedicated facilities would make sense if there is substantial coastal maritime trade, which is currently not the case. But it is not the case because there are no dedicated facilities. One of the few cabotage initiatives that have recently emerged was developed by the Mexican shipping company TMM between the ports of Manzanillo, Mazatlan, Guaymas and La Paz; ten vessels move empty MSC containers and national cargo between the northeast and the centre of the country. This initiative was facilitated by an agreement with Customs on dedicated areas within container terminals for cabotage activities.

A development law to stimulate coastal shipping is under review. The likely aim of the law is to extend the commodities and routes for coastal shipping. This law would provide a good vehicle to stimulate dedicated areas ("control-free") in terminals for coastal shipping.

Various countries have engaged in liberalisation of maritime cabotage. Generally, the range of maritime cabotage regimes is wide, ranging from very restrictive in the US and Japan to very liberal in New Zealand and Australia (Brooks, 2009). The regime in the United States, regulated by the Jones Act, requires not only US-flagged vessels and US crews, but also that the vessel is built in the US. Many countries are less restrictive and do not include the "built in" requirement. The regimes of Australia and New Zealand are very liberal and aim at creating a level playing field between international and coastal shipping. The regime in Mexico could be placed somewhere between restrictive and moderately restrictive on this continuum. The framework has the domestic flag and crew criteria but it also provides possibilities to circumvent these; notwithstanding, cabotage trade in practice only exists for bulk cargo. Although cabotage legislation is sensitive and difficult to reform, various countries have over the last decades liberalised their legislation, one of the more recent liberalisations was conducted in China.

Mexico could consider liberalisation of maritime cabotage in various ways. One step could be to resolve the inconsistency that Mexican companies with more than 49% foreign capital cannot acquire cabotage permits, whereas foreign companies can. Another measure could be to relax the priority given to Mexican crews or bring their emoluments and fringe benefits closer to international practice, in order to improve the competitiveness of coastal shipping. A condition that could be added is that foreign vessels operating in cabotage would need to make a commitment to train Mexican seafarers as part of their operations.

On the other hand, the current system of renewable 3-month permits could be replaced by renewable one-year permits so as to reduce the red tape. Mexico could also consider the introduction of an international shipping register, which is a common practice in many countries to attract shipping activity from foreign ship owners. One of the advantages for ship-owners is that it would allow for cabotage trade in Mexico, considering that these ships are registered in Mexico so they would qualify for cabotage trade.

Efficiency issues

Port efficiency

There are various studies focusing on the efficiency of container terminals in Mexico. The most recent study on the subject, in 2010, indicates that Mexican ports in general have low technical global efficiency with the exception of Manzanillo and Lazaro Cardenas (Delfín-Ortega, Navarro-Chávez, 2013). This study can however be criticised for the limited number of input factors that are taken into account; only quay length and number of employees, but not the number of container cranes and terminal surface as is usual in many port efficiency studies. Older studies indicated that the efficiency of Mexican ports improved after the port reform of 1993 that liberalised the port sector (Estache et al. 2002 and Estache et al. 2004). Merk and Dang (2012) have assessed the efficiency of oil ports and terminals and they conclude that the oil terminal of Cayo Arcas ranked 26th out of 41 ports in terms of efficiency, just after Freeport in Jamaica. No other Latin or Central American Ports were included in this analysis.

Yard turnaround times

The average turnaround time for full containers in the container yards of Mexican ports was 5-6 days in 2009 with some variation in the different ports (Figure 4.10), which is a significant improvement since 2000 when containers stayed on average more than 10 days in container yards (Martner and Martínez, 2011), although it was increased to 7 days recently. International best practice is approximately three days; e.g. this represents the average container dwell time of containers in Hamburg (Germany). The still fairly long turnaround time of containers might be explained by the time it takes to get containers cleared by customs and other inspection bodies. Note in this respect the poor score of Mexican Customs in the World Bank Logistics Performance Index (LPI), which is based on a survey of perceptions of service levels by foreign freight forwarders. Whereas Mexico was overall ranked 50th on the LPI in 2014 with a score of 3.13, it ranks 70th of the world with respect to the quality of customs with a score of 2.69.[7]

Figure 4.10. **Turnaround time in container yards in selected ports in Mexico, 2009**

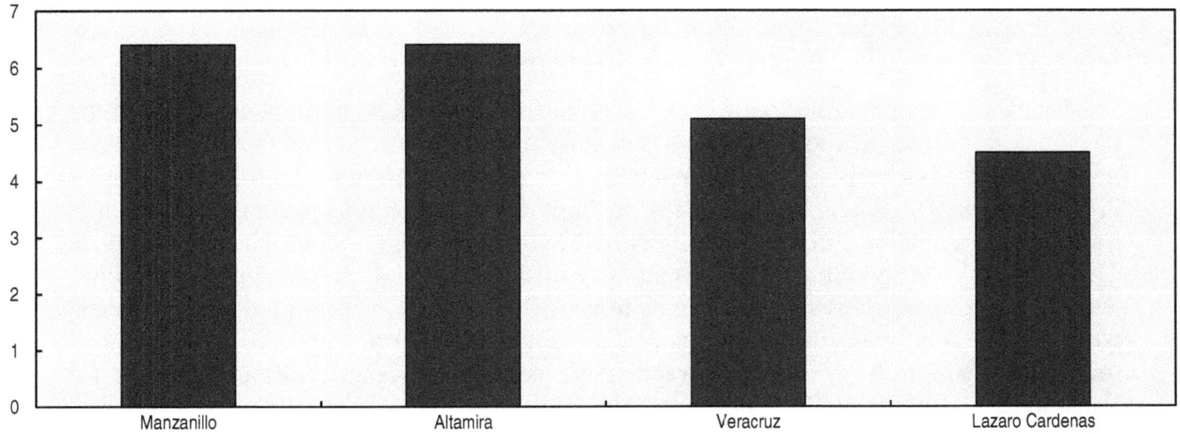

Note: Unit: days.

Source: Peyrelongue and Martínez, 2011.

Overall, port performance in Mexico can be considered fairly well. Ship turnaround times are in line with those in the United States and Canada, berth productivity indicators are high in some containers, but the situation with dwell times in container yards might be more of a challenge. A complete assessment of port performance would also have taken into account ship waiting times and truck turnaround times in the different ports, but such information was not made available.

Cargo release time

Main bottlenecks in ports are linked to the release of cargo due to various controls and administrative procedures. There are various projects in place to reduce administrative burdens, such as paperless port and one single window but these initiatives are not implemented in similar approach across ports and do not encompass all procedures. Reform of the customs law has increased the number of free days in yards from 5 to 7 days. Although it reflects the long time needed for goods clearance, it nevertheless provides no incentive for shippers to get their goods quickly out of the port. The treatment of abandoned containers is regulated in the Customs Law, but the relevant by-law has been in preparation for the last 9 years.

Finally, various port terminals are open 24 hours per day, which is not the case for customs and other inspection agencies. Requests can be submitted to have customs work at night but reportedly, almost all these requests are refused. A more extensive analysis of the issues highlighted here is conducted in the chapter on borders and customs.

Transhipment

Pacific ports as Manzanillo and Lazaro Cardenas could be well placed to capture a share of the sea-to-sea transhipment activity of Central America and the Caribbean. The advantage of these ports is that they are on the crossroads of several shipping routes such as the East-West flows from Asia to Los Angeles/Long Beach to the Panama Canal and the North-South flows of the West Americas. The Panama Canal expansion, finished in June 2016, could stimulate the rise of transhipment ports in the Pacific, in addition to the large transhipment ports that already exist in Panama (Colon) and the Caribbean (Kingston, Freetown) and Cartagena, Colombia. Advantages of developing transhipment functions could be more direct maritime routes between Mexico and Asia, lower handling costs due to the larger ships, more terminal activity and more demand for maritime services, with the related positive economic spill overs.

Thanks to this potential, sea-to-sea transhipment in Mexican ports is emerging in the Pacific ports of Lazaro Cardenas and Manzanillo, but various issues remain that constrain transhipment functions, such as excessive controls. Customs controls and other inspections on containers apply equally to import and transhipment containers, even if transhipment containers do not actually enter Mexican territory—other than the port area. These controls resulted in containers that have missed their connections with feeder ships and damaged cargo. This situation seems to be the consequence of internal guidelines and work practices of the customs agencies, more so than certain provisions in laws or regulations. Similarly to cabotage trade, there are no dedicated facilities or lanes for transhipment containers. This has particularly impacts in the port of Lazaro Cardenas, where the military is in charge of the security of the port, in order to battle organised crime. The lack of cabotage trade in containers in Mexico has possibly negative impacts on the creation of a Mexican hub port. Restrictive cabotage legislation in China has been associated with limited feeder connections in the port of Shanghai (Zheng et al., 2014). A similar situation might exist in Mexico.

Current regulation constrains the development of sea-to-sea transhipment activities. The LNCM states that foreign ocean-going vessels may only carry empty containers among Mexican ports, for the purpose of using this equipment for goods exports (Article 468), prohibiting liner shipping companies to carry out transhipment of full containers between the country's ports. In addition, Article 469 prohibits coastal shipping vessels from transhipment of goods from or to ocean-going vessels (Martner, 2002). So this means, that the domestic coastal shipping industry cannot offer feedering services, whereas foreign companies cannot do this either.

In order to facilitate the development of transhipment, customs offices should be instructed to come up with special rules to facilitate transhipment so as to avoid excessive controls of transhipped containers. This would imply information systems that can identify transhipment containers, group these containers separately in terminal yards and make sure that these are not subject to checks and controls, unless very strong overriding reasons. An alternative, but heavier measure would be to create a free trade zone in the ports that would be most likely candidates to develop into important transhipment hubs.

Facilities and access issues

Road access to the port

The majority of Mexican port hinterland transport relies on road transportation with approximately 80% of cargo moving by road,[8] and 20% moving by rail nationwide (mostly bulk commodities). Some ports however differ substantially from the national average as they enjoy good rail hinterland connection. The Mexican road sector, as discussed in the corresponding chapter has some of the problems of fast developing countries: an ageing fleet, great diversity in terms of equipment and infrastructure at the limit of congestion.

In the specific case of ports major issues related road hinterland movement are associated with:

- Increasing congestion at the gate
- Schedule reliability
- Increasing relevance of environmental externalities.

One of the critical issues in port accessibility is ensuring that port access gates are managed in the most efficient way as possible. The current regime of double gates with inspections and other security procedures both at the entrance of the port and at the entrance of the terminal that seems to be dominant in most of the ports, does not favour the movement of trucks to and from the port efficiently. In several ports, such as Manzanillo and Altamira, trucks are required to station in a waiting area away from the port before being called (*patios reguladores*). While such solution is effective in resolving short-term peaks, it does not provide adequate incentives for port gate systems to improve port accessibility. Those waiting areas are essentially parking lots and do not allow any logistics operations to be performed on the cargo. In the case of Manzanillo, it also contributes to the level of urban road congestion.

Outgoing trucks also seem to suffer delays. The major issue seems to be related to customs inspections procedures. It should be noted, that truck management is one of the main challenges for terminals in global terms. Systems exist to reduce waiting times, expedite gate procedures and resolve terminal gate congestion. Common policies include extended gate times, modal shift often in combination with the development of dry ports, lane prioritisation and IT solutions, ranging from palm recognition to vehicle scanning and automatic identification. It would be recommended that an accurate study of the gate congestion is carried out for all major ports and solutions are likely to require, in addition to investment, policy intervention at a state or federal level, e.g. in relation to opening hours or inspection hours.

Up to date, there have not been policies with the objective to improve the arrival distribution of trucks during the day. Such policies have been implemented with relative success in other parts of the world, which have allowed for a better use of gates, port infrastructure and hinterland connections. Appointment systems can be developed on a voluntary basis, couples with the application of penalties for operators that do not appear at the terminals at the right time (Huynh, 2009; Guan and Liu, 2009). Notwithstanding some successful examples (e.g. Southampton), the implementation of an appointment system in practice has been met often with scepticism. This is partly because the effectiveness of an appointment system around the world depends on the opening hours of distribution facilities and warehouses, and to some extent on labour and road regulation, so the effectiveness could be limited, if for example, trucks are not allowed to drive in weekends or if warehouses are closed at night (Giuliano and O'Brien, 2007). The PierPASS programme, applied in Los Angeles and Long Beach, was effective in reducing daytime truck arrivals from 90% to 66%, within a few months after introduction (OECD, 2014).

Gate operations are only part of the infrastructure necessary to guarantee schedule reliability. At this stage no reliable statistics could be found on the efficiency of trucking operations, travel times, supply chain disruptions and other metrics relevant to assess the performance of the trucking system from and to the ports. In general, Mexico is placed just above world average and in a comfortable position in terms of the World Bank logistics performance index (in position 50 out of 160 countries, and position 46 in terms of shipment timeliness, just below Chile and Panama). The position of the country has remained rather constant in the last survey, slightly deteriorating between 2012 and 2014. As volumes are expected to grow substantially in the coming decade, maintaining logistics performance will become increasingly challenging.

Even if the largest urbanised areas in Mexico are not located in the proximity of ports, port-related trucking has important impacts in some areas with higher population densities (Altamira/Tampico, Veracruz/Boca del Rio, Guaymas, Acapulco, Puerto Vallarta, Tecoman/Colima/Manzanillo) and along the major transport arteries, often close to large conurbations. It is advisable therefore to consider the external effects that derive from trucking operations in terms of congestion, accidents, pollution and health related risks.

Rail access to the ports

An alternative to reduce reliance on trucking is to provide stronger incentives for cargo to be moved by rail. Such strategy requires the development of rail corridors connecting the ports and demand areas and a strengthening the position of railroads serving ports. At the moment it seems that bulk cargo is prioritised, as it is characterised by a more regular scheduling, larger more predictable volumes, and longer-term contractual agreements between railroad companies and cargo owners.

Although ports appear generally well connected to railroads and an investment programme is currently in place to improve this connectivity (*Programa Sectorial de Transportes y Comunicaciones 2013-2018*), most ports have a connection to only one railway concessionaire (Ferromex and Kansas). The exception is Veracruz where the port has recently completed an investment to connect to the lines of the second concessionaires. Port users would benefit from a choice in railway service providers. Trackage rights exist to provide for interline services, but the rail concessions have generally been reluctant to make use of them. Requests for access rights by railroad operators have resulted in legal battles that have prevented the development of competing offers to move rail cargo to and from ports. The negative outcome of such situation is worsened by very high switching costs in inland junctions that make *de facto* unlikely to move cargo across operators. Reforms to the railway law, amended in December 2014 aim to facilitate use of access rights (see Chapter 2).

Port authorities could take a lead in developing hinterland strategies together with the main stakeholders, identifying opportunities for investments to improve efficiency where federal government funds might be attracted to complement investments. In general, there seems to be limited information being collected by the central administration, in order to develop a strategy addressing the real issues of ports.

An option that has been successful internationally is the development of dry-ports inland, allowing for congestion to be relieved at the port and ensuring volumes are sufficient to attract railroads on non-core traffics. The railroad network appears suitable for the developing such infrastructure that would require however the central government to take the initiative at least until volumes are such that dry-ports can be run profitably. The development of dry-ports could also relieve pressure on customs operations at port freeing capacity on terminal yards and improving the efficiency of gate operations.

Modal split

Lazaro Cardenas has been successful in developing a modal split between road and rail that favours rail (around 50%).[9] The good accessibility of rail terminals to the container terminal has favoured a balanced modal split. Manzanillo has much less favourable rail access, with current infrastructure poorly adapted to large trains with double stacks of containers as the tracks pass through the city centre. There are plans to improve access through construction of a railway tunnel. Although new infrastructure is key to resolving access issues, efficiency at ports is not only a matter of infrastructure, but also co-ordination among various stakeholders. In absence of such co-ordination, the cheaper and more flexible trucking is likely to remain the dominant mode of transport to and from most of the major ports, decreasing the attractiveness of railroad operations.

With the exceptions of Altamira and Lazaro Cardenas, the majority of infrastructure projects are road investments, planned in the absence of a comprehensive vision for improving connectivity and the competitiveness of the logistics and port system, and in particular the need to complement road transport with rail services to resolve increasing external costs. While in general, competition between rail and road is beneficial because it tends to moderate transport prices, the advantages that road transport enjoys in terms of gaps in regulation (no regulation of driving time and rest hours for example—see Chapter 1) and limited accountability of external costs, could put railways at a disadvantage.

An additional problem is related to the limitation of the space at the port and near the port, deriving from alternative uses of urban spaces and infrastructure, as in the cases of Veracruz and Manzanillo, where tourism development could pose a threat to port and hinterland infrastructure expansions. Some ports have port-related road congestion in the city, e.g. in Manzanillo. In many cases train connections also cross city centres where the city has encroached upon the port area, increasing the possibility of future port-related congestion in the city. There have been investments to solve some of these bottlenecks (e.g. the planned railway tunnel in Manzanillo, new rail link for Veracruz; new highway bypasses, truck parking areas), but the problem is likely to remain especially if new investments do not take into account traffic growth projections. Railroad crossings are also a source of delays and avoidance of potential accidents and investments in grade-separated crossings (bridges and tunnels) should be prioritised.

Economic and institutional issues

Competition in port services

Since the 1993 port reforms in Mexico, the port system has been characterised by decentralisation, privatisation and competition. The privatisation process implied the promotion of competition between ports and private operators, but also the liberalisation of tariffs for port services and the elimination of cross subsidies and barriers to market entry. Regulation of tariffs is limited to cases where there is only one operator or only one service provider. This regulation requires the establishment of maximum prices (price-caps) and inflation adjustment mechanisms. The maximum prices are based on information of operating costs, capital costs, traffic and prevailing tariffs in Mexico and internationally. The price regulation could be eliminated if the Federal Competition Commission considers that there is a fair competition environment (OECD, 2011). The 1993 LP stipulates that the tariffs for so-called infrastructure services (meaning access channels, dockage and wharfage) need to be set by SCT, as these services are only offered by the APIs. Pilotage services are also regulated by the SCT, but for all other services tariff regulation or free tariff setting is applied (see Box 4.2). Ports services in Mexico are similar to those in other countries and refer to infrastructure maintenance (including dredging of access channels and maintenance of docks and wharfs), pilotage,[10] towage,[11] mooring[12] and bunkering services.[13] In case of complaints on tariffs for which no tariff regulation is required, there exists the possibility of intervention by the Federal Competition Commission. Its intervention has so far focused mainly on port terminal operations and to a lesser extent for port service providers (OECD, 2011).

There is competition for cargo handling services in the large ports, but many port services are monopolies, which is not uncommon across the world. As was mentioned in the section on port organisation, there are various global terminals active in the main Mexican ports. In the container sector, most of the terminals are dominated by Hutchison Port Holdings (HPH), but competition is increasing as new terminals have been awarded to competing terminal operators, such as APM Terminals and ICTSI. Most of the oil terminals are operated by PEMEX, expression of their dominant position in the national petro-chemical industry. Whereas cargo handling in the main Many port services around the world, such as pilotage, towage and mooring, are offered by only one service provider, in some cases public, in some cases private. Mexican ports are not exceptional in this respect: in most ports across the world, pilotage services are monopolies. For the other port services, competition is more common, at least in the largest ports. Considering that the main Mexican ports use several tug boats (indicating large enough size), it would be possible to envisage competition in towage services and possibly other port services.

Box 4.2. **Tariff regulation and tariff setting in ports in Mexico**

The basis for tariff regulation is formed by Article 16 of the Ports Law, which states that the SCT can establish the basis for tariff regulation if in any port only one terminal exists, or only one terminal for specific merchandises exists, or only one service supplier exists. In such cases SCT can ask for the intervention of the competition commission.

In addition, Article 26 of the Ports Law states that the concession must contain the basis of tariff regulations and Article 60 mentions that SCT can establish in concessions and permits the basis for prices and tariff regulations for the usage of certain assets in ports, marines, shores and services providers, when there are no other port options or means of transport which can promote competition, which will remain in place until competition arises.

Article 61 of the Ports Law indicates that regulation can set maximum and minimum prices for specific and joint services and also the updating mechanisms and periods of applicability. In case that regulated firms consider that there are no reasonable grounds to establish tariff regulation, they can ask the opinion of the Competition Commission and if this Commission finds that competition conditions do not justify the regulation, the regulation must be modified within 30 days.

This tariff regulation has been established for services such as handling services, storage services and pilotage in the ports of Lazaro Cárdenas, Manzanillo, Mazatlán, Veracruz, amongst others.

Source: Port Law and SCT.

Increasing ship size will make existing terminals less suitable for operation, but incumbent operators could always bid for new port development projects. The LP stipulates that port terminals can extend their area up to 20% and if they would like to exceed such limit, they would need to bid for a new terminal (Art. 25 of the LP). According to some observers, this limits the possibilities of incumbent operators to increase the scale of their operations, considering the rapid pace with which ships have increased, e.g. the doubling in the average size of a containership over the last decade. This has dramatic implications for terminals that would need longer quays, more storage space and deeper berths to be able to accommodate these larger ships.

Co-ordinated investment for hinterland infrastructure

Hinterland connectivity differs from port to port with some being characterised by increasing congestion (e.g. Manzanillo) while others by their underutilisation (e.g. Lazaro Cardenas). Although, for every port the needs and requirements in terms of hinterland development can differ substantially, the following common themes can be identified as relevant for the country:

- Lack of capacity of hinterland connections
- Issues with road access to the ports
- Challenging rail access to the port
- Conflict for road and rail for port traffics and modal split issues.

The competitiveness of a seaport depends on the extent that cargo handled in such port can reach its hinterland destination (e.g. Acciaro and McKinnon, 2013). The importance of hinterland connections has been recognised as one of the most critical issues in port competitiveness and development in most ports around the world. One of the main issues related to the development of adequate hinterland connections in ports is the need to co-ordinate multiple actors often with conflicting mandates, that constitute the group of private and public institutions governing port hinterland infrastructure development.

Ports around the world have developed multiple strategies to improve their hinterland connections in response to the challenges imposed by increasing traffic, shrinking public budgets, competition for road and rail usage from passengers, and the proximity of many ports to densely urbanised areas.

These strategies have resulted in a variety of policies such as:

- Development of dry-ports. The benefit associated with dry ports include: cost-efficiency, environmental performance and logistic quality. These benefits are usually enjoyed by a big spectrum of stakeholders. Dry ports are usually associated with improved competitiveness of local and regional businesses, increased attractiveness of the region and sustainable logistics development. (e.g. Bergqvist, Wilmsmeier and Cullinane, 2013a; 2013b; Roso, Woxenius and Lumsden, 2009)
- Improving stakeholder management (e.g. Bergqvist, 2012)
- Extending operation times: this policy option has helped in reducing traffic congestion during the week days in Los Angeles, and it has been implemented as well in Vancouver and New York. As traffic has smoothed including expansion during the weekends, it helped in reducing emissions as the truck traffic is better organised, helping to mitigate environmental risks. (e.g. Giuliano and O'Brien, 2008)
- Extending the borders of the port beyond the port precinct (Veenstra, Zuidwijk and van Asperen, 2012) or
- Influencing the port modal split. Monios and Lambert remark the virtues of bringing together the public and private actors to allocate efficiently investment in port infrastructure improvements, this way there will be tangible benefits for the private sector. In order to achieve a successful project there is a crucial need of co-ordination among the private and the public sector (e.g. Monios and Lambert, 2013).

The problems faced by Mexican ports in fostering the efficiency of their hinterland transportation networks are not unique, although the specific geo-economic characteristics of Mexican logistics networks make some of those issues more urgent. The geography of Mexican production chains, concentrated in a few areas away from the coast, the configuration of Mexican rail networks, and the overall policy that has governed the country transport system in the last decades, among other factors, all have favoured the development of freight corridors and a heavy reliance on trucking.

Development of ports

The National Infrastructure Plan 2014-2018 establishes the main policy framework for ports policy in Mexico. It foresees approximately port investments of MXN 70 billion over 2014-18 in the main 20 ports. Its aim is to promote an integral and complementary port system, with four world class ports at its core (Manzanillo, Lazaro Cardenas,

Veracruz and Altamira). The philosophy behind this implicit port strategy is that ports mainly compete with foreign ports, not so much with each other.

This assumption of competition with foreign ports might be somewhat correct for transhipment functions, but much less so for gateway functions, which are much more substantial in the current Mexican context. As was mentioned before, the four main ports in Mexico can be considered to compete for the same hinterland, the metropolitan area of Mexico City; this competition is particularly real between the ports on the same coast (Manzanillo-Lazaro Cardenas and Veracruz-Altamira). Sea-to-sea transhipment functions are limited on the Mexican Pacific Coast and non-existent on the Mexican Gulf Coast. Ports such as Manzanillo and Lazaro Cardenas could be gateway ports for the US Mid-West and as such, compete with US West Coast ports such as LA/Long Beach and Seattle/Tacoma, but for the moment this represents a negligible cargo flow. Although policy support might indeed be needed to expand the transhipment functions of selected Mexican ports, this should not mean that competition between Mexican ports be avoided. In fact, the incentive of competition between main Mexican ports could reduce logistics costs and should thus be stimulated. As competition between the gateway ports in Mexico is mainly determined by the rail corridors related to the ports, more competition between ports would imply increasing the inter-operability of the freight railway networks.

Despite the policy discourses with focus on four main ports, investment portfolio for ports in Mexico is fairly fragmented. Investment projects are foreseen for the twenty largest Mexican ports, including substantial projects in smaller ports like Mazatlan and Tuxpan. One can wonder how this aligns with the stated ambition to develop four Mexican ports into world-class ports. The situation of relative fragmentation of port investments might be related to the function of SCT as a national port authority. A more delegated form of port governance, in which ports would be more self-financing, would be less subject to inter-regional equity concerns and might be helpful in concentrating efforts to achieve the ambition to develop Mexico's four main ports into world-class ports.

Although Mexico moved to a landlord model with the 1993 port reforms, in practice the autonomy of the port corporations is fairly limited. As part of these reforms, ports were granted with autonomy in administration and finance through the creation of 24 different APIs. Their main functions are the management and exploitation of the Mexican ports. However, the port authority functions in policy formulation, supervision, concessions and penalties, remain within SCT, in particular the General Coordination of Ports and Merchant Navy. APIs are the holders of concessions granted by the SCT, and in turn provide many port services through private companies.

Mexico should consider moving towards a next stage of the port landlord model (in which port authority functions are public, but separate from terminal operations which are in private hands), in which more of the regulatory functions could be transferred to the APIs. In comparison with many ports in the OECD countries, the APIs are still very dependent on the federal ministry. As part of the suggested delegation of functions, APIs should acquire larger financial autonomy, which could include keeping part of the revenues they bring in and the possibility to engage in partnerships with financial institutions. By means of example, the port of Rotterdam – Europe's largest port – is corporatised, with the municipality of Rotterdam and the State as shareholders; it is free to use its profits apart from an agreed dividend to its shareholders. In Mexico, although the 1993 port reforms aimed at limiting cross-subsidisation of ports, the substantial national port investment programmes could be considered to be effectively doing this.

The role of the federal government could be to make sure that the main Mexican ports are well connected to national hinterland infrastructure networks and promote and supervise deals with the main railway companies on port connectivity.

Relations with cities could be improved with more efforts for joint planning. The main Mexican ports are urban ports, and constrained by urban development that is encroaching on port activity. As a result, ports and their cities have become heavily interlinked; for instance, port truck traffic has led to urban congestion; environmental impacts have deteriorated the health of urban citizens; and urban development around ports has limited the possibilities to expand the current facilities. Even if there are some efforts to long term planning, as the new container terminal in Veracruz, that will take place at some distance from the city centre, still remains the necessity to align port and urban planning.

At this moment, the municipality in which the port is located has one seat in the board of its API, which is generally dominated by federal representatives. This provides a functional link, but additional mechanisms would be needed to improve the relations between ports and their cities, in order to increase the alignment of urban policies and port policies, and also sustain the long term "license to operate" ports in an urban environment despite the impacts for the local population. The additional port-city mechanisms might take the form of regular contacts between mayor and port director, joint planning exercises, and port-city forums.

Recommendations

Stimulate the establishment of dedicated areas and free of border controls in terminals for coastal shipping. Mexican ports hardly have any transhipment traffic due to cabotage legislations, which allows foreign ocean-going vessels only to carry empty containers between Mexican port (not full containers) which evidently limits the possibilities for transhipment and coastal shipping.

Considering opening up the maritime cabotage market; Mexican companies with more than 49% foreign capital could be allowed to acquire cabotage permits. Another measure could be to relax the priority given to domestic crews, as in Australia or New Zealand, possibly in parallel with an obligation in cabotage permits to train Mexican seafarers.

The current system of renewable three-month permits could be replaced by renewable one-year permits, in order to reduce red tape. Mexico could also consider the introduction of an international shipping register; one of the advantages for ship-owners of such an international register could be that it would allow for cabotage trade in Mexico.

The coastal shipping provided by cabotage permits represents around one third of the total domestic shipping in Mexico, the other two thirds is concentrated by Mexican ships transporting gas for PEMEX. The cabotage permits are widely used. In 2009, it was estimated that nearly 500 permits are granted or renewed every year.

The customs service should be instructed to introduce a specific regime to facilitate transhipment, avoiding excessive controls on bonded containers in transit. Mexican ports hardly have any transhipment traffic due to cabotage legislations which allows foreign ocean-going vessels only to carry empty containers between Mexican ports, not full containers, which evidently limits the possibilities for transhipment and coastal shipping.

Investments in ports and hinterland connections should be more concentrated to achieve the ambition to develop Mexico's four main ports into world-class ports by focusing on the implementation of the national infrastructure plan 2013-18 and by focusing investment on these four ports. The ports system in Mexico is relatively concentrated compared to similar sized countries, despite the large number of ports and terminals. This concentration is particularly visible in containerised cargo and oil products. Approximately, 95% of the total container volume of 4.9 million TEUs is handled in four hub-ports.

Customs and other inspection agencies should more often be open 24 hours per day, in line with the working hours of several port terminals. Several port terminals are open 24 hours per day, which is not the case for customs and other inspection agencies. Requests can be submitted to have customs work at night but reportedly, almost all these requests are refused.

Envisage introducing competition in towage services, and possibly other port services. Mexican ports are not exceptional in this respect: in most ports across the world, pilotage services are monopolies. For the other port services, competition is more common, at least in the largest ports. Considering that the main Mexican ports use several tug boats (indicating large enough size), it would be possible to envisage competition in towage services and possibly other port services.

Transfer more of the regulatory functions to the APIs, which should acquire larger financial autonomy. In comparison with many ports in the OECD countries, the APIs are still very dependent on the federal ministry, hindering the best investment decisions for each individual port. Although the 1993 port reforms aimed at limiting cross-subsidisation of ports, the substantial national port investment programmes could be considered to be effectively doing this. The role of the federal government could be to make sure that the main Mexican ports are well connected to national hinterland infrastructure networks and promote and supervise deals with the main railway companies on port connectivity.

Opportunities for joint planning between port authorities and municipal governments should be sought. This might take the form of regular contacts between mayor and port director, joint planning exercises, and port-city forums. The main Mexican ports are urban ports, and constrained by urban development that is encroaching on port activity. As a result, ports and their cities have become heavily interlinked; for instance, port truck traffic has led to urban congestion; environmental impacts have deteriorated the health of urban citizens; and urban development around ports has limited the possibilities to expand the current facilities.

Develop policies with the aim to simplify port gate operations: investigate the development of appointment systems for trucks to reduce waiting times and port gate congestion, explore IT solutions for driver and vehicle recognition, and investigate the possibility of better exploiting waiting times for trucks at the *patios reguladores* by relocating some controls to these areas. Main bottlenecks in ports are linked to the release of cargo due to various controls and administrative procedures. There are various projects in place to reduce administrative burdens, such as paperless port and one single window but these initiatives are not implemented in similar fashion across ports and do not encompass all procedures.

Develop an integrated logistics strategy for the main four Mexican ports to determine the potential for the consolidation of cargo at inland dry ports, in order to increase the volume of containers that could be carried on railroads instead of road and improve efficiency. The lack of capacity of hinterland connections is a widely-recognised issue and infrastructure expansion is well underway in several ports and critical links. Ports are clearly identified as critical nodes in the logistic infrastructure of the country and, as it is often the case, road connections appear more developed than rail. Several sections of the road, however, need to be upgraded and as cargo volume increases, it is likely that road congestion will become an issue.

The resources available for enforcement should be increased. The number of SCT inspectors for roadside checking of heavy goods vehicles needs to be substantially increased. Police resources for vehicle inspections also need to be increased and consideration given to establishing a dedicated unit charged only with enforcement of heavy vehicle regulations.

Notes

1. Art. 3 and 5. Law of Ports.

2. Art. 16, LP.

3. Art 16, Frac VIII. Law of Ports.

4. Calculations of ship turn-around times are based on vessel movement data over May 2014 and May 2011 from Lloyds Intelligence Unit. The estimated coverage of this database is > 95% of all vessel movements. For the purpose of this analysis only fully cellular container ships with GT >100 were taken into account. The database has per vessel call an arrival time at berth and a departure time from berth, allowing for calculation of duration of port stays. For the analysis all port stays were excluded that were smaller than 0.20 days and longer than 7 days. In this way, bunkering calls and extreme values were excluded. The database that resulted included 38 843 port calls in May 2014 and 25 989 port calls in May 2011.

5. Permisos temporales de navegación.

6. Cabotage is defined as the navigation between two ports or spots within the Mexican maritime zones.

7. The overall LPI score of Mexico of 3.13 is slightly above the relevant peer groups: the Upper middle income countries that scored 2.82 and the Latin American and Caribbean countries with a score of 2.74. Mexico has improved its score on the LPI since 2007, when it scored 2.87, but its score and ranking has been relatively stable since 2010. The LPI consists of different indicators; the indicator on which Mexico scores worst is "Customs" where it ranks 70th of the world with a score of 2.69. On the other indicators (infrastructure, international shipments, logistics quality and tracking and tracing), Mexico consistently ranks around the 50th position. This is more or less in line with the ranking of the Mexican port infrastructure (62nd position) in the 2014 World Economic Forum Competitiveness Report.

8. Information gathered as part of the interviews to stakeholders to prepare this report.

9. Traffic in the port of Lazaro Cardenas has decreased, however, for reasons attributable to external factors, i.e. security issues in the region.

10. Generally the pilot acts as advisor to the Master or Captain regarding the route into (or out of) the port, berthing and un-berthing, drawing on his experience and knowledge of the local maritime area. In many countries, the requirements of the pilot while on board are set out in the pilotage rules or regulations regarding the advice that he can give, the relationship between the pilot and Master and his duties with regard to reporting of the pilotage mission (PWC, 2012).

11. An act by which one vessel, known as the tug, supplies power in order to draw another vessel, called the tow.

12. To secure a ship with cables or ropes.

13. Bunkering services refer to the practice and business of refuelling ships. Bunkering operations are located at seaports, and they include the storage of "bunker" (ship) fuels and the provision of the fuel to vessels.

References

Acciaro, M. and A.C. McKinnon (2013), "Efficient hinterland transport infrastructure and services for large container ports", Position paper for the OECD/ITF Round Table Port Investment and Container Shipping Markets, Santiago de Chile, 7-8 November.

Bergqvist, R. (2012), "Hinterland logistics and global supply chains" in *Maritime Logistics: A Complete Guide to Effective Shipping and Port Management*, eds. D. Song and P. Panayides, Kogan Page Publishers, pp. 211-232.

Bergqvist, R., G. Wilmsmeier and K. Cullinane (2013b), "Introduction—A Global Perspective on Dryports" in *Dry Ports: A Global Perspective, Challenges and Developments in Serving Hinterlands*, eds. R. Bergqvist, G. Wilmsmeier and K. Cullinane, Ashgate Publishing Ltd., Farnham, pp. 1-10.

Bergqvist, R., G. Wilmsmeier and K. Cullinane (eds) (2013a), *Dry Ports: A Global Perspective, Challenges and Developments in Serving Hinterlands*, Ashgate Publishing Ltd., Farnham.

Brooks, M. (2009), "Liberalization in Maritime Transport, International Transport Forum", *Forum Papers* 2/2009, International Transport Forum, Paris.

Delfín-Ortega, O. and C. Navarro-Chávez (2013), "Technical Efficiency in the Container Terminals in Mexico, 1982-2010: Through Data Envelopment Analysis (DEA)", *iBusiness*, Vol. 5, pp. 154-160.

Ducruet, C., H. Itoh and O. Merk (2014), "Time Efficiency in World Container Ports", *ITF Discussion Paper 2014/08*, International Transport Forum, Paris.

Enriquez, D. and C. Moran (2009), "Mexico", in Lux (ed.) *Shipping in 30 jurisdictions worldwide*, www.gettingthedealthrough.com (assessed: 15 December 2014).

Estache, A., M. González and L. Trujillo (2002), "Efficiency Gains from Port Reform and the Potential for Yardstick Competition: Lessons from Mexico", *World Development*, Vol. 30/4, pp. 545-560.

Estache, A. et al. (2004), "Sources of efficiency gains in port reform: a DEA decomposition of a Malmquist TFP index for Mexico", *Utilities Policy*, Vol. 12, pp. 221-230.

Giuliano, G. and O'Brien, T. (2008), "Extended gate operations at the ports of Los Angeles and Long Beach: a preliminary assessment", *Maritime Policy and Management*, Vol. 35/2, pp. 215-235.

Giuliano, G. and T. O'Brien (2007), "Reducing port-related truck emissions: The terminal gate appointment system at the Ports of Los Angeles and Long Beach", *Transportation Research*, Part D: Transport and Environment, Vol. 12/7, pp. 460-473.

Guan, C. and R.R. Liu (2009), "Container terminal gate appointment system optimization", *Maritime Economics and Logistics*, Vol. 11/4, pp. 378-398.

Huynh, N. (2009), "Reducing truck turn times at marine terminals with appointment scheduling", *Transportation Research Record: Journal of the Transportation Research Board*, Vol. 2100/1, pp. 47-57.

ITF (2014), "Freight Railway Development in Mexico", International Transport Forum, *Country-Specific Policy Analysis*, ITF/OECD, Paris.

ITF/OECD (2015), "The Impact of Mega-Ships", International Transport Forum, Paris.

JOC Group (2014), "Berth Productivity: The Trends, Outlook and Market Forces Impacting Ship Turnaround Times", JOC Group Inc.

Martner, C. (2002), "Hub ports in Mexico: limitations and opportunities", *CEPAL Review*, Vol. 76, pp. 117-133.

Martner, C. and M. Martínez (2011), "Competencia, Eficiencia y Regulación de las Cadenas de Carga Contenedorizadas por Puertos Mexicanos", IAME 2011 Conference Paper, Santiago de Chile, 25-28 October.

Merk, O. and T. Dang (2012), "Efficiency of World Ports in Container and Bulk Cargo (oil, coal, ores and grain)", *OECD Regional Development Working Papers*, No. 2012/09, OECD Publishing, Paris, http://dx.doi.org/10.1787/5k92vgw39zs2-en.

Monios, J. and B. Lambert (2013), "Intermodal Freight Corridor Development in the United States" in *Dry Ports: A Global Perspective, Challenges and Developments in Serving Hinterlands*, eds. R. Bergqvist, G. Wilmsmeier and K. Cullinane, Ashgate Publishing Ltd., Farnham, pp. 197-218.

Moran, C. (2013), "The Legal Treatment of Vessels and Offshore Installations Under the Mexican Foreign Investment and Navigation Frameworks", *Newsletter of the Maritime and Transport Law Committee of the Legal Practice Division of the International Bar Association*, Vol. 9/1, International Bar Association, London.

OECD (2014), *The Competitiveness of Global Port-Cities*, OECD Publishing, Paris, http://dx.doi.org/10.1787/9789264205277-en.

OECD (2011), "Competition in Ports and Ports Services", OECD, Paris, www.oecd.org/daf/competition/sectors/48837794.pdf (accessed 22 November 2016).

OECD/CAF/ECLAC (2013), *Latin American Economic Outlook 2014: Logistics and Competitiveness for Development*, OECD Publishing, Paris, http://dx.doi.org/10.1787/leo-2014-en.

Oliveira, G. de and P. Cariou (2011), "A DEA study of the efficiency of 122 iron ore and coal ports of 15/17 countries in 2005", *Maritime Policy & Management*, Vol. 38/7, pp. 727-743.

PWC in partnership with Panteia (2012), "Study on Pilotage Exemption Certificates", prepared for the European Commission.

Roso, V., J. Woxenius and K. Lumsden (2009), "The dry port concept: connecting container seaports with the hinterland", *Journal of Transport Geography*, Vol. 17/5, pp. 338-345.

SCT (2012), "Plan Nacional de Desarrollo: Programa Sectorial de Transportes y Comunicaciones 2013-2018" (National Development Plan: Sectorial Program of Transport and Communications), Government of the Republic, United States of Mexico.

UNCTAD (2014), "Review of Maritime Transport 2014", United Nations Conference on Trade and Development, Geneva.

Veenstra, A., R. Zuidwijk and E. van Asperen (2012), "The extended gate concept for container terminals: Expanding the notion of dry ports", *Maritime Economics and Logistics*, Vol. 14/1, pp. 14-32.

WEF (2013), "Global Competitiveness Report 2013-2014", World Economic Forum.

World Bank (2014), "Connecting to Compete; Trade Logistics in the Global Economy", World Bank, Washington, DC.

Zheng, J., Q. Meng and Z. Sun (2014), "Impact analysis of maritime cabotage legislations on liner hub-and-spoke shipping network design", *European Journal of Operational Research*, Vol. 234, pp. 874-884.

Chapter 5

Regulation of border management in Mexico

In Mexico, several government agencies share the responsibility of managing trade-related cross-border regulatory requirements. The regulatory reforms that have been introduced across the various border management agencies are designed to reduce red tape, improve co-ordination and facilitate the movement of freight. However, difficulties are being experienced in the implementation of the regulations. Challenges include: full functionality of the single window VUCEM system; to undertake a review of risk management practices on inspections by border management agencies; to develop national standards and operating procedures in order to achieve national uniformity of practice, to co-ordinate management and investment in road border crossing facilities so that priority gates for registered carriers are accessed by reserved lanes sufficiently long to bypass queues for non-priority gates.

In Mexico, as in most economies, a number of government agencies share the responsibility of managing trade-related cross-border regulatory requirements which include, but are not limited to, revenue collection, food security, biosecurity (sanitary and phytosanitary), health, national security, immigration, environmental protection, trade facilitation, community protection and consumer safety.

The principal agencies that operate at Mexico's points of entry (including seaports, airports and border crossings) include Customs, SAGARPA, the Navy and the Ministries of Health, Environment and Security. Of these, the key border management agencies that influence the levels of regulatory intervention and trade facilitation are Customs,[1] SENASICA (which is an arm of SAGARPA) and General Directorate of Merchant Navy of SCT.

International standards

Mexico's National Development Plan 2013-18 outlines a range of strategies designed to enhance economic growth, including trade facilitation reform, where Customs and other border management agencies play a key role. Central to these reforms is the need to ensure consistency with relevant international commitments and instruments.[2]

The International Convention on the Simplification and Harmonization of Customs Procedures, as amended (Revised Kyoto Convention)[3] was developed by the World Customs Organization (WCO) in the face of mounting pressure from the international trading community to minimise the level of customs intervention in cargo movements and to maximise the level of trade facilitation. It provides a standard for modern and efficient customs procedures through its promotion of trade facilitation and effective controls, and incorporates important concepts of contemporary compliance management, including a willingness to establish mutually beneficial partnerships between customs authorities and the private sector.

While Mexico is not a contracting party to the Revised Kyoto Convention, it has expressed its commitment to implement the policies and practices espoused in the Convention, which have been the source of several modernisation initiatives in Mexico in recent years. In this regard, a number of significant legislative reforms were introduced in December 2013, in an effort to increase the level of trade facilitation across all modes of transport, the principal amendments being:

- Introducing provisions to enable (and mandate) the electronic transmission of all documents relating to imports and exports
- Removing the mandatory requirement for traders to use customs brokers (*agente aduanal*) in their dealings with Customs. This amendment is consistent with international good practice, as reflected in the World Trade Organization's recent Agreement on Trade Facilitation.[4] Under the new arrangements, traders are able to deal directly with Customs in relation to the import and export of goods, or alternatively employ a legal representative to manage the transaction on their behalf, subject to certain conditions
- Providing the ability for traders or their representatives to make amendments to declarations and other documents after they have been submitted to Customs, even though Customs may have commenced their validation process
- Progressing the use of non-intrusive inspection techniques: this includes the use of large-scale X-ray and gamma-ray machines and radiation detection devices.

Further, as a member of the WTO, Mexico is a signatory to the Sanitary and Phytosanitary (SPS) Agreement, which provides an international framework for ensuring food safety and mitigating the risk of pests and diseases being introduced into the country through trade. Under the SPS Agreement, Mexico is entitled to maintain the level of protection it deems to be appropriate, but must also ensure that the measures it employs do not result in unnecessary barriers to international trade.[5] It is this latter aspect which is of particular relevance to the current report.

In Mexico SENASICA has regulatory responsibility for food security and the application of sanitary and phytosanitary measures, and as such exercises control over domestic and international trade in goods of plant and animal origin. Controls that are exercised by any regulatory agency will inevitably impact on trade and transport, particularly those involving the physical inspection of goods. Consequently, the policies relating to trade controls, including SPS and food security, and the manner in which they are applied, can have a significant impact on the flow of freight through seaports, airports and border crossings.

Recognition of compliant traders

Mexico has also introduced a programme designed to provide customs-certified companies[6] with streamlined processing procedures, which is also based on the principles of the Revised Kyoto Convention. The original programme, which was introduced in 2003, provided facilitated clearance arrangements to trusted traders who utilised customs-registered carriers. To become a certified company, traders were required to demonstrate high levels of regulatory compliance. The programme also integrates safety provisions and provisions to facilitation trade, following guidelines set by the SAT.

Since that time, the WCO introduced its SAFE Framework of Standards to Secure and Facilitate Trade (SAFE Framework). For customs administrations, the SAFE Framework represents the principal international instrument with a focus on supply chain security. First published in 2005, it has subsequently been revised in 2007, 2010 and 2012. In the latest edition the stated aim of the SAFE Framework is to:

- Establish standards that provide supply chain security and facilitation at a global level to promote certainty and predictability
- Enable integrated and harmonised supply chain management for all modes of transport[7]
- Enhance the role, functions and capabilities of Customs to meet the challenges and opportunities of the 21st Century
- Strengthen co-operation between Customs administrations to improve their capability to detect high-risk consignments
- Strengthen Customs/Business co-operation
- Promote the seamless movement of goods through secure international trade supply chains.

The SAFE Framework incorporates the key concept of Authorised Economic Operator (AEO), which applies to companies that are able to demonstrate high levels of both trade compliance and supply chain security—in the case of Mexico, through the SAT's New Scheme of Certified Firms (*Nuevo Esquema de Empresas Certificadas*, NEEC).

The SAFE Framework defines an AEO to be "a party involved in the international movement of goods in whatever function that has been approved by or on behalf of a national Customs administration as complying with WCO or equivalent supply chain security standards" (World Customs Organization, 2012, p. I/1). The AEO concept represents a partnership arrangement between Customs and Industry that is designed to provide incentives for businesses that meet defined supply chain security standards. According to the WCO, "AEOs will reap benefits, such as faster processing of goods by Customs, e.g. through reduced examination rates… These processes will ensure that AEOs see a benefit to their investment in good security systems and practices, including reduced risk-targeting assessments and inspections, and expedited processing of their goods." (World Customs Organization, 2012, p. 6)

Mexico is one of the 169 countries that have adopted, or signalled their intention to adopt, the SAFE Framework, and in 2012, Customs replaced its programme for certified companies with its own AEO regime, the New Scheme of Certified Company Programme (*Nuevo Esquema de Empresas Certificadas*, NEEC). Members of NEEC are deemed to be low-risk. According to Customs, NEEC members have a 1% likelihood of being selected for examination, and in the event that their shipment is targeted, there is a 50% chance that the inspection will be non-intrusive in nature.[8] NEEC members are also entitled to priority processing (by way of priority lanes, or 'head of queue' treatment, for example), and to date special lanes have been identified at six border crossings, as well as at the Port of Manzanillo. However, as discussed below, the available physical infrastructure and current processing procedures do not always allow for the intended benefits of facilitated clearance to be realised.

The importance of Mexico's decision to replace the previous customs-certified programme with an AEO programme lies in another key element of the SAFE Framework, that is, the establishment of Mutual Recognition Agreements (MRAs) between countries that have implemented AEO programmes. These agreements have two primary features: co-operation between the customs administrations of the two countries, and collaboration in providing defined benefits to AEOs certified under one country's programme when their consignments are processed at the border of the other. Importantly, Mexico is currently negotiating an MRA with the United States, whose C-TPAT[9] programme is currently under review to incorporate trade compliance as a criterion for membership (it currently relates solely to supply chain security).

Single window

A Single Window is essentially a national ICT system that provides the international trading community with a single point of communication with those government agencies that have border management responsibilities. Such agencies generally include those responsible for customs, quarantine and security, together with other permit-issuing authorities. The objective of a Single Window is to enable traders and other members of the trading community (for example, customs brokers and other service providers) to make a single electronic submission of all information required by regulatory agencies relating to import, export and transit; and to receive a single, consolidated government response.

This obviates the need to send multiple sets of documentation to different agencies, thereby eliminating the considerable amount of duplication that is traditionally associated with government communication. The use of a Single Window also facilitates the introduction of cross-agency risk management arrangements, which in turn will assist in achieving a more co-ordinated national approach to border management, including profiling and targeting through the application of risk-based intelligence.

The World Trade Organization made particular mention of the Single Window concept in its recent Agreement on Trade facilitation, including the following:

Members shall endeavour to establish or maintain a single window, enabling traders to submit documentation and/or data requirements for importation, exportation or transit of goods through a single entry point to the participating authorities or agencies. After the examination by the participating authorities or agencies of the documentation and/or data, the results shall be notified to the applicants through the single window in a timely manner.[10]

Those economies that are currently advancing the concept of a Single Window are adopting a phased approach to implementation, and all are in different stages of development. Typically, the initial stages of implementation involve electronic submission of customs- and quarantine-related information, and individual electronic responses from the relevant agencies.

The development of the Mexican Single Window, known as VUCEM,[11] has been co-ordinated by SAT and the Ministry of Economy, under the supervision of an Inter-Secretarial Commission for the implementation of the Single Window. The VUCEM currently operates with nine federal public agencies and two regulatory agencies (Tequila and Coffee). VUCEM is accessed via the Government website, www.ventanillaunica.gob.mx. It was first opened for registration in September 2011, and in early 2012 commenced the rollout of electronic goods clearance arrangements. The system, the use of which is now mandatory for all imports and exports, has been designed to process import, export and transit transactions electronically, including all authorisations, approvals and direct debit of taxes—the business can submit the information directly to the VUCEM or submit the traditional formats to the offices where public officials will feed the information to the VUCEM. Alternatively, a system named SAAI-WEB under the responsibility of SAT, enables transport companies to present a simplified customs declaration which a customs inspector reads by way of a handheld device and releases the goods.[12]

When fully operational across all seaports, airports and border crossings, VUCEM should serve to facilitate the movement of freight by automating the relevant application, declaration, reporting and authorisation processes. In addition, it will assist in achieving a more co-ordinated approach to border management through consolidated risk analysis and the scheduling of joint agency inspections, thereby minimising the degree of regulatory intervention. Other benefits should include improved transparency and national uniformity of practice, which will provide the international trading community with greater certainty and clarity in their dealings with the various regulatory authorities.

Port Community Systems (PCS), which are generally owned and operated by members of the port community, have not yet been introduced in Mexico, although some steps in this direction have been taken in the major ports. International experience indicates that PCS can contribute significantly to the efficiency of port and airport operations, including regulatory processes. The most effective PCS also provide services which most government Single Windows do not, that is, Business-to-Business information exchange. [13]

Operational practices and procedures

Submission of documentation for import, export and transit does not differ significantly from other countries and, with the phased introduction of VUCEM, the processes and procedures are becoming increasingly streamlined. For traders, the task of submitting documentation was undertaken by a customs broker, although the recent legislative amendments enabled traders to deal directly with Customs or employ a legal representative to perform this role on their behalf.

Prior to submission of the Customs declaration into VUCEM, the data undergoes two authentication processes, both of which are automated. First, the declaration is submitted for "pre-validation", a process which essentially involves electronic verification of the data to identify potential anomalies that must be rectified—made by the applicant. A further "validation" is undertaken on the final document, incorporating any amendments, prior to final lodgement.

Sea and air cargo is held in bonded warehouses that are located within the port or airport pending formal clearance. Road cargo is cleared at the border crossings, while rail cargo is generally cleared away from the border at bonded industrial parks.[14]

The Import controls exercised by SENASICA are essentially intended to minimise the risk of pests or diseases entering the country, and to ensure that relevant food standards are met. In Mexico, all importations[15] are subject to physical inspection for the purposes of SPS and food safety, and in cases where multiple container loads are reported on a single declaration, a sample of the containers is inspected. This would generally represent 20% or less of the total shipment, depending on the particular country of export.[16] In addition, some consignments undergo pre-shipment inspection by SENASICA-certified inspectors, and these too may be re-examined on arrival in Mexico at the discretion of SENASICA.

SENASICA's export controls are designed to ensure that the regulatory requirements of the importing country are met, and to maintain Mexico's reputation in overseas markets in order to safeguard market access. Consequently, the regulatory controls applying to export consignments differ, depending on the nature of the shipment:

- For exports of aquatic products, the exporter is required to submit laboratory test results to SENASICA demonstrating that the goods meet the particular requirements of the country of destination. Based on this evidence, no physical inspection is conducted
- Exports of animal products (zoo sanitary products) are subject to physical inspection prior to export certification.[17] The controls that apply to such products are particularly stringent, in line with accepted international practice
- For Exports of plant products (vegetal products), the exporter is required to present an inspection report from a Verification Unit (private bodies approved by the General Directorate of Plant Protection) which certifies that all requirements of the country of destination are met. Following receipt of the report, SENASICA

will issue an International Phytosanitary Certificate (*Certificado Fitosanitario Internacional*, CFI) if required by the country of destination.[18]

No physical inspection of transit shipments is required, other than the application and subsequent check of container seals to mitigate the risk of unauthorised access during transit.

All requests for import authorisation of goods that are subject to SAGARPA controls are required to be made through VUCEM, which generates the relevant import permission, including the scheduling of inspection requirements.—Previous to the application of import permit through the VUCEM, the importer must print the health requirements through the requirements module in the webpage of SENASICA. Such permissions include:

- Import permission for zoosanitary products (*Permiso de importación de productos zoosanitarios*)
- Import permission for phytosanitary products (*Permiso de importación de productos fitosanitarios*)
- Import permission for aquatic products (*Permiso de importación de productos acuícolas*).

Contingency procedures, known as the System of Information of Phytosanitary Inspections (*Sistema de Información de Inspecciones Fitozoosanitarias*, SIIF), are also in place to deal with potential VUCEM system outages. Under these procedures, which solely address SAGARPA requirements as opposed to broader regulatory requirements, the importer must register the transaction with SAGARPA electronically, and subsequently deliver the relevant documentation to the SAGARPA office. Similar arrangements exist for obtaining export clearance of goods that are of interest to SAGARPA.

Other agencies that may wish to examine the documentation or physically inspect shipments include Merchant Navy,[19] Human Health, Environment, Police, Army and others. In addition, customs brokers undertake their own physical examination of shipments to verify that the contents are in conformity with the relevant shipping documentation. The level of such pre-examination practices is particularly high, with some 20% of containers being selected for broker-initiated inspections. It is understood that brokers generally inspect all shipments imported by new clients, and up to 20% of those imported by existing clients.

Customs clearance formalities are completed following satisfaction of all SENASICA and other agency requirements, the exception being shipments that are the subject of a specific alert, based on intelligence holdings. With the exception of rail cargo, all documentary examinations and physical inspections are conducted at the point of arrival or departure (that is, within the confines of the seaport or airport, or at the border crossing in warehouses at the custom clearance area), and payment of all taxes is required prior to release. While the policy intent is to conduct joint inspections where possible, there is little evidence of this occurring in practice. Consequently, it is not unusual for shipments to undergo multiple inspections while being held in the bonded warehouse and re-inspected by Customs at the final inspection point.

Customs has advised that approximately 10% of import containers and 6% of export containers are required to be inspected by their administration,[20] and that selection of cargo for examination is made on the basis of risk analysis. It is further reported that inspection of transit cargo is by exception, and is also risk-based. These figures are consistent with the feedback received from industry.

In addition to any physical inspections that are undertaken, Customs requires all import containers to be screened upon exiting seaports via Fiscal Lanes for final Customs clearance. This is performed through the use of non-intrusive devices.[21] However, this procedure is not standard across all ports, as some do not have access to the relevant equipment.

In relation to land border crossings, Customs has advised that a real-time exchange of data with US CBP is currently being piloted which is designed to improve their targeting capabilities and provide greater facilitation for low-risk shipments.

Findings

In many cases the practices and procedures adopted by the various regulatory agencies appear to differ quite markedly from the policies espoused by them. The regulatory reforms that have been introduced across the various border management agencies are designed to reduce red tape, improve co-ordination and facilitate the movement of freight. However, difficulties are being experienced in the implementation of the regulations, which not only detract from the intended benefits of the recent modernisation initiatives, but also fail to provide the international trading community with the commercial certainty and clarity they require.

Co-ordinated border management

The lack of co-ordination among border management agencies is adding to the clearance time, cost and uncertainty of freight movements. Despite claims that co-ordinated cargo inspections are the norm and that, in some cases, the co-ordination of examinations is a legal requirement this is not reflected in practice. It is not unusual for shipments to undergo multiple inspections by different agencies, particularly in relation to sea cargo. However, other modes of transport are equally impacted. For example, it was reported that it is common for rail freight "to be opened by SENASICA in the morning, and by Customs in the afternoon".

Progress is, however, being made. The organisational statements of SENASICA specifically identify the need to facilitate trade while also ensuring compliance with its regulatory responsibilities. A significant initiative that is currently being progressed in this regard is a project to facilitate the clearance of perishable products at seaports, with the target of ensuring a maximum turnaround time of 36 hours. The initiative, which commenced in late 2013, is being conducted in co-operation with Customs.

Under the project, importers are required to lodge all declarations electronically via VUCEM at least 24 hours prior to arrival at the seaport. This provides the opportunity to risk-assess the shipment prior to its arrival, determine the necessary regulatory interventions that may be required, and to schedule the joint inspection if required. In this way, the physical inspection of perishable goods is conducted only once, with both SAGARPA and Customs in attendance, as required.

It is proposed to introduce a further facility within VUCEM to improve the level of co-ordination among border management agencies. It is understood that VUCEM-2, which was scheduled for full implementation in 2016, will include a national automated scheduling system that will result in joint inspections by Customs and SENASICA, thereby eliminating multiple intrusive inspections, at least those involving these two agencies.

While this is an encouraging development, there is a need for further progress in this area to include Merchant Navy and other agencies in joint inspections to further improve the level of border management co-ordination. The need for further development is supported by the OECD's recent recommendation that Mexico should embrace a 'whole of government' culture for regulatory improvement policy (OECD, 2014). Indeed, in the border management environment there is a particular requirement to pursue a whole of government approach to the implementation of the policy, as the administrative practices and procedures which deliver the policy at the operational level are equally critical to the achievement of policy objectives, see Box 5.1.

Box 5.1. **Effective co-ordinated border management in New Zealand**

Since 2011 the New Zealand Customs Service has operated an Integrated Targeting and Operations Centre (ITOC) to support the command and co-ordination of border sector operations across New Zealand's various border management agencies.

The ITOC is a multi-agency border sector headquarters with well-trained staff to support the command, planning, and co-ordination of border operations. A number of key agencies have a presence in the ITOC, and work together closely and efficiently in planning and executing operational activities. These include:

- New Zealand Customs Service
- Ministry of Agriculture and Forestry (MAF) Biosecurity New Zealand
- Immigration New Zealand
- Maritime New Zealand
- New Zealand Police
- The Security Intelligence Service, and
- Other agencies as required on an operational basis.

The ITOC brings together targeting, operational planning, and co-ordination functions and provides all information necessary for effective border security management in one location, 24 hours a day. The intelligence gathered by ITOC is used to target risks to the border and to provide planning, co-ordination and threat assessment processes to ensure operational activity is properly co-ordinated and focused on risks and priorities, which serves to facilitate the clearance of legitimate travellers and trade.

Source: Elaboration by the OECD Secretariat based on Contraband, New Zealand Customs Service, October 2011, Issue 119.

Regulatory practices

At first sight, the level of regulatory intervention appears high, but not overly so. However, while the combined import inspection rates of 15% by regulatory agencies are high by international standards,[22] it is apparent that these rates may fluctuate significantly. For example, it was reported that in April 2014, some 90% of containers at the Port of Manzanillo were opened for inspection on the instructions of Merchant Navy.

In relation to exports of plant and animal products, it is to be expected that a relatively high level of physical checks will be undertaken by SENASICA in order to safeguard access to overseas markets. However, the reported 6% of export containers that are inspected by Customs is particularly high compared to international practice.[23] The fact that Customs has indicated that all inspections are risk-based suggests that its approach to risk management, including its profiling and targeting policies, may need to be reviewed.

It should be noted, however, that regulatory practices vary depending on the particular port, border crossing or inspection point, which indicates a general lack of national uniformity. As previously noted, this is not a reflection of the regulatory policy, but rather the implementation of the policy at an administrative level. This lack of national uniformity of practice leads to a lack of clarity and certainty for traders and service providers.

In this regard, a number of interviewees pointed to the need for publicly available national standards, guidelines and operating procedures in order to improve national consistency and provide industry with a clear understanding of their rights and responsibilities. The need for a focus on the training and development of officials from all agencies was also identified, with both regulatory agencies and industry representatives suggesting that many officials lacked the necessary knowledge, skills and competencies to effectively perform their duties. This also extends to the need for a greater understanding of commercial practices and constraints, particularly in relation to rail cargo. Implementation of VUCEM also helps to achieve a greater level of national uniformity and in this context the need for training in the VUCEM system for both government officials and industry was raised as a specific priority.

A general practice which customs should review is the benefit of the pre-validation process, which costs about $16 to $20, but does not appear to reduce exposure to inspection or regulatory sanctions in any way. Customs has indicated that the process serves to combat fraud, but there is no evidence of this, or of the effectiveness of the system in improving rates of compliance. The service is currently operated by the customs broker association but as previously noted, the opportunity of providing the service will soon to be extended to other parties. In the event that pre-validation is assessed to be a worthwhile process, and that the practice should continue, consideration should be given to providing it as a free service as an adjunct to VUCEM.

The treatment of transit and transhipment goods is another aspect of regulatory practice that should be reviewed. There have been reported instances that both transit and transhipment goods have been treated as separate import/export transactions, and physical inspection of such shipments is also reported to be commonplace. Once again, clear national directives should be developed and training provided to ensure that such consignments are dealt with in accordance with the principles of the Revised Kyoto Convention of the World Customs Organisation.

Finally, the particularly high level of broker-initiated inspections, which occur despite the pre-validation and validation processes that are in place, is worthy of further examination. Initiation of such inspections is claimed to be driven by the penalty regime that applies in the event of irregularities in the customs declaration. If this is in fact the case (and not simply an opportunity to charge additional service fees, consideration should be given to reviewing the penalty regime with a view to placing a greater regulatory onus on the trader. At the same time, it would be useful to examine the results of broker-initiated inspections to determine their effectiveness.

Performance monitoring

In most other OECD countries customs services have a clear mission to facilitate trade, backed by performance indicators. This has been taken furthest in countries highly dependent on trade, such as New Zealand and Australia. More than 20 aspects of service quality are monitored in Australia, for example, with performance against headline targets published regularly (Table 5.1). Mexico's customs and other inspection procedures should develop performance targets suited to the environment in which they operate but designed to stimulate re-orientation of their services towards an emphasis on facilitating trade.

Table 5.1. **Australian customs and border protection service performance against trade facilitation targets in 2010–11**

Key performance indicators	Target	Actual
Availability of electronic cargo systems to Customs and Border Protection clients (excluding scheduled outages)	99.7%	99.7%
Proportion of electronically lodged cargo documents where a response message is transmitted within five minutes	98%	97.9%

Source: Australian Customs and Border Protection Service, Annual Report 2010-11.

Infrastructure

Regardless of how good the future regulatory framework may be, it is unlikely to meet its desired objectives of enhancing controls and facilitating trade in the absence of improved infrastructure. The new certified company, or trusted trader, NEEC programme, is a case in point. The intention of the scheme is to provide NEEC members with facilitated clearance arrangements, and to achieve this, priority lanes have been introduced at border crossings. In practice, however, NEEC members are failing to receive priority treatment due to the congestion of the roads leading to the priority lanes.

Also, at the Port of Manzanillo, where two of the ten Fiscal Lanes have been designated NEEC priority lanes, those eligible to use the lanes are still required to wait in line until reaching a point at which they are able to enter a priority lane. Consequently, it is not unusual for the two priority lanes to be vacant even though NEEC members are seeking to exit the port.

Dwell time

The dwell time at seaports was estimated to be 5-6 days in 2009, and the government reform process is seeking to reduce this. Interestingly, however, the recent customs legislative reforms provide an increase in the number of days that imports are able to be stored free of charge – from five to seven days, which does not appear to encourage a reduction in dwell time.

Many countries undertake a Time Release Study (TRS) to determine the relative contribution to the overall dwell time by the various parties, both public and private sector. The TRS, which has been developed by the WCO, measures relevant aspects of operational procedures that are carried out by border management agencies when processing imports, exports and goods in transit. The study measures the average time taken between the arrival of the goods and their release, which helps to identify both the problem areas and potential corrective actions to increase their efficiency. It is also a useful tool for measuring improvements in trade flows.[24] Mexico would benefit from undertaking such a study.

A specific regulatory practice that affects the clearance time of cargo is the failure to differentiate between those issues that must be addressed at the point of arrival and those that may be pursued post-transaction. While certain regulatory matters must be dealt with prior to the release of goods, others may be resolved following their release. A case in point is detention for revenue purposes, particularly in situations where the importer has a good record of compliance. The standard practice in Mexico is to detain all such goods at the terminal, regardless of the circumstances. It would therefore be appropriate to examine such practices in the context of a general review of its risk management policy.

The hours of business and the availability of personnel, both during and outside those hours, is another issue that can have a significant impact on dwell times, and several interviewees identified the restriction of many border clearance and inspection services to standard office hours as a significant impediment to trade.[25] For example, it has been reported that, in those ports which operate 24 hours per day, requests for customs and other inspection agencies to provide services after normal working hours are generally refused. Similar issues are encountered in relation to other modes of transport.

Recommendations

A time release study and review of border agency operating hours should be undertaken to identify problem areas and potential corrective actions.

Based on the time release study, an assessment of the effectiveness of agency and broker initiated inspections should be undertaken with a view to curtailing this function.

Full functionality of the single window VUCEM system should be implemented as a matter of priority.

Pending full implementation of the VUCEM system, initiatives should be developed to improve border management co-ordination between agencies, including rationalisation of risk profiles and joint inspections.

Border management agencies should undertake a review of their risk management practices.

National standards and operating procedures (including SAT procedures) should be developed and made publicly available on friendly basis to avoid misinterpretations, including those relating to the treatment of transit and transhipment goods, in order to achieve national uniformity of practice.

The customs service should be instructed to introduce a specific regime to facilitate transhipment, avoiding excessive controls of bonded containers in transit.

Regulatory agencies should provide training in national standards and operating procedures to both their operational staff and members of the trading community.

A review of the pre-validation requirements should be undertaken with a view to making it a free of charge service.

A review of penalty provisions should be undertaken to ensure an appropriate balance between the responsibilities and accountabilities of traders and customs brokers.

Regulatory processing requirements should be taken into account when reviewing infrastructure needs and infrastructure investments made to ensure that investment in clearance facilities deliver the trade facilitation benefits intended. Specifically, management and investment in road border crossing facilities needs to be co-ordinated so that priority gates for registered carriers are accessed by reserved lanes sufficiently long to bypass queues for non-priority gates.

Operating hours for customs services should be adjusted to facilitate the relief of key bottlenecks, in particular they should match train operating hours for block-train and intermodal traffic.

Notes

1. The Customs General Administration ("Customs") is an arm of the Tax Administration Service (SAT), which is a department of the Ministry of Finance.
2. See Montes, C 2014, WTO Trade Facilitation Agreement: a potential catalyst for equality of opportunity, WCO News, No. 74, June 2014, pp.12-15.
3. International Convention on the Simplification and Harmonization of Customs Procedures (as amended) 1999, adopted 26 June 1999, (entered into force 3 February 2006).
4. WTO Agreement on Trade Facilitation Article 10: Formalities connected with importation and exportation and transit; Section 6: Use of Customs Brokers.
5. See www.wto.org/english/tratop_e/sps_e/spsund_e.htm, "Understanding the WTO Agreement on Sanitary and Phytosanitary Measures".
6. *Empresas Certificadas.*
7. This aim relates to the WCO's Supply Chain Management Guidelines for the transfer and sharing of trade data.
8. For example, gamma-ray or X-ray screening.
9. Customs-Trade Partnership Against Terrorism.
10. WTO Agreement on Trade Facilitation Article 10: Formalities connected with importation and exportation and transit; Section 4: Single Window.
11. *Ventanilla Única de Comercio Exterior de México.*
12. See: https://www.ventanillaunica.gob.mx/envucem/AboutVU/Operation/index.htm.
13. Long, A 2009, Port Community Systems, World Customs Journal Vol. 3, No. 1.
14. According to Customs, about 90% of rail cargo is cleared away from the border.
15. Here the term "importation" relates to all goods that are reported on a single customs declaration.
16. Note, however, that SAGARPA does not provide aggregate reports on the volume or percentage of consignments or containers that are inspected.
17. TIFF certification.
18. A fee applies for this service.
19. Merchant Navy charter includes interdiction of drugs and explosives.
20. Customs has reported that 9.49% of import containers and 5.85% of export containers were required to be inspected by Customs 2013.
21. Gamma-ray screening devices.
22. Physical inspections in the order of 5% is generally considered to be appropriate.
23. Physical inspections in the order of 1% to 2% is generally considered to be appropriate.

24. See www.wcoomd.org/en/topics/facilitation/instrument-and-tools/~/link.aspx?_id=709aa955423a430cb97a02f5d1c11c3e&_z=z.

25. However, detailed information on the availability of regulatory services has not been gathered during the course of this review.

References

Australian Customs and Border Protection Service (2011), *Annual Report 2010-11*, Canberra, Australia, https://www.border.gov.au/ReportsandPublications/Documents/annual-reports/ACBPS_AR_2010-11.pdf (accessed 19 November 2016).

Long, A. (2009), "Port Community Systems", *World Customs Journal*, Vol. 3/1.

Montes, C. (2014), "WTO Trade Facilitation Agreement: a potential catalyst for equality of opportunity", *WCO News*, No. 74, June.

New Zealand Customs Service (2011), "Contraband", Issue 119, Wellington, www.customs.govt.nz/news/resources/publications/Documents/contrabandissue119october2011.pdf (accessed 22 November 2016).

OECD (2014), *Regulatory Policy in Mexico: Towards a Whole-of-Government Perspective to Regulatory Improvement*, OECD Publishing, Paris, http://dx.doi.org/10.1787/9789264203389-en.

World Customs Organization (2012), "SAFE Framework of Standards to Secure and Facilitate Global Trade", World Customs Organization, Brussels.

ORGANISATION FOR ECONOMIC CO-OPERATION AND DEVELOPMENT

The OECD is a unique forum where governments work together to address the economic, social and environmental challenges of globalisation. The OECD is also at the forefront of efforts to understand and to help governments respond to new developments and concerns, such as corporate governance, the information economy and the challenges of an ageing population. The Organisation provides a setting where governments can compare policy experiences, seek answers to common problems, identify good practice and work to co-ordinate domestic and international policies.

The OECD member countries are: Australia, Austria, Belgium, Canada, Chile, the Czech Republic, Denmark, Estonia, Finland, France, Germany, Greece, Hungary, Iceland, Ireland, Israel, Italy, Japan, Korea, Latvia, Luxembourg, Mexico, the Netherlands, New Zealand, Norway, Poland, Portugal, the Slovak Republic, Slovenia, Spain, Sweden, Switzerland, Turkey, the United Kingdom and the United States. The European Union takes part in the work of the OECD.

OECD Publishing disseminates widely the results of the Organisation's statistics gathering and research on economic, social and environmental issues, as well as the conventions, guidelines and standards agreed by its members.

OECD PUBLISHING, 2, rue André-Pascal, 75775 PARIS CEDEX 16
(04 2016 19 1 P) ISBN 978-92-64-26827-2 – 2017

www.ingramcontent.com/pod-product-compliance
Lightning Source LLC
Chambersburg PA
CBHW061213240926
51846CB00006B/1212
* 9 7 8 9 2 6 4 2 6 8 2 7 2 *